Isaac Bird

Bible work in Bible Lands

Or, Events in the History of the Syria Mission

Isaac Bird

Bible work in Bible Lands
Or, Events in the History of the Syria Mission

ISBN/EAN: 9783337170554

Printed in Europe, USA, Canada, Australia, Japan

Cover: Foto ©ninafisch / pixelio.de

More available books at **www.hansebooks.com**

IN

BIBLE LANDS;

OR,

EVENTS IN THE HISTORY OF THE SYRIA MISSION.

BY THE
Rev. ISAAC BIRD.

FULLY ILLUSTRATED.

PHILADELPHIA:
PRESBYTERIAN BOARD OF PUBLICATION,
1334 CHESTNUT STREET.

Entered according to Act of Congress, in the year 1872, by

THE TRUSTEES OF THE

PRESBYTERIAN BOARD OF PUBLICATION,

In the Office of the Librarian of Congress, at Washington.

WESTCOTT & THOMSON,
Stereotypers and Electrotypers, Philada.

EDITOR'S PREFACE.

WHEN the great and good work yet in its infancy in Syria shall have ripened into maturity, and when the various religions of its mingled yet severed races shall have melted into one in the blessed gospel of Jesus Christ, the question will be asked, "Who were the planters of these churches? Whence came the beginnings of these glorious results? Under what circumstances did the truth return to these lands, hallowed by the footsteps of the apostles and of the Lord himself?" To preserve the records of this memorable story has been a labor of love to the author of "Bible Work in Bible Lands," himself one of the earliest laborers in the Syria mission field. But while a labor of love to him, it is to the Church of the present as well as of the future an invaluable boon. Already is the dawn of a new spiritual day breaking upon those historic lands. Its rays are glittering on the summits of Lebanon and Hermon, and glancing thence into the valleys and over the plains of Syria. The gaze of many is drawn thither, and gladly will they welcome this first chapter, though not, as we trust and believe, the *last*, in the story of the bringing to Christ's feet of the dwellers in Bible lands.

J. W. D.

CONTENTS.

CHAPTER I.

                                                       PAGE

Introductory remarks—Mohammedans to be specially benefited—First laborers—Operations commenced at Smyrna—Residents friendly to the object—Studies and labors in Scio—Tour to the "Seven Churches" 15

CHAPTER II.

Separation of Messrs. Fisk and Parsons—Voyage of Mr. Parsons to Jaffa—Doings at Jerusalem—Greek rebellion—Destruction of Scio—Visit at Samos—Mr. Parsons ill at Syra—At Smyrna—Voyage to Egypt—Death of Mr. Parsons......................... 33

CHAPTER III.

The war in Smyrna—Reflections—Mr. Fisk—Bible labors in Egypt—Sails for Malta—Is joined by Messrs. King and Wolff—The three visit Egypt—Pass the desert—Reach Gazza, Jaffa and Jerusalem—The morals of Jerusalem............................ 49

CHAPTER IV.

Journey to Beirut—Messrs. Way and Lewis at Sidon—Lady Hester Stanhope—Beirut—Emeer Besheer—Antoora—Convents of Lebanon—Baalbec—Patriarch Jarwi—Residence of Mr. King at Deir el Kommer—Arrival of Messrs. Goodell and Bird. 64

CHAPTER V.

Bishop Monsignor Gandolfi at Beirut—A Maronite priest—Departure of two of the brethren for Jerusalem—Visits at Sidon, Tyre, Acca, Nazareth, Nablus and Jerusalem.................. 86

CHAPTER VI.

Preaching at Jerusalem—Papas Esa—Deacon Cæsar—Sale of Scriptures—Bible men arrested—Omar Effendi—Congratulations at our release—Arrival of the Jaffa consul's son—Visit to the governor and the moollah—Our rooms opened—Rapid sale of Testaments... 106

CHAPTER VII.

Visit to Bethlehem and Hebron—Cave of Machpelah—Jews—Sheikh Mohammed—Frank Mountain—Cave of David and Saul—Governor of Jerusalem removed—At Jaffa—Beirut...... 118

CHAPTER VIII.

Mr. Goodell alone at Beirut—First patriarchal denunciation—Letters from Rome—Mr. B. Barker, Bible agent, and Lady Stanhope—Mr. King revisits Deir el Kommer—Conversations with priests—Journey to Damascus, Hums, Hamah and Aleppo—Firman against the Scriptures—Three months in Aleppo—Eventful journey through Antioch and Tripoli to Beirut 132

CHAPTER IX.

Reply to the patriarch's bull—Mr. Fisk robbed—Patriarch Jarwi roused—Mr. King with Mr. Fisk at Jaffa and Jerusalem—Pasha collecting taxes at Jerusalem—His cruelties—Journey to Beirut—Robbers—Assad Shidiak—His casting a lot about the pope—Mr. King leaves Syria......................... 159

CHAPTER X.

Shidiak and the patriarch—Sickness and death of Mr. Fisk—Shidiak in custody of the patriarch—Escapes by night—Describes in writing his sojourn with his holiness—Is visited by his acquaintances and relatives—Priest Girgis mocks at him—He is recaptured by the patriarch—Plot against the Bible men—The Lord of Hosts breaks it up—Attack of Greeks on the city—Mr. Goodell's house plundered before his eyes........ 184

CHAPTER XI.

Phares Shidiak driven from home—Letters from Assad—He is taken to the clutches of the patriarch, never again to be free—Additions to our communion—A second papal bull—Excommunications—Sheikh Naameh Lattoof—Two youths of the Trodd family—Imprisonment and trial of Tannoos el Haddad—Mr. Smith's arrival—Priest Girgis—Bishop Zachariah friendly—Bishop Gerasimus and the schools.......................... 207

CHAPTER XII.

Sick child taken to the mountains—Excommunications—Removal from Eh-heden to Ba-whyta—Negotiations with the patriarch—Sheikh Girgis of Besherry intercedes—Interview of the sheikhs with his holiness—Sheikh Naameh exasperated and indomitable; the others pardoned............................ 232

CHAPTER XIII.

Convent of Belmont—Monks afraid of the Bible—Worshipers of Mary—An eclipse of the moon—Famous Greek preacher, Miniati—Battle of Navarino and panic—Account of events at Beirut and vicinity in various letters—Return to Beirut—Retirement to Malta.. 250

CHAPTER XIV.

Operations in Malta—Messrs. Whiting and Dwight—Visit to the coast of Africa, to Greece, to Armenia—Labors at Beirut resumed—New curses—Patriarch excommunicated by Jos. Wolff—Death of Assad Shidiak—Brummana village—Druzes—Messrs. Parnell and Hamilton—Wortabet's labors in Sidon—His death—two Jesuits—Lamartine eulogizes them—Outrage of soldiers—Traits of Ibrahim Pasha.......................... 274

CHAPTER XV.

Mr. Thomson sets off with his family for Jerusalem—Becomes isolated at Jaffa by war—Terrible earthquake—Horrors in Jerusalem—The city taken by the Arabs and retaken by the pasha—Mrs. Thomson's death at Jerusalem—Mr. Thomson returns to Beirut... 298

CHAPTER XVI.

Work in Beirut—Arrival of a press—Decease of Consul Abbott at Eh-heden—Station at Jerusalem resumed by Messrs. Whiting and Dodge—Death of the latter at Jerusalem—Druze excitement with little present result—Mrs. Bird's ill health compels the family to leave Syria—Mr. and Mrs. Smith's shipwreck—Death of Mrs. Smith—Triumph at Brummana—Earthquake at Safed—Jerusalem abandoned—Good reasons—Death of Mr. and Mrs. Hebard—New war at Beirut—Death of Mrs. Wolcott... 312

CHAPTER XVII.

Patriarch's ambition and defeat—Dr. and Mrs. DeForest—Death of Mrs. Smith—Case of Raheel, tried for her faith—Abeih occupied—Hasbeiya waking up—Fierce persecutions assail the inquirers—Alarming threats—Temporary retreat to Abeih

—Dishonorable meddling of the Russian consul—The persecutors become advocates—The Protestants, after severe trials, fence off a cemetery, have a church of seventeen members and regular supply of preaching... 348

CHAPTER XVIII.

New flames of war in 1845—Druzes prevail—Maronite princes driven from Abeih—Greeks killed at Hasbeiya—Death of the patriarch—New election ends in quarrel and sacking of Canobeen—Greek patriarch in trouble at Beirut—Meshaka and his patriarch in discussion—Messrs. Wilson and Foote at Tripoli—Yanni—Messrs. Wilson and Foote driven from Ehheden—Yanni unites with the church at Beirut—Abdallah Zeidan—Ishoc el Kefroony—Safeeta............................... 382

CHAPTER XIX.

Sidon—Messrs. Thomson and Van Dyck, laborers with helpers, Tannoos el Haddad and Eleeas Fuaz—Sabbath services—The hearers are laid under ban—A Jesuit preacher—Meetings in Lady Stanhope's joon—Petitions from Deir el Kommer—Church of seven members organized—Calls from Birteh, Kana, Alma, Rasheiya—Cruelty of the governor of Tyre—Deir el Kommer—Ain Zehalta out-station—Druzes attack Deir el Kommer June 1, 1860, and on the 22d utterly destroy it—Letter of Mrs. Bird—Wholesale butchery—A few saved by the missionary—Attack and massacre at Hasbeiya—Destruction of the city of Zahleh—Rush of people, wounded and impoverished, to Beirut—Task of feeding them—The part performed by the Americans—The mission transferred to the Presbyterian Board—Its present state—Letter of Rev. D. Stuart Dodge.. 403

ILLUSTRATIONS.

	PAGE
1.—MAP OF THE SYRIA MISSION FIELD..........FRONTISPIECE.	
2.—MODERN THYATIRA..	23
3.—MODERN PHILADELPHIA...	29
4.—JOPPA, THE MODERN JAFFA.......................................	35
5.—JERUSALEM FROM THE EAST......................................	54
6.—THE EMEER BESHEER..	69
7.—REV. JONAS KING, D.D., IN ORIENTAL COSTUME........	87
8.—NAZARETH..	93
9.—BETHLEHEM..	113
10.—MODERN HEBRON...	121
11.—DAMASCUS...	148
12.—THE MARONITE PATRIARCH.......................................	159
13.—CANA...	180
14.—ROBBING THE HOUSE OF DR. GOODELL, AT BEIRUT...	203
15.—MT. LEBANON, WITH THE CANOBEEN CONVENT.........	211
16.—LATTOOF'S WIFE AND DAUGHTER RESISTING THE PERSECUTORS.	235
17.—A SYRIAN GENTLEMAN..	269
18.—SAFEETA, NORTHERN SYRIA......................................	333
19.—BETHLEHEM..	335
20.—DEIR EL KOMMER..	351
21.—ABEIH SEMINARY, MT. LEBANON................................	359
22.—HASBEIYA..	371
23.—MODERN SIDON..	405
24.—HASBEIYA, ITS LOWER PORTION................................	421

BIBLE WORK IN BIBLE LANDS.

CHAPTER I.

Introductory remarks—Mohammedans to be specially benefited—First Laborers—Operations commenced at Smyrna—Residents friendly to the object—Studies and labors in Scio—Tour to the "Seven Churches."

IN the autumn of 1819, two young ministers of the gospel embarked at Boston on a Christian enterprise in behalf of a needy race of people on the eastern shores of the Mediterranean. The American churches had sent forth men to the far East to teach and reclaim from idolatry the degraded heathen of India; they had done the same for the savages of the far West and among the islands of the sea, and they were now directing their efforts, as was fit, to a prominent and populous nation *nearer by*—a nation who, though they had found their way out from the sottish idolatry of their ancestors, still had need that some man should guide them as truly as the heathen themselves. Taking their stand on the great fundamental truth that "there is no god but God," the Mohammedans had strongly condemned all idolatry, and finding images in Christian temples, had hastily classed all the professed followers of Jesus among the nations who were to be put under tribute or be destroyed. Bloody wars, for century after century, had been waged between the two parties, without any apparent prospect of an end. Christians still continued to use their images, and their antagonists to follow their false prophet. It was high time that the former should make a better choice of weapons, and exchange their sword of steel for that of the gospel.

It seemed probable that, if by any means the adversary could be convinced that the *true* disciples of "Esa" (Jesus) believed in only one God as truly as himself, and that his prophet was under a gross mistake in supposing that Christianity had anything of idolatry in it, he might easily be persuaded to become a defender instead of a persecutor of the Christian name, and this change of attitude between those so long at variance would be the gaining of a great nation.

To commence measures for the introduction of so happy a change, Messrs. Fisk and Parsons set out on an expedition to the Turco-Christian population of Western Asia. They came to a landing first at Smyrna, the great commercial emporium of the country, where they began their labors. The plan before them was first to obtain the sympathy and co-operation of the nominally Christian population, and through them to reach, in the end, their long-avowed and oppressive enemies.

But before the native Christians could be made of use in this desired capacity of co-workers it was necessary, for their *own* sake as well as for that of their neighbors, that they should themselves be persuaded to adopt certain changes. It was necessary that they should remove out of their neighbors' way those very prominent stumbling-blocks consisting of church images and pictures, that they should cease to invoke the help of dead men and dead women, that they should cease to imitate the heathen in giving to heaven a queen and to God a mother, and, more than all, that they should hold and teach that all hope of salvation for man rests on Christ alone as the Saviour, and not on the priest or the sacraments or ceremonies of any Church.

To effect such a change in the native Christians of the country would require much time and labor and patience, but the two brethren, in the name of their Lord and Master, who is Head over all things to his Church, immediately put their hands to the work, grasping languages, distributing Scriptures and other books, preaching the gospel and conversing with the people according to ability and opportunity.

They were not left without friendly assistance in beginning their work. The representatives of English societies, the Rev. Messrs. Jowett and Wilson, furnished them from Malta with reading matter for distribution and valuable advice for themselves. At Smyrna itself the Rev. Mr. Williamson, Mr. John Lee, the Messrs. Van Lennep and the Messrs. Perkins, with other foreign residents, gave them their countenance and influence. Mr. Williamson was the English chaplain for the city. He warmly recommended the establishment of a press at Smyrna especially for the Greeks, who were very fond of reading, and another press at Jerusalem with Arabic type, for he said that among all the thousands of readers, Greeks and Arabs, in the Turkish dominions, there was found for them no such thing as a native newspaper or any other periodical publication.

Mr. Lee was a native of Smyrna, a brother of the British consul at Alexandria, somewhat advanced in years, a great reader and a man of evident piety. He requested his American friends to make free use of his large library and to look to him freely for any aid which he could bestow, whether in the way of information about the country or of financial credit. The Messrs. Van Lennep were three brothers, merchants, also born in the city and doing business together. They welcomed the brethren into their large family circle, and manifested a continually-increasing attachment both to them and to their work.

The Messrs. Perkins were two brothers from Boston, trading in partnership, and the two new-comers were not disappointed in the friendly reception they experienced from these their own countrymen.

In the enjoyment of such a circle of friends, and confident of the divine approbation, they were greatly encouraged by their prospects. But before they could enter into the heart of their work they must have the gift of tongues. For this purpose, especially for the acquisition of the modern Greek, after a short stay in the city, they repaired to the island of Scio. Here was a famous Greek seminary, the chief college of the nation, having fourteen instructors and six or seven hundred students. At the head of this fountain of knowledge for the Greek nation was Professor Bambas, a man the like of whom for learning, for religious sensibility and freedom from sectarian prejudice might be looked for in vain through all the ranks of his co-religionists.

To this gentleman the brethren went with letters of recommendation from the Rev. Mr. Jowett, of Malta, and the British chaplain of Smyrna. He received them with open arms, and immediately promised to give his own time for their instruction. Some hours each day were his own, and he might spend them upon his friends. This special attention he was induced to pay them, in consideration, as he said, of the "sacred cause to which they were devoted."

Further to illustrate the spirit of this excellent man, the following facts may be mentioned. He took for a text-book in the instruction of one of his higher classes a volume presented him by his new American pupils, called the "Young Minister's Companion," a compilation specially prepared for the use of the theological students at Andover in America. The professor would dictate a translation from the English book, and the pupils would write it from his lips in Greek. On his first receiving this book, he exclaimed,

"Oh this must be excellent! I may make a selection from it to print for the use of the ecclesiastics."

Of another book which these friends gave him he said,

"I shall read this attentively, both for my own advantage and for the benefit of my pupils."

He had read the entertaining tract, "The Dairyman's Daughter," it being one of the exercises of his little American class to translate the book under his supervision into Greek. One day, as they were out with him examining the apartments of a very splendid mansion in the city, he observed,

"This is indeed elegant, but the chamber of the Dairyman's Daughter was still more splendid."

When in the course of their translation exercises they had come to the account of the last sickness and death of the subject of the story, he remarked, "I have never been able to read this account without weeping," and while making his remarks upon the translation, he was so much affected that he could not go on without pausing several times to recover himself. While the brethren were distributing their tracts to the pupils in the college, he stood by and added his strong recommendation to the gifts. When, at a certain time, Mr. Fisk was ill, he called early in the morning to see him, and expressed the solicitude and tenderness of a father. During his call they read to him portions of the last Report of the British and Foreign Bible Society, which he translated into Greek. Afterward they read and sang the hymn:

> "Kindred in Christ for his dear sake
> A hearty welcome here receive."

He was so much interested in this hymn that he wished them to transcribe both the hymn and tune for his own use.

It was a rare chance to meet with a man like this in Western Asia, and a rare privilege to enjoy his instructions and his patronage. It was also esteemed by our friends to be a rare privilege to have the opportunity to stimulate such a man in his Christian zeal, and by their warm sympathy in their intercourse with him to add something to the stability of his faith. They looked forward with joyful hope to the immense improvement which he, if his life was continued in his present station, would effect in the character of his countrymen. But, alas! how little man can know what a day may bring forth! Even cities and institutions may, like men, be compared to a flower of the field: "the wind passeth over it, and it is gone."

During the six months' residence of Messrs. Fisk and Parsons on this island they paid visits to four monasteries containing more than four hundred priests and monks, and two other establishments for females having between two and three hundred nuns. These latter were generally able to read, but of the former one hundred and twenty only out of the four hundred could read. Forty of the readers were priests. One is inclined to ask how it could ever have entered into the heart of man to believe that by building half a dozen spacious houses on this island, and taking from the community six hundred men and women and confining them in these prison-houses, the glory of God would be promoted! Among all this crowd of men professedly devoted to religion there appear to have been in use only two New Testaments, and these had been printed in Germany, two hundred years before, in ancient Greek—unintelligible to them. One copy also of the Old Testament they possessed, safely locked up in a box. A great many schools were visited where children were taught to read, parrot like, in the ancient Greek psalter. The introduction by the missionaries of thirty-five modern Greek Testaments and thirty-seven hundred intelligible tracts must have been to these destitute islanders of Scio as the rising sun after a long and dreary night. To many they may have proved a warning voice unto salvation against the day of approaching calamity.

Immediately on the return of the brethren to Smyrna they made preparations for visiting the places where once stood and flourished

THE SEVEN CHURCHES OF ASIA.

These places were once among the most populous and famous cities of the western part of Asia Minor. Smyrna was one of them; the others lay around it in a semicircular line three or four hundred miles in extent. These cities naturally had very early their important churches, and no one who has ever read that wonderful composition, the Book of the Revelation, can easily forget the messages sent them by Jesus Christ through his servant John in Patmos, each particular message being accompanied by that solemn charge, "He that hath an ear let him hear what the Spirit saith unto the churches." And every serious-minded reader is inclined to ask, "What is the state of these churches now? Have they heeded their message, and do they still exist and flourish, or are they swept from the face of the earth?"

The Rev. David Lindsay, English chaplain at Constantinople, had visited these places in 1815, carrying with him a few scriptures, but our travelers were going with the additional advantages of having more and better books and a better knowledge of the language of the people. Of the church at Smyrna little need be said. The message of the Lord to it contained no rebuke nor threat: "I know thy works and tribulation and poverty (but thou art rich). Fear none of those things which thou shalt suffer. Be thou faithful unto death, and I will give thee a crown of life." So Smyrna has survived the general desolation that has come upon the other cities.

After leaving Smyrna the brethren first visited the site of the "church in Pergamos," fifty miles north of Smyrna. Here they found ruins of theatres, and of temples, Christian and heathen, and particularly the vast granite foundations of the defensive wall of an old castle. All these antiquities showed that Pergamos was once a strong and populous city. It was supposed to have still a population of more than fifteen thousand souls, mostly Turks. The Greeks and Armenians had each a church, and the Jews a synagogue. The first of these had a school of twenty boys connected with it, taught by one of the priests. The explorers visited also the other

MODERN THYATIRA.

priests, and one, to whom they gave a New Testament, read to them what the Spirit had said "to the angel of the church at Pergamos."

From this northern extremity of their circuit the travelers take their course in a south-east direction to examine the remains of the church in Thyatira, the city of Lydia, the seller of purple. Acts xvi. 14.

They reached the place at the close of the second day from Pergamos, after crossing an extensive plain and seeing a number of villages.

Mr. Fisk writes: "We had a letter of introduction from a Greek in Smyrna to Economo, the bishop's procurator, and a principal man among the Greeks in this town. This morning we sent the letter, and he immediately called upon us. We then conversed some time respecting the town. He says the Turks have destroyed all remnants of the ancient church, and even the place where it stood is now unknown. At present there are in the town one thousand houses for which taxes are paid to the government.

"Thyatira is situated near a small river, in the centre of an extensive plain. At the distance of three or four miles it is almost completely surrounded by mountains. The houses are low, many of them of mud or earth. Excepting the governor's palace, there is scarcely a decent house in the place. The streets are narrow and dirty, and everything indicates poverty and degradation." *

The prevailing language of the place among all

---

* Since the time of this visit there has been instituted in Thyatira a growing Protestant church with an educated preacher. We may hope that the Master will be able to say at the last, "I know thy faith, and thy patience, and thy works, and the last to be more than the first."

classes was Turkish. The modern Greek was, however, understood by some of that nation. Economo spoke with gratitude of the copy of the Greek Testament which Mr. Lindsay left with them five years before. The Turks had nine places of worship, and the Greeks and Armenians one each. Of the schools, one of fifty boys was taught by a priest, another of twenty, by a layman, to each of which were given a few tracts. For two or three other private schools were also left tracts, and a copy of the Testament for the priests.

On the morning of November 11, after calling in a while upon the thirty worshipers in the Armenian church, the two travelers began their journey to Sardis.

Passing the village of Marmora, containing five hundred houses, and having crossed a vastly extended plain, they reached, at the foot of Mount Tmolus, the great capital of the Lydian kings, the city of the far-famed Crœsus and scene of the private quarrel between the two Roman republicans, Brutus and Cassius.

It was the last day of the week. They had traveled ten hours from Thyatira, and the best place for this company of five men to lodge in for the Sabbath was a room ten feet square in the hut of a Turk—a hut whose floor and walls were earth, and its roof of the same material, with grass growing upon it. Not a chair or table was to be seen, and the proprietor seemed to have nothing to live upon but his pipe and his coffee!

In the morning, after their devotions, they took some tracts and a Testament, and went to a neighboring mill where three or four Greeks were living. The mill was in full operation, as on a week day. They found two of the men, with whom they read and conversed, and in the upper part of the mill they had their usual Sabbath-day service, attended, as it would seem, by these native Greeks and their own traveling company. They wept as they prayed among the ruins of this great and famous city and while they sang the seventy-fourth Psalm,

> "How long, eternal God, how long,
> Shall men of pride blaspheme?"

Here were once a few names which had not defiled their garments. These are now walking with their Redeemer "in white." But, alas! the church as a body had only a name to live while they were dead. They had not an ear to hear the voice of the divine admonition. They did not strengthen the things that were ready to die, wherefore their candlestick has been removed out of its place.

The next morning the brethren went out to view more particularly the ruins of the place. They saw the decayed walls of two churches, of the market and of an ancient palace. Two marble columns were still standing, thirty feet high and six feet in diameter, and fragments of similar pillars lay scattered on the ground. Mr. Chandler, who was there sixty years before them, found five pillars then standing instead of two. On a high hill were the remains of an old castle whose walls were still very strong.

There is not now a single Christian family in the village. Three grist-mills are kept in operation by nine or ten Greek men and boys, but none of them with families.

The fourth of the "Seven Churches" visited by our travelers was Philadelphia.

But the Turks did not like this name. It had too much Greek in it, and so they called it Ala Shehr—Beautiful City. It was still honored by being the residence of a Greek archbishop. This prelate had been in office but a few years, although himself an aged man. Formerly he had a bishop under him, but at this time not one. His diocese included Sardis on the west and Laodicea on the east, but in it there were not more than six or seven hundred Greek houses, and about twenty priests. In Philadelphia there were only five churches in use, but twenty others which were either too small or too old to be used for worship. The houses in the city numbered three thousand, two hundred and fifty of them Greek. The visitors gave the archbishop some tracts and a Testament. He had had a Testament years before from Mr. Lindsay, but had given it away. They afterward dined with the archbishop. It chanced to be on a fast day, when the Greeks eat no meat. "The dinner consisted of rice, soup, boiled beans, several plates of herbs and a rich variety of fruits, with bread and cheese, and a plenty of rakee (brandy), rum and wine"—a somewhat singular dinner for a fast day.

A school of thirty boys was taught in the place by a young man. A small library was connected with the school, in which was an old copy of the Greek Testament, the date and title-page lost, also a translation of Goldsmith's "Greece," in modern Greek. The Turkish was the prevailing language of this place, so that the tracts in Greek were not much in demand.

One of the six mosques of the place was pointed out not only as having been a very ancient church, but as the very one occupied by the Christians of the time of

MODERN PHILADELPHIA.

John. A sad relic of barbarous antiquity was found about a mile west of the town—a wall built of human bones. The structure was near thirty rods in length, eight feet thick and ten high. According to tradition, there was once a church dedicated to St. John near this spot, and when a vast multitude were assembled there to celebrate his festival, the enemy suddenly fell upon them and slew them all. Their bodies were not burned nor buried, but piled up in a long line as the bones now lie. The wall now remaining seemed to be principally if not wholly composed of bones. On breaking off pieces, some small bones were found almost entire.

The last place to be visited in this direction was the site of the church of Laodicea. But on account of illness, under which Mr. Parsons had been suffering for more than a week, the travelers reluctantly gave up their hope of completing their attempted excursion. The disappointment, however, was felt the less keenly, as they were assured that Laodicea was at that time almost nothing but ruins, and that that part of the country presented very little opportunity for evangelical labor. They therefore turned their course directly toward Smyrna, where in four days more they arrived in health, having accomplished their journey in just three weeks.

To complete the account of the seven churches, it may properly be added here that Mr. Fisk on a subsequent occasion made a visit to the ruins of Ephesus.

At the mean Turkish village of Aiásaluk, a quarter of a mile from the old city and built from its fragments, Mr. Fisk visited a building now called the Church of St. John, supposed to have been once a church, afterward a mosque, but now a perfect wreck. He saw within its walls some immensely large and high pillars of red granite, said to have been taken from the temple of Diana. The ancient city itself seems to have been bounded on the east by a small hill, on the northern side of which was the circus or stadium, having a length from east to west of forty rods. The north or lower side was supported by a wall on arches which still remain. The area where the races were run was now a field of wheat. At the west end was the gate. The walls adjoining it were still standing, and of considerable height and strength. The same was true of the gateway of the famous theatre (Acts xix. 29), the site of which was still plainly visible only a few yards southward. Many columns and finely sculptured ornaments of buildings lay heaped among the ruins, but not a single inhabitant was visible.

CHAPTER II.

Separation of Messrs. Fisk and Parsons—Voyage of Mr. Parsons to Jaffa—Doings at Jerusalem—Greek rebellion—Destruction of Scio—Visit at Samos—Mr. Parsons ill at Syra—At Smyrna—Voyage to Egypt—Death of Mr. Parsons.

MORE than a year had gone by since our two travelers and sojourners among strangers set out upon their great work of benevolence. They had labored together with one heart and one mind, by sea and by land. Not for a single night or a single day had they been separated. But now they felt themselves irresistibly drawn in different directions. It was time that a movement was made toward Jerusalem, the place of their ultimate destination. But on the other hand, as Paul felt himself bound to tarry yet a while at Ephesus because of the effectual door that the Lord had opened before him, so these brethren regarded the opening for labor in the city of Smyrna and vicinity as pleading strongly for a continuance of the work at that place. It was therefore decided that Mr. Fisk should remain in Smyrna, and that his colleague, with a native attendant, should proceed directly to Jerusalem. The separation took place on the 5th of December. A passage had been engaged for Mr. Parsons on board a Greek vessel carrying pilgrims to Jaffa. The two brethren went on board together. There they sang, "Guide me, O thou great Jehovah," united in prayer, commended each other to the divine protection and gave the parting hand.

The vessel touched at the harbor of Scio, and afforded Mr. Parsons another and last opportunity of seeing the good Professor Bambas, who received his old pupil most affectionately, listened attentively to the narrative of his late tour among the churches, and dismissed him with his renewed blessing on the work in which he was engaged.

The pilgrims proceeded onward in their voyage in the same path that was traversed by Paul in his last voyage toward Jerusalem, passing in sight of Ephesus, and Miletus, and Patmos, touching at Samos, Rhodes and the coast cities of Cyprus, viewing, at short distance, Mt. Lebanon, Beirut, Sidon, Tyre, Ptolemais, Mt. Carmel, Cæsarea, and at last reaching Jaffa, their destined port, on the 10th of February. The voyage had been long and somewhat tedious, from contrary winds and frequent detentions in harbor. But the gospel laborer went on with his work, reading, preaching and discussing the truths of God's word, and he had an attentive audience, for they had nothing to do but to listen. Some of them received lasting impressions, which they manifested by searching out the preacher after they arrived in Jerusalem and putting themselves in the way of obtaining additional instruction.

At Jaffa, where they landed, the English consul, having heard of Mr. Parsons' approach, sent his son and his dragoman to receive him at the beach and conduct him to his house, offering him a place in his family and every assistance he could render. Mr. Parsons also made the acquaintance of the Russian consul, to whom he brought letters of recommendation. That gentleman showed himself very kind and friendly, gave him liberty to occupy, while at Jerusalem, a room which he had at his disposal in one of the convents, and invited him to accompany him in the spring in a tour which he intended to take in Mount Lebanon. He also offered to take charge of all letters and packages from abroad directed to his care for Mr. Parsons, and forward them immediately to Jerusalem.

JAFFA, THE MODERN JOPPA.

Jaffa or Joppa* was always the seaport of Jerusalem, and nothing but the lack of a good harbor for ships prevented it from being one of the most splendid cities of the coast. It is still the most common landing-place for pilgrims on the way to the holy city, and at the time

---

* This place is often alluded to in the Scriptures, both of the Old Testament and the New Testament, though in the former it is written Japho and the latter Joppe. The cedars from Lebanon for Solomon's temple came from Tyre to Japho. Jonah fled from the presence of the Lord to Japho. Peter raised Dorcas to life at Joppe by the seaside. Cornelius sent men to Joppe to invite him to Cæsarea.

of Mr. Parsons' visit offered strong inducements to be made a missionary station and dépôt. The English consul was favorable to the distribution of the Scriptures, as were also the Russian consul and his protégés, the Greek inhabitants, and besides, the annual stream of pilgrims might there be supplied with the saving word both before and after their visit to the holy city.

After some detentions by the rain, Mr. Parsons, in company with the dragoman of the Russian consul as a guide, set off on his way to Jerusalem. As they were crossing the plain of Sharon, the path led them amid cultivated fields of wheat and barley. Numerous herds of cattle and flocks of sheep and goats were seen feeding in every direction. Four hours' ride brought them to the ancient Arimathea. On the north, in plain sight of the pilgrim coming from Jaffa, was the village of Lydda, where Peter cured Eneas of his eight years' palsy, the consequence of which was that "all the inhabitants of Lydda and Saron (or Sharon) turned to the Lord."

The travelers were invited to lodge in the Greek monastery. They found its president a man of more than common intelligence who had spent many years at Jerusalem, and was now stationed in this place to provide for pilgrims. The village had two other monasteries, a Greek church and several mosques.*

* Dr. Edward D. Clarke, in 1801, writes: "There is not a spot in the holy land more fertile than the plain around Rama (Arimathea). It resembles a continual garden. Rama and Lydda were the two first cities of the holy land that fell into the hands of the Christians when the army of the Crusaders arrived. Rama was then in its greatest splendor, a magnificent city, filled with abundance of all the luxuries of the East. It was exceedingly populous, adorned with stately buildings and well fortified with walls and towers. The count of Flanders was sent with five hundred cavalry to reconnoitre the place and demand its surrender. He found the gates open. The in-

During the evening several friends of the president called to see Mr. Parsons. As Mr. Parsons was the first man they had seen from the New World, they had a great many inquiries to make of him, especially on the subject of religion. Most of them listened with attention, and said, "It is well."

The next morning they resumed their way toward Jerusalem. They had yet three hours to go before leaving the plain to enter upon the "hill country of Judea." At twelve o'clock they came to the village of the noted Abu Goosh, a powerful sheikh of these mountains who demands tribute from all the native pilgrims, as well as from the Jerusalem convents on their account. The convents are dependent to such an extent on the patronage and gifts of such as come to them from abroad, and the sheikh can so easily close up the passage between these convents and their port of entry, that they are obliged to pay even large sums, at times, to keep up the good understanding between them. Mr. Parsons, on the present occasion traveling with an imperial firman, the protection-paper of the sultan, and in company with a consul's interpreter, was readily excused from paying the tribute money. The sheikh even invited him to tarry and take some refreshment, by which, however, the wily Arab may have expected to obtain a few piasters as a *present* which he did not dare to demand in the character of tribute.

habitants had all fled. The place became a rendezvous to the Christians, who remained there three entire days, regaling themselves upon the abundance which was left to them by the absentees. During this time Robert of Normandy was elected bishop of Rama and Lydda, the whole army joining in thanksgiving to St. George, the martyr and patron saint of Diospolis (Lydda) and Rama, to whom the auspicious commencement of the enterprise was attributed."

4

They passed on a couple of hours and began to ascend a high mountain, and in two hours more the guide exclaimed, "*The Mount of Olives!*" The holy city itself was yet covered from sight by intervening hills. "The mountains are round about Jerusalem." Whether coming from the west or from the north, the traveler does not discover the city till he is close upon it. In half an hour more, having been eleven hours on the way, the company entered the city. They found Bishop Procopius, to whom Mr. Parsons had letters, and by him were directed to the lodging-place kindly offered him by the Russian consul at Jaffa.

Procopius was a sort of vice-patriarch at Jerusalem. He was president of all the Greek convents or monasteries, and was one of the foreign agents of the British and Foreign Bible Society. In kindness and Christian sympathy he seems to have been another Professor Bambas. He called on Mr. Parsons early the following day, welcomed him to all the privileges of the monastery where he was, and repeated his readiness to aid him in his work to the extent of his power. Mr. Parsons presented him an excellent copy of the New Testament in Persian, translated by the lamented Henry Martyn, which he took and read with fluency.

Within a few days Mr. Parsons visited the Church of the Holy Sepulchre. The church is large, and covers not only the sepulchre, but different apartments or chapels for five or six separate sects of Christians— Latins, Greeks, Armenians, etc. Near the middle of the building is a large open area surrounded by a circle of columns, in the centre of which is the small edifice containing the tomb, and directly over it is the immensely high and spacious dome of the church. The small edifice measures on its outside twenty-nine feet by eighteen and a half. Within it are two apartments. In the inner one, on the right hand, is the tomb or sarcophagus, covered by a slab of marble two or three feet in height; on the left is a space where three or four men may stand or kneel and meditate upon the marble coffin beside them. The apartment is lighted by burning lamps. Mr. Parsons seems to have entered alone, and while he was standing there a pilgrim entered who, at the sight of the tomb, wept and sobbed as over the grave of a parent.

Mr. Parsons visited the Mount of Olives. Crossing the Kedron, he observes, "The bed of the stream was perfectly dry, notwithstanding the late copious rains." Passing through the place where must have been the Garden of Gethsemane, he says, "In fifteen or twenty minutes we reached the summit of the Mount of Olives. Here we had a delightful view of the city, and also of the Dead Sea. Perhaps no place in the world commands a finer prospect or is associated with events more sacred and sublime. 'David went up by the side of Mount Olivet, and wept as he went up, and had his head covered, and he went barefoot.' On the east side of it our blessed Saviour raised Lazarus from the grave, and on the west he endured the agony of Gethsemane. Here he beheld the city and wept over it. From this mount he was at one time conducted to Jerusalem with shoutings of 'Hosanna to the Son of David!' and at another with the cry of 'Crucify him! crucify him!' From this spot he gave his last commission: 'Go ye into all the world and preach the gospel,' and then ascended and 'sat down on the right hand of the majesty on high.'"

Procopius estimated the number of Jews in Jerusalem

at ten thousand, and that of Christians at two thousand. An Armenian of distinction told him there were in Jerusalem sixty families of Armenians, and in Palestine four monasteries for that people, one each in Jerusalem, Bethlehem, Rama and Jaffa, and that there was an Armenian church on Mount Zion, outside of the city.

Mr. Parsons found and visited thirteen Greek monasteries within the walls of the city, besides four others, Catholic, Armenian, Syrian and Coptic. In Bethlehem and other places in the neighborhood were found six or seven more.

Under the Greek patriarchate of Jerusalem were thirteen bishoprics, viz., those of Petrea or Petra, Nazareth, Lydda, Gaza, Philadelphia (all the five bishops of these places reside at Jerusalem), Cæsarea, Bashan, Ptolemais, Bethlehem, Neapolis (Nablus), Jaffa, Mount Tabor and Mount Sinai. (The bishop of the last place resides at Constantinople.)

On Friday, April 20, were services suitable for the anniversary of the crucifixion. The following day, the Saviour being supposed to be lying in his grave, there was celebrated around that spot the disgraceful exhibition of

THE HOLY FIRE.

"The afternoon," says Mr. Parsons, "was a memorable season. Every apartment of the church was crowded with Turks, Jews, Christians and people 'from every nation under heaven.' These assembled to witness the supposed miraculous descent of the Holy Spirit under the similitude of *fire*. It is estimated that at least five thousand people were present. The governor of the city and the Turks of rank were there. A very convenient place was allotted to me to observe distinctly every ceremony. About twelve o'clock a body of Arab Christians, natives of Palestine, were admitted to perform their part in the duties of the holy week. They began by running round the holy sepulchre with all the frantic airs of madmen, clapping their hands, throwing their caps into the air, cuffing each other's ears, walking half naked upon the shoulders of their companions, hallooing or rather shrieking to the utmost extent of their voices. This was the exhibition to five thousand people who were in expectation of soon witnessing the descent of the holy fire.

"About one o'clock the Turks entered the small apartment of the Holy Tomb, extinguished the lamps of the church, closed the door and set a watch. I was determined myself to enter the sepulchre with the Russian consul, to see from what direction the fire proceeded. But they replied: 'The Turks will not give permission to strangers to enter.' Shortly after, the principal Greek priest entered the sepulchre, attended by the Armenian patriarch, and also by the Syrian patriarch. The first, however, entered the second apartment unattended. Every eye was fixed as the time approached. As we stood waiting, suddenly there darted from the sepulchre a flaming torch, which was carried almost instantaneously to a distant part of the assembly. I stood among the first to receive the fire, and to prove that, as to its power of burning, it contained no extraordinary qualities. The zeal of the pilgrims to get a part of the fire before the superior qualities departed, as they say that, in a few minutes, it burns like other fire, endangered the lives of many. Several were wellnigh crushed to death. Some lighted candles, others tow, with a view to preserve a part of its influence. Some held the blaze to their faces, saying: 'It does not burn.' Others said, 'Now, Lord, I believe; forgive my former unbelief.' After this the pilgrims retired, abundantly satisfied with what they had seen and heard."

Among the last things, Mr. Parsons with a company paid a visit to the Jordan. They set out from Jerusalem at nine o'clock, and "at four P. M. pitched their tent on the plains of Jericho." The village was then inhabited by about three hundred Arabs. They were awaked at two in the morning, and at five stood upon the banks of the Jordan. "The current, in consequence of the great rains, was rapid and violent. The banks of the river were ten feet at least above the level of the water. The pilgrims all rushed into the stream and plunged themselves beneath the sacred waters." From the point where they struck the river they proceeded three or four miles to the south, through a desert of sand, to the Dead Sea, satisfied themselves with the taste of its bitter waters, and then set their faces again toward Jerusalem.

Procopius kept a depository of the Scriptures, and had them for sale in the different monasteries. Besides what he might have disposed of in the city, Mr. Parsons had sold about a hundred Greek psalters, and he had sold since leaving Smyrna near fifty Greek Testaments. Many applications had been made for Armenian Testaments, of which unfortunately he had almost no supply. He had distributed more than three thousand tracts, some of which were destined to go a thousand miles from the Holy City. In every instance the books had been received not only without hesitation, but with a smile of gratitude. A pilgrim from Caramania (ancient Lycaonia) engaged to carry a supply to school teachers and priests, saying they would be received with thankfulness. To some Armenians who applied for tracts Mr. Parsons said, "Perhaps some of my friends will pass through Armenia with Bibles and tracts for sale." "We shall rejoice," said they, "and all will rejoice when they arrive."

Whilst the pilgrims were preparing to start on their return journey, there burst upon them the news of the great rebellion of the Greek nation against the Turkish government. The Greeks in Palestine were thrown into the greatest confusion by an order from government to surrender their arms, as also by the arrest of the Russian consul at Jaffa. Mr. Parsons hoped to find a place of quiet in some one of the islands of the Archipelago. On the 8th of May he bade adieu to the Beloved City, hoping and praying, in the words of David, "If I shall find favor in the eyes of the Lord, he will bring me again, and show me both it and his habitation." In six hours he was at Rama, and at Jaffa before sunset. At the gate of the city he was stopped by two Turkish soldiers in front of several cannon. One of the two men stood at his right hand, the other at his left, with pistols and swords. In half an hour came an order from the governor for him to enter.

The English consul received him into his family, and invited him to tarry till some fuller information should be received respecting the disturbances. He called immediately on the family of the Russian consul, and found it in a most distressing situation. The consul himself had, only a few hours before, secretly fled from the city and set sail for Constantinople. This he did, as they said, "to save himself from the bloody knife of the Turk."

Mr. Parsons embarked the next day in a Greek vessel bound to Scio, having for his fellow-passengers the presiding priest of the church at Gethsemane and a multitude of pilgrims. Among these great alarm had been excited by the report that the Russian consul at Acre had been beheaded. The next morning they were in the port of Paphos, in Cyprus. Two miles distant was the residence of the bishop, who, hearing of their arrival, sent bread and cheese and wine for their refreshment. They passed the day and night on shore, sleeping upon a bed of beanpods. Some days after this they met with a vessel (Greek) having a flag entirely black, with the exception of a white cross in the middle and a red crescent beneath it.

"We were soon hailed," says Mr. Parsons, "and ordered to lower our sails. The captain of the vessel, with a number of soldiers, came on board, ordered our flag (which was the Turkish) to be taken down, and then, with the utmost contempt, trampled it under foot, pronouncing a curse on him who should ever raise it. 'We do not take your vessel,' said they, 'nor do we wish to molest Greek pilgrims, but *we seek the blood of Turks*. They have executed our patriarch and our bishops, and we are determined to stand in defence of our lives and of our religion. All the Greeks in the Morea and on the islands are in arms. If you are arrested by a Turkish vessel, you must expect immediate execution.' It is impossible to describe the consternation which now prevailed among the pilgrims. The women especially lifted up their voices and wept. From our vessel the black flag ship went in search of another pilgrim vessel which had accompanied us from Jaffa. There they found two Turks and about thirty Jews. They were all arrested and put in confinement. The Turks were to be beheaded immediately and the Jews reserved for trial. Our pilgrims stood on deck to witness the dreadful scene, but we were soon at too great a distance to see what took place. During the day we saw many other vessels with a similar flag. Preparations were now made on deck for self-defence. The cannons were loaded and the marines supplied with arms."

Soon after, they came to anchor in the port of Stamphalia. The same day arrived two other vessels, one of which was a prize taken by the Greeks from the Turks. The next day Mr. Parsons visited a school in the island and distributed fifty tracts among the scholars. He had never observed so great a desire to receive religious books, and never had more pleasing evidence that they would be read with attention. "Send us books," said these poor islanders; "we want a supply for our families—for our children."

As they proceeded on their voyage they were hailed by another man-of-war, the captain of which assured them that they could not enter the harbor of Scio nor the harbor of Smyrna, that *the college of Scio was broken up, and that Professor Bambas had fled just in time to save his life.* The fate of Scio was one horrible to relate. The sultan of the Turks had much of the lion in his nature, and when he became fully assured of the extended plot of the Greeks against his government, he was transported with the feeling of revenge. He determined on giving a blow which might strike dismay into every Grecian heart. He began by cutting off the head of his chief interpreter and those of ten of the most noted and influential Greeks of Constantinople. Next he fell upon the priesthood. The venerable Patriarch Gregory, universally respected for his blameless life and reputed piety, was seized on coming out of his church on Easter Sunday, dragged to his palace and hung up like a dog over the gate, after which his body was taken down, trailed by the heels through the streets and thrown into the sea. Priests and bishops followed in their turn, and the promiscuous murder and burning of houses and villages of all Greeks was inaugurated. This, of course, wrought up the Greeks to a fury.

But the people of Scio, being comparatively prosperous and happy, were unwilling to engage in a struggle where success was so very doubtful, and where failure would, *to them*, be unavoidable ruin. Nevertheless, a war party came to them from the island of Samos, by whose persuasions and acts the people became at length compromised, and war was declared by the Turks against them. Suddenly, on the 11th of April, the Turkish fleet was seen steering toward the port, consisting of seven ships of the line and twenty-five frigates and corvettes. With these the captain pasha approached the town, and immediately opened his broadsides upon it. Most of the inhabitants fled; only about five thousand remained, trusting to the mercy of the Turks. The pasha, with six thousand men, took possession of the town, and, with assurances of safety, invited all the fugitives to return to their homes and their occupations. Many complied, and about one thousand entered into the convent of St. Meenas. On the fourth day the pasha ordered the thousand men of that convent to be brought out, one by one, before him, and each one, as soon as he appeared, was put to death. Then came an order for the general slaughter of all that remained in the city and island. Some hid themselves in caves, some fled to the mountains and some found means to escape to the neighboring islands. Some well-favored men, women and children were saved to be sold as slaves. Out of eighty thousand persons, it was estimated that twenty thousand were slain. The dwellings of the people, the churches, the convents and the *flourishing college* were broken open and pillaged, and plunder in immense quantities was taken on board the ships. Among those who escaped the sword of the Turks was the noble-minded, kind-hearted *Professor Bambas*, who, though driven from his high station in Scio, still lived a powerful advocate of the Bible and of its universal distribution.

Thus the prospects of Mr. Parsons became more and more beclouded and embarrassing. The vessel touching at Samos, Mr. Parsons reported himself to the English consul, and accepted an invitation from him to remain a few weeks in his family.

Mr. Parsons stayed at Samos four weeks, and then sailed in a Genoese vessel to the island of Syra. Here again he was welcomed into the family of the English consul, and as the island was under the protection of the French, he rested from the turmoil and perils of war. But he had not enjoyed the privileges of his situation many weeks before he was seized by a disease which brought him to the gates of the grave, and from which he was not sufficiently recovered to be removed until the middle of November. On the 21st of that month he set sail for Smyrna. He remained in Smyrna more than a month, without, however, that improvement in health which was hoped for, and a threatening cough coming on, the physician recommended to him a voyage to Alexandria and a trial of the air of Egypt. Accordingly, the two brethren embarked together on the 9th of January, and accomplished the voyage in five days. The weather had been boisterous and uncomfortable. The invalid arrived in great weakness, and two men took him in a chair to his lodgings. He himself writes, five days after his arrival: "It seems that this shattered frame will not long endure so great weakness. With Brother Fisk I talk freely of finishing my work and of meeting my final Judge, the Lord of missions. Heaven looks desirable—to obtain the perfect image of God, to know more of the existence of God as Father, Son and Holy Ghost, to see without a glass the exceeding love displayed on the cross, to observe the stations, orders and employments of angels, to know how saints are employed in relation to this and to other worlds, to see how God overrules sin, and why it is *through great tribulation* that he brings his children to glory,—in a word, to see God in all his attributes and his angels and saints in all their glory."

In this devout frame of mind he continued for twenty days, his thoughts soaring upward, his prayers ascending without ceasing, his body in great weakness, a tabernacle ready to be dissolved and exchanged for the house not made with hands eternal in the heavens. His final departure as well as burial took place February 10, 1822.

CHAPTER III.

The war in Smyrna—Reflections—Mr. Fisk—Bible labors in Egypt—Sails for Malta—Is joined by Messrs. King and Wolff—The three visit Egypt—Pass the desert—Reach Gaza, Jaffa and Jerusalem—The morals of Jerusalem.

MR. FISK, during the previous year, while his fellow-laborer was at work among the pilgrims, found himself shut up to the city and suburbs of Smyrna. He was near the centre of a bloody civil war. "His ear was pained, his soul was sick, with every day's report of wrong and outrage" that filled that hapless city. To the Turk all Greeks were made outlaws. They were hunted like wild beasts. They were shot at for sport to show the skill of the marksmen. Neighbor would meet neighbor with a smile, and with a stab lay him dead at his feet. The assassins would count up their victims and glory in their numbers as the American Indian glories in the number of his scalps.

When, in the good providence of God, his associate from Jerusalem was restored to him, their hearts melted together in new affection, and each found the other as before, fervent in spirit, serving the Lord. From this time it is obvious to remark how their mutual attachment increased. They were both made keenly sensible how much they owed, not only to their divine Master, but also to each other, for spiritual strength and comfort in their work. The invalid in his weakness leaned upon his brother, and was happy in a strange land to enjoy the help and sympathy and prayers of a long-tried friend. The other was happy in feeling that whatever he did for this his languishing fellow-servant he did for his Master himself. And when the sad hour of separation came, it is evident not only from his emotions at the time, but from his frequent recurrence to the event afterward, how heavy a blow he had himself received.

But yet he in no wise permits his calamity to hinder his diligence in business or his fervor of spirit in regard to his work. His room is open to all callers, and wherever there is Roman, Greek or Jew he seeks to approach him, find out his sentiments, call his attention to the Scriptures, and, if he can read, beg his acceptance of a tract or purchase of a book.

Having remained in Egypt more than two months, one of which he spent in a visit to Cairo, Mr. Fisk embarked for Malta, a friendly captain having offered him his passage free. Here, in the society of Mr. and Mrs. Temple from America, and of the two English missionaries, Messrs. Jowett and Wilson, he found that rest and solace which he so much needed.

In this fortified island, filled with one hundred thousand souls ground to the dust by Romish ignorance and superstition and guarded by English cannon, Mr. Fisk continued between eight and nine months, preaching in public and in private, studying the Arabic and perfecting himself in other languages. Meantime, he was joined by his old acquaintance, the Rev. Jonas King, from Paris, and by the Rev. Joseph Wolff, a converted Jew under the patronage of the English. These, all having the same destination, sailed together for Egypt and Syria at the beginning of January. The voyage was one of seven days. They occupied themselves in Egypt for three months, preaching in the large cities, visiting villages up and down the Nile, and disseminating as widely as possible the truth of God as contained in religious tracts and in the Holy Scriptures. After this, in company with a caravan, they hastened to make the journey of the desert toward the holy land. On the eleventh day they reached Gaza of the Philistines. At this point their caravan, which had had a number of accessions on the way, consisted of seventy-four persons, forty-four camels and fifty-nine other animals.

In two days' more travel they came to Joppa, having seen on the way neither stream of water nor smiling village, thrifty field, vineyard nor olive grove.

Moving onward from Jaffa toward Jerusalem, Mr. Fisk writes: "In about two hours we saw a Bedawin horseman sitting on the ground, a little distance before us, with his horse feeding by his side. As we advanced he rose and boldly put himself in front of us all. The Christians who were with us, and who rode forward, stopped and turned from him as if he had been a lion. As soon as Mr. Damiani, son of the consul, told him who we were, he let us pass quietly, but tried hard to get something from the rest of the company. But all he got was a trifle from the mule-drivers to keep him good-natured for the future. At 8 o'clock we crossed a hill and then entered a valley, which we were half an hour in passing. We next came among the mountains. Here we saw at a distance a camp of Bedawin. As soon as they saw us one of their horsemen rode on swiftly, as if to intercept our path. He came into the road before us, halted and looked at us again, and then rode off Had we been Rayahs (*i. e.*, Christian subjects of the grand signor), he would not probably have left us without money. For some time our road lay along the bed of a brook in a deep ravine, with mountains of rocks rising up like pyramids on each side of us. By degrees the ascent became more steep till we reached the height of these rugged mountains, where we had a good view of the plains between us and Jaffa. It was often with difficulty that our beasts could walk, on account of the roughness of the road and steepness of the ascent. These mountains are covered with small shrubs suitable for goats, of which we saw several large flocks. There are no forests, but in the valleys and on the sides of the hills are many olive and fig trees. At a place called Sareen two or three fierce-looking armed Bedawin appeared and began to demand tribute. We rode on very carelessly, bid them good-morning and inquired after their health. They began to talk loudly and ordered us to stop, but we rode on, and they did not attempt to stop us by force. When the native Christians and Jews pass such places, they have no way to get on but to satisfy the rapacity of these plunderers.

"At 12 o'clock we reached the village of Ibrahim Abu Goosh, a sheikh who has under his command great numbers of Bedawin, and who generally exacts tribute from those who pass this road, but for some reason we were permitted to pass in peace. We continued our course among the hills over a road impassable for camels and very difficult for mules and asses. After crossing a high mountain we passed through a deep valley where is a small village called Kaluna. The mountains here are of a peculiar formation. They seem almost as if built by the hand of man, and rise gradually, step by step, like pyramids. Each step, however, is so fastened into the 'everlasting hills' as to show that it was placed there by the hand of Him who existed 'before the mountains were brought forth.' On these steps, which are sometimes three or four rods wide and sometimes only a few feet, you see soil which produces shrubs, and, when cultivated, vines, figs and olives. The country continued the same till we were within half an hour of Jerusalem, when all at once Mt. Olivet and the holy city opened to our view.

"As we drew near the city we remembered how our dear brother Parsons, when wars and rumors of wars obliged him to leave the place, turned back his eyes as he ascended the hill west of Jerusalem and wept and said, 'If I shall find favor in the eyes of the Lord, he will bring me again, and show me both it and his habitation.' Alas for us! these words were fulfilled in a much higher sense than he then anticipated. Though he was not permitted to return to the earthly Jerusalem, yet his divine Saviour has given him an infinitely higher felicity, even that of entering and enjoying that *upper* Jerusalem where dwells the divine glory.

"With feelings not to be described, about 4 o'clock we entered JERUSALEM. The scenes and events of four thousand years seemed to rush upon our minds—events in which heaven, earth and hell had felt the deepest interest.

"Jerusalem seems, in a *general* view, to be situated on the side of a mountain descending gently toward the east, where it is divided from Mt. Olivet by the brook or valley of Kedron. The summit of the mountain on which it stands is considerably higher than the city, so that in coming from Jaffa you arrive near the place before you discover it.

"On taking a *nearer* view of the city, you perceive that it is built on several hills, viz.: Zion on the south-western part, Calvary at the north-west, Moriah at the south-east and Bezetha at the north-east. According to the ancient descriptions of Jerusalem, it included another hill called Acra. This hill it is not now easy to distinguish; at least, we see nothing now which corresponds entirely to the description given of it by Jo-

JERUSALEM FROM THE EAST.

sephus. Before Titus besieged Jerusalem it had been captured five times, and was once demolished by the Babylonians. Titus spared the west wall and three towers, 'but for all the rest of the wall it was so thoroughly laid even with the foundation that there was left nothing to make those that come thither believe that it had ever been inhabited.' And since the time of Titus the city has been often plundered, and at least partially destroyed. In the space of so many ages it is to be expected that some valleys should be filled up and some hills leveled. The south wall passes over Zion near its summit, so that a great part of the hill is left without the city. South of the hill is the deep valley of the son of Hinnom. The same valley, turning north, bounds Zion likewise on the west. The valleys which separate it in the city from Calvary on the north and Acra on the north-east are not deep. The valleys north and west of Moriah at present are not at all steep. Calvary, which is not called a mountain in the Scriptures, was perhaps only a small elevation on a greater hill which is now the northern part of the city; but the name is now given to the whole hill. Bezetha is separated from Calvary by a wide valley, and east of Calvary is also the dividing valley between Moriah and Bezetha, in which is the pool of Bethesda.

"We have viewed Jerusalem from different stations, have walked around it and within it, and have stood on the Mount of Olives with Josephus' description of it in our hands, trying to discover the hills and valleys as laid down by him nearly eighteen hundred years ago, and after all our research we compare Jerusalem to a beautiful person whom we have not seen for many years, and who has passed through a great variety of changes and misfortunes, which have caused the rose on her cheeks to fade, her flesh to consume away and her skin to become dry and withered and have covered her face with the wrinkles of age, but who still retains some general features by which we recognize her as the person who used to be the delight of the circle in which she moved. Such is the appearance of this holy city which was once 'the perfection of beauty, the joy of the whole earth.'"

The population of Jerusalem is differently estimated, but may well enough be considered as equally divided between Jews, Mohammedans and Christians, reckoning five thousand to each. In general they are poor, ignorant, bigoted and deceitful.

The Muslims are distinguished for their pride and cruelty. They are of the ruling class, and consequently expect deferential treatment from other sects and partial favor from the government. If the foreigners walked into the Mohammedan streets, the boys pelted them with stones; if they walked outside the walls, they met armed men looking sternly at them as if marking them for plunder. Very little good was expected from religious discussion directly with Muslims. Few of them had knowledge enough, and fewer had the desire, to attempt a defence of their religion.

The Jews were somewhat better instructed and more accessible, but not less hardened against the truth than the Muslims. The latter believed in the divine mission of Christ as a prophet of the highest eminence next to Mohammed, but the Jews rejected him altogether. A Mohammedan effendi, a teacher of Mr. Fisk at Jerusalem, had a great aversion to the Jews. "Once," he said, "a Jew called on me at my house, and in conversation I asked him what he thought of *Said-na Esa* (our Lord Jesus). He said, 'He was a vile impostor.' I was so enraged at him that I was ready to stab him with my hanjar on the spot. As he was my *guest*, however, I could not do that, but I railed on him most angrily, called him an unclean beast and other foul names, and sent him away."

The Jews at Jerusalem are never offended at being addressed on the subject of their faith. They often affect great wisdom about it, such as they—that is, the learned among them—have got from the commentaries of their rabbies. Here is a specimen by Mr. Fisk: "The young Rabbi Isaac ben Schloma and Rabbi Yoosef Marcovitz, an old man of eighty, called at my room. Mr. Wolff was present, and acted as interpreter. I asked the Rabbi Marcovitz when he thought the Messiah would come. He looked very wise a little while, and then, changing his position, began to move his body backward and forward, as is customary with Jews in their synagogues and boys in their schools when they read. He then said there were two things about which it was not permitted to inquire: one was what took place before the foundation of the world; the other was *when the Messiah will come.* Daniel said, 'The time is sealed,' and what fool would presume to be wiser than Daniel?

"'But are there not Jews who *do* endeavor to ascertain the time when the Messiah will come?'

"'Yes; there are some such. But they are not upright. They are wicked Jews."

"'What is your opinion of the words of Israel in Gen. xlix. 10, the sceptre shall not depart from Judah till Shiloh come?'

"'Shiloh is the name of a place,' Rabbi Isaac said. 'The word in Genesis means the Messiah. When the word means a place, it is differently spelled.'

"The old man replied angrily, 'I have more understanding than you.'

"The Hebrew Bible was then brought and examined, and from more than twenty places the old man was proved to have less understanding than the younger."

A Caraite Jew of Jerusalem, one of the sect who follow the Scriptures alone, rejecting tradition, to whom Mr. Wolff had presented a Hebrew New Testament, afterwards came and expressed his gratitude, declaring that he really loved Jesus Christ. The Rabbies received the visits of the brethren kindly, but without any apparent desire either to convert or to be converted. They, as well as a large portion of their people, seemed to wish to die at the holy city, expecting some great spiritual advantage from having their dust mingled with that of David and Solomon and the holy prophets.

STATE OF MORALS IN JERUSALEM.

It would seem as if men endued with reason and reflection, dwelling in a place whose very name is holy, and where so many circumstances are fitted to keep alive a sense of the divine presence, would be remarkable for holy and devout living. But it is disappointing and distressing to every feeling heart to know that the very opposite is the case. Our friends had not sufficient time and experience at this their first visit to the city to become qualified to speak with full authority of the state of morals in the place. But beside what they had been told by others, a few specimens fell under their own observation. A Mohammedan, belonging, as many think, to the most honest class of the natives in Turkey, had sold them a certain manuscript for a few dollars and was paid on the spot. But thinking he might manage to obtain something more from the strangers, he went before the authorities of the city and accused them of keeping by force a book which he had only lent them to look at. The defendants were able to produce very credible witnesses that the bargain was fairly made and the article honorably paid for, so that the judge was ashamed to entertain the complaint, and would have subjected the man to the bastinado had not the strangers plead him off.

At another time, a man who was a Romanist was hired by them for a single week, and at the end of the time was paid his wages. In a day or two he re-appeared and told sorrowfully how he had found a hole in his pocket and his money was all lost. They pitied the man, and in whole or in part made up to him his misfortune. Soon after this an article of furniture was missing from one of the rooms and was found in this same man's possession. He steadfastly denied the theft and used many devices to clear himself, but at last made a full confession, laying all the blame upon the devil who had made him do it. Papas Esa, the tract and book translator, was applied to for a good trusty boy whom he could recommend to be employed for work about the house. He answered, "You can't find such a boy in all Jerusalem. They are all devils." A company excursion was arranged for visiting the Dead Sea and the Jordan. Men of Jerusalem were engaged at a rate of expense well understood by both parties. But these hired men contrived so to annoy the party who engaged them that by intimidation or otherwise they forced from the company a considerable sum above what was bargained for.

But what our travelers failed to discover in this present short stay in the city appeared from subsequent experience. The next year's visit of Mr. Fisk to Jerusalem was made in company with the Rev. William Jowett, of Malta. When that gentleman had finished his short visit in the city, he agreed with a respectable Muslim muleteer to take him and his baggage to Beirut, specifying how many and just what kind of animals he must have. The man understood it, and swore by his head it should be done as he wished. At the appointed hour Mohammed was at the door with his animals below waiting for the baggage. This was duly laid outside the door for him to take down to the yard and lash upon his animals. This done, he sent them forward with an attendant, while he himself would wait and follow on with the traveler. When Mr. Jowett overtook the animals and saw what sorry things they were, half angry at the cheat, he wheeled about and rode straight into the city without saying a word. Mohammed soon arrived at the door and found him resting at his ease on the sofa. One word was all he needed to explain the difficulty, and he disappeared. In about half an hour the Howadji was again called down, and finding all things set right, resumed his journey. In about twenty days Mohammed was again in Jerusalem. He brought to Mr. Fisk two papers, one of which was a recommendation for the bearer to future travelers, and the other a line to Mr. Fisk, in which Mr. Jowett, among other things, remarks: "I find Mohammed to be a very kind and serviceable ass when once you get the bits fairly in his mouth."

At a still later date, when Mr. Thomson, our missionary, commenced the building of a wall to enclose the American cemetery on Mt. Zion, he found the utmost difficulty in getting men to commence the work. He wrote that it was only after a desperate effort on their part to carry their point, and after being convinced to their full satisfaction that neither by flattery nor by threats nor by any deception they could cheat him out of his money, that they would go seriously to their business. "They showed a depth of depravity to which he never before supposed human nature could sink." He had with him a pious native assistant to oversee the work, who more than once came in expressing his utter astonishment that any such men could be found on the face of the earth.

But all this will seem a matter of less surprise when we consider the lack of preachers in Jerusalem and the example of the ecclesiastics. One of the Greek priests made the astonishing confession to Mr. Fisk that they had in Jerusalem a hundred Greek priests and monks, but among them all not a single preacher.

But this lack of preachers would not be so disastrous were it not for the demoralizing influence of the priestly example. Such were the abominations existing in the large Armenian convent in Jerusalem, that two of its chief bishops were constrained to leave it and repudiate their own vows of celibacy by marrying wives. The convent owed them for services debts of thousands of dollars, debts which the convent people repeatedly acknowledged before the government to be honestly due them, but payment was refused under the false plea of poverty.

The celebrated Greek fire, sent forth every year by the chief Greek bishop in Jerusalem, is manifestly an impious cheat on a large scale. It is a foul blot on the fair name of Christianity, and is enough to destroy all reverence for truth and honesty in the whole city. What marks this disgraceful exhibition as a dishonest farce is the fact that even the Greeks themselves, in Jerusalem, never put forth this pretended miracle as a proof of the divine character of the Christian religion, nor even as a proof of the orthodoxy of the Greek Church. It is only for the rabble. The thinking part of the people among them are ashamed of it. The character of the Latin convent has long been that of dark and bloody treachery. The leading men there have been Spaniards, and have a most unenviable reputation among the French and Italian members of their own fraternity. French and English travelers, however, make this convent their most common resort. Mr. Fisk was informed of a case in which an American traveler, coming from Marseilles in feeble health, took lodgings at that establishment, and was visited by a French physician either professionally or as a friend. One day this friend called and found the sick man had just received a letter from abroad which he was about to open and read after taking a little rest. He conversed as usual. Two hours after this the physician called again, and behold the man was dead and buried.

The monks pretended that the man had renounced Protestantism and become a good Catholic, not the least intimation of which had he given to his French friend. The latter disbelieved the whole story, and said if the man had really become a Catholic the mere funeral services could not have been performed in the short time that elapsed between his last two visits. But the monks prepared a tombstone with an epitaph, which is still read over the man's grave, informing all readers that this man, "repudiating all the errors of Luther and Calvin, died in the bosom of the Holy Roman Catholic Church." It had been noticed as remarkable, and not without unfavorable suspicions, that the reverendissimos and superintendents of the Propaganda convents had died one after another in very rapid succession. Plain hints of foul usage were frequently expressed by monks of other nationalities and Romish deputies themselves. A superior of the convent of Harissa, in the vicinity of Beirut, speaking one day of those Jerusalem friars, said as he put his hands upon his gaunt sides, "I should be loth to trust my poor body in their hands." Yet it so happened that that same body was, shortly after, summoned to Jerusalem, passed through the hands he had so much dreaded, and in not far from a twelvemonth he was safely lodged in his grave.

"What shall we do with these Spanish monks?" said Monsignor Gandolfi. "If we write to the Propaganda we get no answer to our applications. If we write to the pope neither will he vouchsafe any reply; and we cannot complain to the king of the French—he has become a monk himself."

Poor Gandolfi! After serving as the pope's legate forty years in Syria, and becoming thoroughly disgusted with the people, he was on the point of embarking for Italy. His movements as well as his sentiments were, no doubt, well known at Jerusalem. He would have been a fearful witness of the things he had seen and known in the Terra Sancta had he once reached Rome; but just in the nick of time, as he was about setting his foot upon his waiting vessel at Beirut, he was seized by some malady that suddenly terminated his life. An Italian priest said to Mr. Fisk that before he came into the holy land he had heard much of the Spanish friars as being most holy men without fault or blemish. But on coming among them he had found them the greatest rascals (bisbirri) on the face of the earth. They were a hypocritical and accursed "*nazione.*"

CHAPTER IV.

Journey to Beirut—Messrs. Way and Lewis at Sidon—Lady Hester Stanhope—Beirut—Emeer Besheer Antoora—Convents of Lebanon—Baalbec—Patriarch Jarwi—Residence of Mr. King at Deir el Kommer—Arrival of Messrs. Goodell and Bird.

DURING their visit of two months at Jerusalem the missionaries had distributed, chiefly among the pilgrims, by sale and otherwise, a hundred New Testaments and five thousand or more religious tracts.

The two Americans, leaving behind them their zealous brother Wolff, who thought he had not yet said all his last words to the Jews, commenced a land journey to Beirut by way of Jaffa and Sidon. On coming in sight of the latter place they spied an English ship of considerable size anchored off the town, which proved most unexpectedly to be a *missionary ship* commanded by a pious ex-admiral of the British navy, chartered and employed expressly to bring to these shores two English missionaries. They had come under the auspices of the London Jews' Society. One of them was the Rev. Lewis Way, a gentleman of wealth and engaged with much enthusiasm in the Jewish cause. He had left Sidon by land, and was occupying himself in fitting up an establishment for himself and his fellow-laborers in the vicinity of Beirut. His associate, however, the Rev. Mr. Lewis, was still at Sidon, and with him they spent a very agreeable Sabbath. The Rev. Jonas King, afterward eminent for his labors at Athens, on his way from

Paris to join Mr. Fisk at Malta, had passed through Marseilles, where he had been furnished by the British consul of that place with a letter of introduction to Lady Hester Stanhope, who was known to enjoy a queenly reputation in Syria, and being a niece of the younger William Pitt, was believed to partake of his partiality for Americans. Her residence being near to Sidon, Mr. King now sent a messenger to her ladyship, bearing Consul Turnbull's letter. When the Sabbath was past she sent her dragoman, Luigi Marone, to escort him to her dwelling. "She gave him a very favorable reception. They had a long conversation about America, about Syria, the Bible Society and religion," and finally she furnished him with letters of introduction to some of her native friends.

Whether this kind treatment of Mr. King was owing to his nationality, or to his natural suavity of manner, or to the sincere respect he manifested toward the granddaughter of the Earl of Chatham, certain it is that the interview was of a kind that could not have been calculated upon. Neither the Stanhopes nor the Pitts, with all their fame for statesmanship, seem to have been very friendly to religion, and as for Lady Hester herself, her prejudices were very strong against it. The author of the book *Eothen*, whose mother Lady Hester remembered as "a sweet, lovely girl" of her acquaintance in England, and who, on his mother's account, was indulged with repeated familiar chats with her ladyship at her establishment, represents her as religious in no sense but what consisted with an overruling belief in magic, sorcery and astrology. Her antipathy to the Bible was such that she refused a call from Mr. Benjamin Barker simply because he was in the employ of the Bible Society, while he was of a family for all of whose members she professed the highest respect. Her treatment of Mr. Wolff was an outrage. This zealous convert from Judaism, after finishing his message to the Jews at Jerusalem, followed his two American brethren to the parts about Lebanon. At Sidon he sent a note to Miss Williams, Lady Stanhope's maid of honor, to say to her that the letters she had entrusted to his care, when here before, he had safely delivered into the hands of her friends in Malta, and that those friends were in good health. Without thanking him for his politeness, Miss Williams replied that she had her positive orders not to have any communication with him, and that her ladyship was thinking of issuing a circular to all her friends in the land respecting these " wandering gentlemen," to say that her ladyship *disowned them all.*

But, not fully satisfied with the reply prepared by Miss Williams, her ladyship accompanied it with a note of her own, more adapted, in her view, to the aggravations of the case. It was couched in the following terms:

"I am astonished that an apostate should dare to thrust himself into observation in my family. Had you, whose real name I know not, been a *learned* Jew, never could you have abandoned a religion rich in itself, yet defective, to embrace a shadow of one. Light travels faster than sound; therefore the Supreme Being could never have allowed his creatures to remain in utter darkness for nearly two thousand years, until paid speculating wanderers might think it proper to lift their venal voice to enlighten them.

"HESTER LUCY STANHOPE."

To this note Mr. Wolff mildly replied:

"I have just received a letter which bears your ladyship's signature, but I find it difficult to believe it genuine. As any communication with your ladyship's family proceeded from kindly feelings toward the friends of Miss Williams, I am at a loss to understand the meaning of your ladyship in saying that I wished to thrust myself into observation, as your ladyship's name was not even alluded to in my letter. With respect to my religious views and pursuits, I feel perfectly at rest, and they must be quite immaterial to your ladyship. My religious principles, however, would never permit me to insult persons whom I never saw, and they enable me to assure your ladyship that I always wish your ladyship happiness, and I have the honor to be," etc.

This letter was despatched by a Turkish messenger, unsealed. The Turk was beaten by her ladyship's order and the letter returned.*

Passing on to the important commercial city of Beirut, the two missionaries were accommodated with rooms in the convent of the Capuchins.† They had scarcely become rested, however, in their comfortable

---

* Lady H. was not, as some have supposed, a daughter, but only a distant relative, of the celebrated Philip Dormer Stanhope, commonly known as Lord Chesterfield. The first Earl of Chesterfield was Philip Stanhope, two of whose sons were named, severally, Henry and Alexander. Charles Stanhope, the father of Lady H., was a grandson of Henry, and Philip D. a grandson of Alexander. Charles Stanhope is described as "a *very eccentric man*, a great mechanical genius and a republican." Some of Lady H.'s peculiarities seem to have come to her by inheritance.

† The Capuchins compose a Romish religious order, wearing outwardly a long coarse garment girt round with a rope, and having a peculiar *caput* or hood which gives the order its name. Their convents in Syria are very few.

quarters before there arrived from the same direction the reverendissimo, or padre superior of all the convents belonging to the congregation of the Terra Santa; it was therefore, of course, required that they should give this man place. They had known this Roman dignitary at Jerusalem, and now they took occasion to renew their acquaintance and to hold converse with him on religious themes.

The brethren having made the acquaintance of the Greek bishop at Beirut, and of the English and other consuls, prepared themselves to visit his excellency the Emeer Besheer, the governor in chief of the mountains of Lebanon. They had already seen the prince in Egypt. At that interview he had condescended to invite them to visit him when they should arrive in Syria. And now, as they were expecting to spend some months in Syria among his people, it seemed every way expedient to comply with his invitation.

The prince had some special reasons for showing favor to Englishmen (and such our two travelers were recognized to be by the authorities), for he had once been rescued by an English admiral* from danger, and perhaps from death, when he had fallen under the displeasure of that barbarian Jezzar Pasha. He received their call in a friendly manner, though thronged with callers on business, and gave them passports for traveling or residing in any part of the mountains under his jurisdiction.

The Emeer Besheer was no common man. When a young man, Jezzar Pasha, having heard of him, invited him to Acca, and was charmed with his manners, appearance and address, "for," says his biographer, "he

* Sir Sidney Smith in 1799.

EMEER BESHEER.

was the most noble and majestic-looking prince of his day." His first step toward power displayed an ominous vigor. He gave battle to his uncle at Deir el Kommer, and drove him from his seat of power quite out of the mountain, taking that seat himself in undisturbed possession.

"So complete was the mastery he obtained over the turbulent feudatories of Lebanon, and so strict the etiquette he exacted, that all the emeers and sheikhs, both Druze and Christian, who came to pay him their respects, stood with folded arms before him until he invited them to be seated, and until the invitation was repeated a second or third time. The effect produced by his personal appearance was of itself sufficient to reduce the most rebellious spirit to abject submission. On entering his divan you would see a venerable-looking man sitting on his heels, leaning against a cushion, with thick, shaggy brows overhanging eyes replete with fire and vivacity, and a broad, massive beard reaching down to his waist. The tone of his voice was deep, hollow and sonorous, and few if any of the great men of the mountain could stand before him without trembling."

Messrs. King and Fisk were next found in company with the Rev. Mr. Way, at the village of Antoora near Beirut. Mr. Way, having come to the belief that the Jews were on the eve of a return to their native or fatherland, had made the voyage hither with the hope of being able, in some capacity, to facilitate this desirable object.

His attention had been directed to an old building at Antoora, once occupied as a Jesuit college, but now quite forsaken and dilapidated. He was fitting it up, at considerable expense, to be a centre of operations for all

Protestant religious societies. It is very questionable whether any important benefit would have resulted from the plan of Mr. Way had he been able to remain and superintend its execution, but his expectations were suddenly cut off by his rapidly-declining health. After a six weeks' visit to the land of which he had thought and spoken so much, and where he had hoped to view with his own eyes some magnificent displays of the divine glory, he found himself obliged to leave it in the same vessel which had brought him.

Mr. King now took a station for study at Deir el Kommer,* while Messrs. Fisk and Wolff—the latter having arrived from Jerusalem—remained a while at Antoora.

This small village belongs to the district of Lebanon called Kesru-án, where, as well as in the mountainous region farther north, there is a multiplicity of papal convents. The brethren were disposed to ascertain by experiment in what estimation the Scriptures were held in these religious establishments and to learn whatever else might be known respecting them. They therefore made visits to several of those in the neighborhood, to Mar Hanna esh Shu-éir, Harissa, Bkoorki, Sharfi, Bzum-már, Bshâra and Mar Elee-as. At some of these places they disposed of some copies of the Scriptures and enjoyed profitable opportunities for religious discussion.

Mar Hanna belonged to the papal Greeks, and was occupied by thirty or forty monks. About the year 1750 this convent became possessed of a printing establishment, introduced by Abdallah Zaw-khir, and by this

---

* An engraving of this interesting spot will be found in the latter part of this volume. See "List of Illustrations."

press have been printed nearly all the Arabic books now used in their churches. Mr. Fisk tried to have a few unobjectionable tracts printed there, but was unsuccessful. Bkoorki was but a short walk from Antoora. It was a somewhat spacious building, but chiefly in ruins, and only remarkable for what it had been. It was erected for a nunnery by a fanatical woman called Hendeeye, who finally lost entirely the confidence of the public, and was obliged to flee the neighborhood to escape the indignation of her own sect. Harissa belonged to the Terra Santa congregation of Rome, and was built with massive stone walls of a sufficient thickness to stand the siege of a castle, having twenty or thirty rooms, but inhabited by a single solitary Franciscan monk. During a late disturbed state of the country the British consul, John Barker, Esq., resorted to it as the safest asylum he could find from surrounding dangers. Sharfi was one of the only two convents on Lebanon belonging to the papal Syrians under the notorious new patriarch Jarwi, who himself was at that time residing at his other establishment, a day's journey distant. Here at Sharfi was the aged metropolitan Simon, late patriarch of the sect, and now seventy-five years of age, together with another bishop and a priest. They said that the press, types and paper procured by Bishop Jarwi in England were now in this convent, but the patriarch had at Mar Ephram the key of the room which contained them. It was the outdoor report that the present patriarch had supplanted Simon, the late patriarch, by means of the money he obtained in England. The brethren here gave away four copies of the Scriptures and had a long discussion on religious topics. A sheikh of the neighborhood, who was present listening, sided with the missionaries, saying a number of times, "that's so." The bishop afterwards wrote to his visitors for more Scriptures.

At Bzum-már the missionaries found the papal Armenian patriarch Gregory, two bishops and two priests, with twenty young men, studying for the ministry. Two or three of the ecclesiastics spoke Italian. The branches studied in this theological school were said to be grammar, rhetoric, logic, metaphysics and theology, but chiefly in books translated from Latin or Italian. Some pupils studied Arabic and Turkish. A long discussion was had with the bishops about popery, in which the patriarch took little or no part. He seemed a jolly sort of man, preferring to shift off the discussion of religious subjects upon his bishops and priests, as if he had done with all such matters, having taken a degree beyond them.* Fifteen books were sold at this convent, but in a private way, lest, as the purchasers said, the patriarch should take offence.

The nunnery of Bshâra was of the papal Greek denomination. It had twenty-two inmates, beside, in another apartment of the building, two priests, who conducted the religious services of the institution. They accepted a Bible, a New Testament and a Book of Genesis. There was a very marked difference between the spirit manifested here and that which appeared in the Maronite nunnery in the immediate vicinity, called Mar Elee-as. This latter had four priests and forty nuns. When a Bible was offered for the use of the nuns, one of the priests objected, saying there were mistakes in the book. Being challenged to prove it, he went and brought

---

* When subsequently the persecuted Shidiak visited this prelate for advice and instruction, one of the priests whispered in his ear, "If you want to know good tobacco, go to the patriarch."

his own Arabic Bible, and found the two were precisely alike. He was confounded and fell into a violent passion, railing vehemently against the Protestants for rejecting the Christian doctrines, particularly the seven sacraments, and often quoting St. Augustine. When Mr. Fisk called his attention repeatedly to the words of Christ and asked, "What need have we of St. Augustine?" he replied, "What need have we of Christ?" The anger of the man was quieted at last by the interference of another priest. The visitors, having made another ineffectual attempt to introduce a copy of the Scriptures, took their leave.

Messrs. Fisk, King and Way made an excursion over the mountains by way of Tripoli, Canobeen and the Cedars. At Tripoli, two days north of Beirut, on the sea-coast, they opened their boxes of sacred merchandise, and the people, after manifesting a good deal of timidity, at last ventured to buy a hundred books for twenty dollars. One Turk bought a Bible, another a New Testament, and a third a New Testament and a copy of Genesis. In the evening the brethren sought an interview with the Greek bishop of the place, who received them kindly. The next day, breaking off at a right angle from the sea-coast, they set out for the mountains, and in nine hours came to the Convent of Kos-hy-a. Its site was on the almost perpendicular side of a mountain, at the bottom of a frightful chasm, and it contained about a hundred Maronite monks. They seemed dirty, stupid and ignorant. Not more than one-fourth of them could read. They had a press with which they printed their church books in Syriac, and in Arabic with Syriac letters. This last they call *Carshoon* printing. They had no Arabic type. When the superior was asked about his belief in the Scriptures, he gave the usual stereotyped reply: "I believe what the Church believes." One of the priests revealed something of the extent of his knowledge of the gospel by asserting that St. Paul, before being converted to Christianity, was a pagan. The travelers spent a Sabbath with this untaught company of people, and had with some of them very long conversations, not without effect, for one of them declared in private his conviction that the Protestant views of Christian doctrine were right.

The next place of interest was the Convent of Canobeen, the summer residence of the Maronite patriarch. "We first ascended a very steep mountain," says Mr. Fisk, "and then descended one of the steepest I ever attempted to pass. The road turns so often as nearly to double the distance, and yet it is almost impassable for steepness. We often crossed narrow ways, with a stupendous precipice above us of immense rocks piled upon each other almost perpendicularly, and with a similar precipice below us." The newly-elected patriarch received them civilly. Simple-minded man! he had not yet learned what ravening wolves were concealed beneath the harmless-looking sheep he was beholding. He even ventured to accept at their hands the gift of an Arabic Bible and a Syriac New Testament.*

From Canobeen the travelers proceeded to the village of Eh-he-den, distant a couple of hours, where they spent the night with the liberal-minded sheikh Lattoof. They found Eh-he-den to be one of the most elevated,

---

* He estimated the Maronite nation at one hundred to one hundred and fifty thousand souls. They had forty or fifty convents and ten or twelve bishops. The priests are by others reckoned to be about one thousand, and the monks and nuns at sixteen hundred.

flourishing and beautiful villages of the mountains, and might well be called what its name rather suggests—the Eden or Paradise of Lebanon. The aged sheikh had in the course of his life been considerably occupied in business transactions with French residents in Tripoli, and was able to hold conversation in that language, but his subjects were all bigoted Maronites. No books were sold here, and no free conversations were had among the people.

The next night the brethren were entertained at the house of Sheikh Girgis, of Besherry, whose generous and cordial hospitality reminded them more than anything they had hitherto met with of the noble treatment of strangers by Arabs of which they had read.

The brethren had now to some extent explored the two extremes of the Maronite population—the Kesru-án district and the Gíb-bee—and had reached the northern boundary of the Emeer Besheer's dominions. And here stands, like a venerable monument, the only clump of ancient Lebanon cedars that has been saved from the devouring tooth of time and the woodman's axe. Other trees of the same kind, of more recent growth, are found in different places, which are freely used, as needed, for timber or for fuel, but these are held by the people in religious reverence, and are likely to continue increasing in size and in number for ages yet to come. They are clustered together within a circumference of less than a mile at the foot of some of the very highest ridges of Lebanon, which sweep around them like the seats of an amphitheatre. Their number, on being counted, was found to be more than three hundred, of all heights and sizes, from the very lowest to those of ninety feet in height and near forty in circumference. The fruit of the trees is a large scaly truncated cone like those of the pine, but barrel-shaped, and grows upward from the upper side of the branches. The body of the cedar is straight and sends out horizontal branches, shortening as they ascend, till the top of the tree is the point of a cone.

Passing eastward, the travelers found themselves in half an hour on the other side of the mountain ridge, descending into Coelosyria, the hollow or plain of Syria, now called by the natives the Bkaá. In the south-east, twenty miles or more distant, were visible the ruins of Baalbec, to which they were now directing their course. They did not reach the place that day, but tarried for the night at a miserable, dirty village called Dyah el Ahhmar, or the red village, and put up for the night in a mean, dirty room with the earth for a floor.

Baalbec, as a village, is at present quite insignificant, and is inhabited by Muslims of the sect called Metawallies. Originally it was called by the Greeks Heliopolis, the city of the sun. It is situated on the eastern border of the vast plain called the Valley of Baalbec. Being watered by a copious fountain gushing forth from the foot of Antilebanon, and having at its door the products of an immense fertile plain, it was once a large and powerful metropolis. Its fame in modern times has been due to the colossal and imperishable ruins of its temple. Mr. Fisk, at his present visit, took an accurate measurement of the walls of this temple and of the stupendous materials of which they were composed. At the north-west corner of the outer wall were twelve or fifteen stones thirty feet long by ten or twelve in breadth and height, or three thousand solid feet or more each. Three other stones were of the same breadth and height and fifty-eight in length, and one other of the length of sixty-eight feet. Moreover, this huge block of stone, of the size of a small farm-house, was found inserted in the wall on the top of three tiers of stones each fifteen feet in height. Who lifted it and adjusted it in its place in the wall forty-five feet above its foundation? The natives said it was the work of angels. A block still larger than any of the above was found at the quarry close by, hewn out on three sides, but never detached from the rock of which it formed a part.

Within the outer enclosure were great numbers of ornamental columns, some of which were yet standing, others lying prostrate, whose pedestals, however, still remained in their places. In the southern part of the enclosed area was a small temple by itself exquisitely adorned with carvings.

From Baalbec the party turned westward by way of Záhh-leh, where they spent a night, and the next day ended the week, Saturday evening, at Deir er Rugm, otherwise called Mar Ephrâm. This convent has already been mentioned as one of the two establishments of the kind belonging to the papal Syrians of the mountains. The new patriarch, Peter Jarwi, was at the time making the place his residence. The precious flock of this "chief shepherd," as he called himself, consisted, so far as Mount Lebanon was concerned, of one ex-patriarch, a bishop and priest at Deir Sharfeh, and eight or ten priests and monks at Mar Ephrâm, a flock of thirteen all told. He, however, professed to have one other bishop in Beirut, two in Aleppo and two more in Mesopotamia. He was building an addition to his convent and pretended that he still expected to put his press in operation. He denied that he went to England to ask help from the Protestants, but said they gave of their own accord and without conditions as to how the money should be expended. He expressed gratitude to Mr. Clymer, the American who gave him the printing press, but none to the English who gave him the money.

In his doctrinal views the patriarch showed himself a thorough-bred papist, saying that under the form of bread the laity receive the blood as well as the body of Jesus Christ, because that which was given them was his true, living body which could not be without blood, saying also that outside the Romish Church there could be no salvation, that the English had no priesthood, and that all these efforts of various societies to convert Jews, Turks, etc., would be found useless. His treatment of these guests of his was nothing more than cold civility. During the Sabbath they had no small disputation with the monks. Sometimes nearly all of them were present. "We told them," says Mr. Fisk, "some plain truths about their popish doctrines and practices, such, I suspect, as they never heard before."

Returning to Antoora the brethren visited the neighboring Armenian convent of Krym* and the ancient Maronite college of Ain Waraka, which is the chief school for the higher branches among the people of that sect, and is under the personal control of the patriarch. In company with the Rev. Mr. Jowett from Malta, Mr. Fisk made a second call at the convent of Bzum-már. They carried with them Bibles and Testaments, of which they sold near twenty dollars' worth. Mr. Fisk says: "I have seen no convent so good or so neat as

---

* This convent also, like that of Bzum-már, had a school for young men. The only other Armenian convent in Lebanon is Beit Kháshbo, an hour's walk or more northward from Krym.

Bzum-már, nor have I anywhere on the mountains met with men of equal talents and acquisitions. They are clever, enterprising and persevering."

Mr. King on arriving in the region of Beirut took up his residence at Deir el Kommer, where he could study and speak and hear nothing but Arabic. This place, though it may fall a little below its rival Záhh-leh in its population, was nevertheless very properly called the capital of the mountains, as being in the immediate vicinity of the seat of government at Bteddeen. The record of the toleration and mild treatment of Mr. King in this large village is interesting as showing in what light Protestantism was viewed by the natives and with what effect it fell upon the mass of popish minds to which it was then first presented. A few incidents only of this record can be introduced here.

Mr. King one day went to the church to witness the baptism of a child. After he had returned home a considerable number of women came in from the church and took seats also with the family. On finding himself in such a company of veiled females he felt out of place and rose to leave the room, but they at once objected, and laying aside their veils begged him to resume his seat. They acknowledged that they were not acting after the stricter social customs of the place, but from what they heard of him they considered him an exception among men, and so they made him no stranger, but a friend. Mr. King improved the occasion to impress upon them some religious truth, and as they had come from witnessing a baptism he took the New Testament and read and expounded to them the beginning of the third chapter of John about the new birth. They all listened with earnest attention, and begged to know if he would not put on the black dress and become their curate.

At another time he took up a church book that contained what was said in the caption to be "The Ten Commandments as they were written on tables of stone and given to Moses." On examination he found that nothing was said in these commandments about making or worshiping graven images or other likenesses. The word "Sabbath" was turned into "the first day and the feast days," and the tenth commandment was divided into two. This to Mr. King seems to have been a new discovery. He was well aware of the perversions which popery had made of other parts of Scripture, but that it would enter the holy of holies, violate the ark and take such liberties with the tables of the covenant, and withal give out that no change had been made, was a piece of audacity of which he had not before suspected even Rome herself to be guilty.

"Soon after I had read this," says Mr. King, "the superior of the convent came in, and I remarked to him what I had read, and observed that these were not the Ten Commandments *as delivered to Moses;* that there was still another commandment not found here. He seemed angry, and tried to make me believe that I was under a mistake. I told him it was in vain for him to try to do that, for I had read the ten commandments in Hebrew, and that everybody knew that there was another commandment which says, 'Thou shalt not make unto thee any graven image, nor any likeness of anything,' etc. I really felt so indignant that any man should dare to take away one of the commandments of God, that I told the priest plainly it was an impious thing and a lie to say that these were the ten commandments of God as *God gave them to Moses* while the second was entirely left out, the fourth one changed and the tenth divided." His teacher then put in *his* voice, saying, "If these were the commandments of the church, they were the commandments of God." Mr. King replied that this was not true, for that some of the popes had said one thing and others had said the opposite, and could they both be from God? But the teacher would not believe that the priests had kept back the second commandment, and said he would bring a Jew and inquire of him whether such a commandment was in the Jewish books. He saw it was in Mr. King's Bible, but that was printed in England; it might be false. He sent for a Bible printed at Rome, which must be true. Mr. King opened it at the place and told him to read, and to his astonishment he found the truth had been told him.

At one time a priest from the village called and introduced the question whether Mary were the mother of any other children beside Jesus. Mr. King gave some reasons to believe that she was. "God forbid!" said the priest; "God pardon us!" Saying this, he left the room in anger and went and took his seat with the family and began to talk against Mr. King in a great rage for attempting to blast the reputation of Mary. Mr. King rose to go to him. His teacher, fearing a quarrel, begged him not to go; but he went, and taking a seat beside him, said mildly, "Aboona, I wish to say one thing. We profess to be disciples of Christ, to be his followers; it does not become us to speak with anger. Christ was humble, and when men opposed him he did not fall into a passion."

"True," said the priest.

Mr. King proceeded: "Here now are Muslims around us and many who do not believe in Jesus Christ. Let us show to them that we are Christians by our love one to another and by our meekness. If I am in the dark I wish to be enlightened. I do not wish to remain in darkness and go to destruction."

"While I said this," says Mr. King, "the eyes of all were fastened on us and the whole house was silent. The padre seemed confused and ashamed, and said, 'What you say is true.'"

Mr. King then added, "I have one question to ask you, Aboona, and then I have done. When the Lord Jesus Christ commissioned his disciples to go and preach, what did he tell them to preach, himself or his mother? and what *did* they preach? They preached Jesus Christ and him crucified, salvation through his blood and intercession alone—*not one word about Mary*. There is not one syllable in all the epistles of Paul and the other apostles about Mary."

All present listened attentively, and the priest said calmly, "When you become well acquainted with Arabic, I shall be glad to converse with you more."

Upon the arrival from America of Messrs. Goodell and Bird with their families at Beirut, Mr. King bid adieu, though not a final one, to his kind friends in Deir el Kommer that he might come to the aid of his new associates. The circumstances attending his departure he thus describes:

"A little before I left them the family appeared very sorrowful, and some of them wept. The mother wept much, and the priest with whom I had often conversed sobbed like a child. I improved this occasion to tell the priest his duty as a pastor, and spoke of the great day of account, the responsibility that rested on him and his duty to search the Scriptures. The family I exhorted to prepare for death and the solemn scenes of eternity, to love the Lord Jesus Christ, to read the word of God and have regard to *all* his ten commandments.

"It was truly an interesting scene, and I was surprised to see the feeling they manifested. As I left the house they loaded me with blessings, and as I passed through the street many commended me to the care and protection of the Lord."

CHAPTER V.

Bishop Monsignor Gandolfi at Beirut—A Maronite priest—Departure of two of the brethren for Jerusalem—Visits at Sidon, Tyre, Bossa, Acca, Nazareth, Nablus and Jerusalem.

AS for us new-comers who were waiting for the arrival of our brother from the mountains, we found it a great gratification and relief, on entering among this people of new customs and of a strange language, to be met by an old acquaintance with whom in our own land we had often taken sweet counsel and gone to the house of God in company. He was dressed in Arab style, with loose robes and a thick, venerable beard, and streams of Arabic were flowing from his lips as he addressed himself to the natives around him. It was quite evident that since commencing his work in the land he had made good use of his time and his tongue.

On the third evening after our landing we had the opportunity of spending an hour in company with the pope's vicar, Monsignor Gandolfi, of Antoora. He had come down from his mountain residence to perform the marriage ceremony of the French consul and his bride. This being over, he had called in for an evening's chat with his familiar friends, Consul Abbott and his lady, at whose house we had been hitherto hospitably entertained. The opinions of this papal high priest and the freedom with which he avowed them astonished us. He was utterly sick of Syria. He was seventy-four years old and had lived in the country thirty-nine years. The sufferings he had undergone during his residence here no one could tell nor would any one believe. Once he was assaulted, threatened and stabbed at by the Druzes; often had he struggles with injustice, hypocrisy and baseness of every kind, such as had destroyed all his confidence

THE REV. JONAS KING, D.D., IN ORIENTAL COSTUME.

in the people. The Spirit of God had long since left them. Various were the sects and parties that had resorted to him as umpire in their endless disputes, and so great had been the numbers whom he had been obliged to entertain at his house that his salary had been quite insufficient to save him from poverty. He sold one farm some time ago to meet his necessary expenses, and now more lately he had been forced to dispose of another. For a number of years past the Catholic missions here had been neglected by the church, and for himself he would leave the country as soon as he conveniently could. The English travelers who had called on him had always given him pleasure, and the American Protestants had been objects of his cordial friendship from the first of his acquaintance with them. But this native people were of a different stamp. This *terra santa*, this land of holiness, had become a *land of devils*. It was no longer the *blessed*, but the *accursed*, land. He had had transactions of various kinds with princes and people of all grades, with patriarchs, bishops, priests, monks and laymen, and *not one man of integrity had he found among them all!*

The intention of the two newly-arrived families had been to push directly on to Jerusalem and at once take up their permanent station at that city. But the winter storms had begun, and our advisers, especially the consul, who knew the country and the climate best, said that for families like ours to undertake a journey of two hundred miles, in such a country and at such a season, was quite out of the question. We accordingly proceeded to obtain a home for the winter at Beirut. Mr. King took up his quarters for a time with us.

One evening, soon after we had entered our new habitation, we received a visit from a near neighbor, a Maronite priest whose name was Simeon. His white beard and solemn demeanor impressed us with veneration. He brought with him, as a sort of introduction, a present for the ladies of two beautiful young pigeons, white as the snow of Lebanon. In return we offered him a copy of the Arabic Bible, but he refused to accept it as a present, saying it would not be right before God to do so; it was a good book and worth paying for, and we were good people for bringing such good books into the country. He then took out a Spanish dollar and said he should feel better to give that for the book than to receive it as a gift. This was probably the first time that he, though a priest and a man of three-score years and ten, had ever possessed the entire Bible, and this was the first time that a native Syrian had been known to insist on paying for it.

The next day it was discovered that the two white pigeons had found means to escape from their place of confinement and had fled. But in the evening, behold, our very reverend neighbor the priest makes a second call, bringing the little escaped prisoners in his arms. When we had thanked him anew for his kindness, he said, in a meek and serious manner, "When the infant Jesus was brought to the temple, and the aged Simeon took him in his arms and blessed him, the parents of the child, being poor, had nothing to bring but a pair of turtle-doves or two young pigeons, and when I heard of the arrival of these two good women I asked myself, 'What have I to bring them?' and being poor, I could think of nothing but these two young pigeons."

As we had had no reason to expect so special a mark of attention from a Maronite priest, we considered it the more binding on us to reciprocate his friendly advances. Accordingly, we called on him a few days after and found him living quite alone in a solitary upper chamber, the entire furniture of which consisted of three old pipes, a native lamp of coarse pottery, a mat on which he was sitting, a small box and two or three other articles of little value. All that we saw might be purchased new in the market for less than five Spanish dollars. According to the ancient custom of his church, and which papal policy connives at in favor of the Maronites, though a priest, he had been married. A son of his was now residing near Antoora, and a daughter in Deir el Kommer. Our call upon him was short, and he was a man so studious of peace that no serious discussion was indulged in. Our acquaintance with the old man thus pleasantly begun lasted unchanged for many years. He was a rare specimen of a Romish priest. In his professions of regard for us we always believed him sincere. Though obliged to conform somewhat to the persecuting measures of his superiors, he evidently sympathized in heart more with *us* than with *them*.

One Sabbath day, on returning from our worship at the consul's, we found the owner of our house, a Muslim, seated on the sofa, having called to pay his friendly respects. His attendant, a papal Greek, had taken up the Arabic Bible he had found upon the table and was reading it to his master. Mr. King, having received the book, turned to the history of Joseph and read a portion of the story, and told the rest in his own words. Seeing the Mohammedan interested he proceeded to give him a brief summary of the true Christian faith, saying we believe truly, as do the Muslims, that there is *no god but God,* that we worship only the one living and true God, that we consider it profane to worship pictures or saints or angels, that we never go to a priest to obtain forgiveness of our sins, but only to God himself, and so on. The Muslim declared it was all good, and turning to the man whom he had brought with him he began to reproach him as an idolater for bowing down before images and praying to saints. "You are all wrong," said he; "all going astray. One Englishman is worth fifty of you." Mr. King frequently encountered Muslims in the streets and at their shops, and had religious conversation with them with uniform good nature and evident good effect.

The Rev. Mr. Jowett, returning from Jerusalem, whither he had gone in company with Mr. Fisk, was invited to a home at our house. In giving us an account of his travels, he said he had made his journey with very little precaution and entirely without arms. Once he was stopped, but without any threatened danger either to life or limb. Turks, he said, were afraid of Englishmen, and intimidation was the only way in which you could obtain good treatment from them; you will not get it by flattery. The English are safe here, but for the natives there is no security for a single day. At Acca constant exactions were laid upon the people, as if the government were making the experiment to see how much they would bear, and it was really astonishing how much they *would* bear. But in these levies upon the people there was no partiality. Muslims had to take their share as well as Jews and Christians. Some few days ago twenty-five Muslims at Acca were soundly bastinadoed for attempting to make their escape from the oppressions of the city. When a new governor lately arrived at Jerusalem many of the most respectable inhabitants went before him in their tattered garments and made such a representation of their distress that the Turk was affected to tears. "But," replied he,

"I can do nothing for you, nor can you expect any better state of things at present, for even your brothers, whom I have just left at Constantinople, are no better off than you." Some of the poor monks at Jerusalem were in great tribulation, and lived as if they had the impression that the government might the next day send for their heads.

That our associate, Mr. Fisk, might not dwell alone at Jerusalem, and that a practical examination might be made to ascertain the feasibility of a removal of one or both of our missionary families to the city or neighborhood of Jerusalem, it was concluded that Mr. Bird with Mr. King should repair for a while to that city.

On the morning of the 2d of January, 1824, we who were set apart for the journey were in readiness. Mr. Jowett read a portion of the 20th chapter of the Acts, and we all kneeled down and prayed; and so, being recommended by the brethren unto the grace of God, we departed. We halted on the Sabbath at Sidon, where we were entertained by the English agent, Yacob Abcarius, or, as he was more commonly called, Yacob Aga. This man had formerly been an archbishop in the Armenian church, and as such was held in high estimation by his sect. He had spent years in the national convent in the holy city, as well as at Echmiazeen, the ecclesiastical metropolis of his nation. Endowed by nature with a fine personal appearance, dignified in his deportment, well gifted in mind and rather fond of public life, he had been promoted to the episcopacy, and had enjoyed the confidence of his church to that extent that he had been selected on some occasions to conduct their diplomatic concerns at the capital. But becoming utterly disgusted with the corruptions of the clergy and convinced of their errors in doctrine he gave them up, married a wife at Beirut and accepted the office of an agent under the English consul.*

At Tyre we were received and "lodged two days courteously" by a brother-in-law of Mr. King's late teacher in Deir el Kommer. His wife was a prodigy in the land because she was able *to read*. Among the ruins of this famous city we observed a magnificent column of red Egyptian granite. It would have been removed long ago to Acca to grace some new structure in that city, but its giant size was too great for any modern Pasha to lift. It formed the best part of a native garden wall. It lay in near connection with the high walls still standing of some vast church or cathedral, conjectured by some to be that known to have been built here by Constantine and consecrated by Eusebius of Cæsarea, father of church history.

Near Acca (or Acre) we found it convenient to spend a night in a small village called Bossa, on the left of the direct road to Acca. In the evening the muleteers

---

* His former life, in one respect, had not been without reproach. But in this particular his conduct would not suffer in comparison with that of his ecclesiastical compeers in the best standing; nor was he complained of for this delinquency until he began his approach toward a reformation by becoming the husband of one wife. For the public services he had rendered to the church he had accepted a reward of two or three thousand dollars. He afterwards lent this money, at high interest, to the convent at Jerusalem and lived upon the income. After paying the interest several years the convent suddenly stopped payment, not because it was not due, but under the sole plea of poverty. Yet a respectable English traveler, who passed this way in 1827, has ventured to characterize this man as "one of the rascally converts of the missionaries who had run away with the money of his convent."

and the people whom the arrival of strangers had attracted together sat and heard with attention what Mr. King had to say to them, while he read the New Testament and expounded it by order unto them. One of our men, an old Muslim, often exclaimed, "truth," "truth," "that's a man of wisdom," "as for us, we are all beasts." Two or three others gave signs of their interest by using the common exclamation, "Lord have mercy upon us."

In the morning we set off for Acca, proceeding directly west. We had scarcely got clear from the houses of the village before we began to hear calls from behind. We turned and saw a little troop of people streaming out from the village in haste to overtake us. One of them was the priest of the village. They had heard that we carried the gospel and other books to be disposed of. They wished to see them. While they were opening and examining them, kissing our hands and gazing at us wonderingly, a poor blind man came picking his way carefully along, and as soon as he came to the crowd he began to exhort his townsmen, saying with lifted voice: "Buy the gospel, my friends, buy it—it will do you good." He reminded us of the blind son of Timeus, who, in the face of the crowd at Jericho, manifested in a loud voice his faith in "Jesus the son of David." The people took a number of copies of the Book of Genesis, the Psalms and New Testament. The priest wanted the entire Bible, but we could only refer him to our dépôt in Acca, telling him the price would be five piasters. He said "all right."

After Mr. King had exhorted them to study the word of God attentively and expressed his hope that it would make them wise unto salvation, we continued on our way. In a very few hours we were in the house over which waved the flag of England in the city of Acca.

The most ancient name of this city was written in Hebrew, *Aco*, the middle letter being marked as double. Judges i. 31. Strabo (B. C. 50) wrote the name in Greek, Ak-e; the native Arabs now call it Acca or Akkeh. Ptolemy I., King of Egypt and Syria (B. C. 300), gave the city the new name of Ptolemais, but this, though common in the time of our Saviour, was probably never fully adopted by the people of the country, and has long since gone out of use.

It is the only well-fortified city on the Syrian coast, and has perhaps the best harbor, though this latter is not much to say. In the history of the Crusades it occupies a very prominent position. The Knights of St. John made it their stronghold. Here, in the year 1291, after having been driven from every other spot in the land, they were besieged by the exasperated Sultan Ashraf, and the whole garrison of twelve thousand men are said to have perished either in the stormy sea as they attempted to get on board their ships, or by being struck down with the sword of their conquerors.*

Our sense of security from the savage-looking men without made some amends for the eccentricities and cold reserve we met with from our sub-consular host, Mr. M., who seemed to take special pains to show his antipathy to everything religious. We visited a school in the city where we found in the teacher another mem-

* Napoleon Bonaparte besieged the place in 1799, but the garrison, aided by the English navy under Sir Sidney Smith, made a successful defence. Ibrahim Pasha took the city by assault in May, 1832, and in the name of the sultan the combined fleets of Austria and England retook it November 3, 1840.

ber of the priesthood. He was seated, cudgel in hand, giving out various orders to a company of forty spirited Arab boys. The clamor of the lads and the still more powerful voice of the teacher were almost deafening. Mr. King begged leave to address a few words to the school, which was granted. He spoke to them briefly on the value of the Bible, which was the word of God, saying that all Christian children ought to read it; that all would be judged by it, and therefore ought to regulate their lives by it; that all persons were bound to love in their hearts our Lord Jesus Christ as our Saviour, and so on. They looked around upon one another at this strange talk from strange lips; some smiled, but others listened thoughtfully. The consular dragoman who accompanied us, as well as the teacher, evidently did not relish the remarks, and we stayed but a short time.

From the school we stepped into the adjoining church and into the chamber of the priests. Here we found three of the inmates sitting in company with three or four of the common people. Mr. King began to speak to them about the Arabic Bible which had been lately printed by benevolent Christian people in Europe and sent to the people of this country for their benefit. He spoke also of the difference there is in the sight of God between that part of religion which was seen in outward worship and that which was unseen in the heart. One of the priests offered a few replies approvingly, but the two others sat as mute and unmoved as if all that had been said to them had been in an unknown tongue or had relation only to affairs of the people of the moon. One of the laymen made a sensible remark or two, and at the close, as we retired, one of the mute priests, to show that we did not depart under his curse or displeasure, followed us to the door, and with special courtesy sprinkled us with rose-water.

In the evening of the Sabbath which we spent here we made a call in company with Mr. M. on the Austrian consul. Conversation turned on some of the doctrines of religion. A Muslim, one of the attendants of the consul, began to find fault with our doctrine of the Trinity. Mr. King of course stood up in its defence, showing by various illustrations that though we could not comprehend it or explain it fully, yet it could not be called an absurdity. The discussion became considerably extended and earnest, though in the utmost good nature. The consul, though a Romanist, was in rapt attention, but Mr. M. rose, saying our call was getting to be too much prolonged. "Oh no, sir," exclaimed the consul. "Do not break off this subject; it is exceedingly interesting." But as we were with Mr. M. in the relation of guests, we considered it impolite for us to trespass farther on his patience, and so, following his move, we took our leave.

The next day we arrived at Nazareth and found a lodging-place in the Romish convent. Probably we were the last of our class of men that enjoyed such a privilege. Orders were even at that time on their way from Rome requiring the monks to exclude from their hospitality all men employed in Bible distribution.

We found in this spacious establishment only six inmates, where in flourishing times they had had twenty. Ali Bey in 1807 reports them to have been thirteen, of whom nine were Spaniards. In the time of Burckhardt (1812) they were eleven. There was a long suite of rooms on each side of the convent gallery entirely empty, and for the most part of the time apparently quite useless. In one room of the building there was a small school, taught by a sprightly young native who had been educated in Rome and who conversed with us fluently in Italian.

One of the monks conducted us round to see the in-

NAZARETH.

teresting objects afforded by the convent—the paintings, the tapestry, and particularly the rich priestly robes, adorned with gold and silver, nicely packed away in several ample chests. As he entertained us the while with conversation in Italian he complained that the establishment had been left to languish very much during these latter years. France particularly had failed to send her usual remittances. Spain had been wanting, too, as it appeared, since her nine monks of 1807 had nearly or quite all disappeared, and if it had not been for Portugal they might have been obliged to abandon the convent altogether, "but Portugal," said he, "*non manca mai*" (never fails).

He showed us the room under the chapel where lived the blessed virgin, and the rocky wall blackened by the smoke of her kitchen fire. Just at the entrance into this room we observed the fragment of a column two or three feet long in a hanging position, being fastened at the top by mason work into the floor of the chapel above it; another corresponding fragment was fixed in the ground below, as if once they had been united, forming but one solid pillar. Two different traditions were handed down respecting this mysterious phenomenon. One was that the rude Saracens, when they conquered the country, wantonly broke the column, and God by a miracle held the upper part of it suspended thus in the air; the other explanation was that when the angel came to announce the glad news to Mary he stood behind this pillar, and his voice shivering the centre of it into fragments these two parts were left in their present situation, and when this convent was built the upper piece of the column was found still hanging in mid-air and the floor of the chapel had to be built around it as we saw it. But the monk, probably believing us to be Protestants and ready to make objections, anticipated us by saying, "For myself, I do not fully believe that this was all one column, for you see the upper piece is granite and the lower one is marble."

We were conducted out to the traditional hill from the brow of which the Nazarenes would have thrown Jesus down. It was a fourth of a mile distant from the present village. Mr. Jowett seems to give credit to this tradition. Other travelers, however, are pointed to a different locality.

Concerning this murderous attempt upon the life of Jesus a most extraordinary account is given in a large Latin book which we found in one of our rooms in the convent. It was a book composed expressly to be a guide to pilgrims visiting the "holy places," and printed probably at Rome. Under the head "Nazareth" was found this entertaining narrative, in which all devout Catholics who never had a Bible would be vastly interested:

"The populace of this village being enraged at a certain speech that Jesus made to them, seized him, dragged him to a neighboring precipice and threw him down headlong. He fell upon a rock. The rock melted at his touch and received him into its soft bosom, from which he rose unharmed and went his way, leaving behind him the exact form of his body and the folds of his dress as if they had been skilfully wrought in the rock by the graver's tool."*

The last place of importance which we passed was Nablus. This is, as the Arabs call the place, a corruption of Neapolis (new city.) Epiphanius changes Nablus into *Anablatha,* as Ramah is changed into Aramathea. Josephus calls the city both Neapolis and Sichem. It was one of the chief cities of ancient Samaria, the ruins

---

* The hill or mountain of Nazareth is an eminence of many miles in extent, coming down from the north-east and terminating rocky and precipitous, overlooking the plain of Jezreel, a little south-west of this village. The present site of Nazareth is probably the same that it always was, not upon the top, but upon the eastern slope of this mountain range, some little distance above its foot, where is found the fountain which gave the town its life doubtless from the very first.

of whose capital are still visible a few miles off. If Sichem is the same place as Sychar, as many suppose, then Nablus was the place of residence of the woman whom Jesus met at the well of Jacob.

This city is the religious capital of the Samaritan nation. We made a call on their high-priest Salami. He was a man of a demeanor rather venerable, of the age, as he said, of forty years, and the only legitimate priest of God in all Palestine or perhaps in the world. He was of the sons of Aaron, and had regularly succeeded his great ancestor in the priesthood, and his only son, who was present before us, was to succeed him, for the line could never run out nor be broken. There were about sixty families of his nation in the city who worshiped in his synagogue. But in other parts of the world there were nations of Samaritans, especially the native Indians of America. Mr. King told him the native Indians were savages; they had no books and no learning. *That*, he said, was a lie, for they had both. Jesus, he said, was the first of infidels, because he called himself the Son of God; however, as his works were good, Samaritans did not think it right to curse him. As to the interview between Jesus and the woman at the well, all that was true about it was that Jesus made some simple inquiries about the well, and the woman informed him that it was the well of our father Jacob; all the rest of the story that is told in the gospel of the Christians was a lie. The Samaritans offer the sacrifice of a lamb once a year, but not on the mountain, for fear of the Mohammedans. (Dr. Robinson understood *seven* lambs on the mountain.) This sacrifice, however, he said, is not for sin, but merely as a memorial of former things: men were not saved by sacrifices nor by a mediator; those who had sinned must *repent,* but for those who, like himself, had never sinned, not even *this* was necessary. On being pressed a little, however, on this point of sinlessness, he seemed to allow the possibility that he might have some particle of sin attached to him, but (putting the nails of his thumb and finger together as if he were pinching a pin's head) he intimated it to be quite an unappreciable quantity; he had always loved God with all his heart and his neighbor as himself!

Mr. King reminded him of the great promises of prosperity made to God's people in case of their obedience, and of the curses that should come upon them if they rebelled, and then told him that the low state of the Samaritan nation was owing to the rejection by his people of the great Prophet, the Messiah, the Lord Jesus Christ.

He admitted that the nation exhibited the appearance of being under a curse, and that their present scattered and depressed condition was from the hand of God, but that Jesus Christ had anything to do with it, *that* was all a lie.

When Mr. King proposed that we should visit his synagogue and look at the ancient copy of the Pentateuch which he possessed in the Hebrew language, he hesitated, as if in doubt whether to consent or not, made some frivolous excuses, and finally he *could not find the key.*

Mr. King said humorously to the rabbi, "I can tell you where the key of your synagogue is: it is *in my purse.*" The rabbi took the hint and joined in the laugh. The key being now discovered, he led the way to the holy place, brought out the sacred manuscript and suffered Mr. King to take it into his own hands to read it—a liberty which Mr. Fisk, when there, was not allowed to assume. The book was found to contain the ten commandments in Exodus just as we have them from the Jews, but a supernumerary one is added at the close, in these words: "Thou shalt make to thee an altar of stones on Mount Gerizim."

Wishing to visit the ruins of the ancient Samaria, we sent a request to the governor for one of his soldiers to go with us as a guard. Word came back that the soldier should be ready, but meantime the governor would be glad to see us at his quarters. We went accordingly and were well received. The governor, finding that Mr. King spoke easily in Arabic, made considerable conversation. He said,

"I hear that you have no pictures in your churches; is it so?"

"It is," answered Mr. King. "Our holy book forbids the worshiping of images and pictures. It says, 'Thou shalt not make unto thee any graven image, or any likeness of any thing that is in heaven above, or that is in the earth beneath, or that is in the water under the earth: thou shalt not bow down thyself to them, nor serve them.' We may have pictures in our *houses* for ornament, but never for worship."

"That," said the governor, "is a very different thing from having them in the churches. Do you believe Christ to be God?"

"We believe that there is but one God, existing as Father, Son and Holy Ghost. This distinction I cannot explain. We do not believe that there are three Gods, neither do we believe that Christ is the Son of God as a son is the child of an earthly father. We believe that

God gave him the Spirit without measure, that God was with him, and that they are one."

The governor listened calmly without any mark of disapprobation, but some of the Turks around him exclaimed, "Istogfr Allah! Istogfr Allah!" (God forbid!)

During the dialogue a collection of people assembled about the door, some of whom came within. Perhaps there were fifty men crowded together to gaze and listen. Before them all Mr. King declared the message of the gospel—that all men are by nature sinners and as such are liable to punishment, that Christ as the Son of man died to redeem us, and that there is no salvation but by his blood.

We left Yoosef, our dragoman, to give the necessary presents to the governor's attendants, who, as he afterward told us, set upon him rudely to get his money, but the governor himself, to the last, showed all politeness, and sent us a request that we would favor him with another interview.

Samaria, now called Sebaste, we found to have occupied a hemispherical eminence quite isolated from other hills that surrounded it. The foundations of its wall of defence were still plain to be seen. One long row of standing columns remained on the southern slope of the hill, with others elsewhere standing or lying separately; the walls of one large building were seen having yet a height of some twenty feet. The remains of an old aqueduct were found in the valley below, with a small stream of water still traversing the broken pipes. A low hut, half under ground, contained all the specimens we saw of humanity in this once strong capital of the idolatrous Israelites. We left with them a copy of the New Testament, which, though none of them could read it, might stimulate them to learn, or which some friend might be found to read to them.

The second day from Nablus brought us to the holy city. As we approached the heart beat high with expectation. The summit of the Mount of Olives began at length to show itself above the surrounding hills, and suddenly the eye caught the broad, green dome of the Mosque of Omar brooding proudly and profanely over the hallowed spot where once rested the ark of God's covenant and his mercy-seat. Then were observed the lesser objects of interest—the mass of the city buildings, the mosques with their high and slender minarets or towers, the broad-walled Christian churches and convents and the perfectly irregular jumble of little domes and terraces of private dwellings. The *kofila* of travelers moved rapidly on. We could not be permitted to halt as we would and enjoy for a few moments the rush of thought and emotion produced by this thrilling sight, but we deeply sympathized with the royal poet when he said, "I was glad when they said unto me, Let us go unto the house of the Lord: our feet shall stand within thy gates, O Jerusalem."

We entered the city with the rest of our little caravan at the western or Jaffa gate and proceeded directly to the Greek convent of St. Michael, where we found our brother Mr. Fisk and associate in good health, and where the friendly superior was very ready to supply us with lodgings.

Mr. King in a few days left us, expecting to be obliged to visit Damascus in order to obtain a competent instructor in the Arabic language, but on arriving at Jaffa he met with such a man as he wished, and concluded to remain in that city till spring.

CHAPTER VI.

Preaching at Jerusalem—Papas E-sa—Deacon Cesar—Sale of Scriptures—Bible men arrested—Omar Effendi—Congratulations at our release—Arrival of the Jaffa consul's son—Visit to the governor and the moollah—Our rooms opened—Rapid sale of Testaments.

MR. FISK had already begun to preach sermons occasionally at his room in the Greek language as well as in the Italian. His audience consisted of six or eight natives at most, but, considering the peculiar state of society in Jerusalem, this number was perhaps as large as could be reasonably expected. On account of the strong sectarian zeal that prevailed in the city every man was well marked and guarded by some spiritual watchman or overseer. This oversight was not as jealous and strict among the Greeks as among some of the other sects, since their depressed circumstances at this time made it a matter of interest to them to cultivate the good-will of the Protestants, to whom they let their convents. Two men of the Greek denomination, men of considerable importance, were always present at the preaching of Mr. Fisk, one a priest, the other a deacon. Papas E-sa Petros (priest Jesus Peter) was a native of the country and a man of more learning, probably, than any other Christian in Jerusalem. He spoke fluently four or five different languages, and could read more or less easily about fifteen. He read and spoke well the French language, and had evidently borrowed many of his ideas, both political and religious, from the

French. He often inquired particularly about the creed and customs of Protestants, and said freely that the English and American churches were more like the primitive Christians than any other churches on earth. He was employed extensively by Messrs. Wolff, Jowett and Fisk as a translator of books and tracts into Arabic, and in this department his services were invaluable.

Deacon Cesar, of whom mention is made in the journals of Mr. Parsons, was connected with the principal Greek convent in the city. He was a young man of uncommon promise, comely in person, easy and modest in manners and of an active, inquiring mind, yet strongly attached to the superstitions in which he had been educated. He came and requested Mr. Fisk to teach him Italian, proposing, in return, to assist him in his Arabic. They two, in consequence, spent a part of almost every day together reading the Scriptures and conversing freely about the doctrines of religion. It was believed that he had begun to understand and practically to feel the difference between real and mere nominal Christianity.

As the pilgrims were beginning to collect at Jerusalem from various parts of the country, our work of book and tract distribution assumed a considerable degree of importance. One day our young man Yoosef went out with his books and in two or three hours' time returned, bringing us five or six dollars for the books he had sold. Still more books had been asked for, and he went out the next day with about the same success.

It appears that tidings of these things came to the ears of certain of the chief priests and scribes which dwelt in Jerusalem, and they doubted of them whereunto this would grow. If they should let it thus alone all Jerusalem might peradventure be filled with the apostles' doctrine, and the English heretics would come and take away both their place and nation. They therefore took counsel together what they might do to stop these proceedings. Their plan was quickly matured and its execution begun. At about one o'clock in the day, as Mr. Fisk and myself were occupied in our different rooms with our teachers, Moosa Beg, the governor's sheriff, with half a dozen attendants, made his appearance in our part of the convent, and after considerable delay, during which he maintained an ominous silence as to the object of his visit and kept up a continual interchange of messages with the Latin convent, he ordered us to accompany him before the authorities of the city.

First he brought us before the moollah or judge. He was occupying his judgment-seat, with two or three assistant judges or scribes at his side and with many surrounding attendants. He spoke to our young dragoman, saying, "Demand of these men who they are and why they assume the liberty of wearing the white turban."

Mr. Fisk replied, "We are English (under English protection), and all Englishmen wear the white turban."

"That is false," said he, and waving his finger threateningly, he added, "you can't do that without a firman."

"Behold the firman!" said Mr. Fisk, pulling it from his bosom.

The judge took the document, cast a hasty glance over it, and, immediately changing his tone, requested us to be seated. "But," said he, still holding the paper in his hand, "this is a *traveling* firman; it gives you no license to be trading in books. Why do you take the liberty to be scattering about such things as these (holding up one of our books), which are neither Christian books, nor Mohammedan, nor Jewish, which contain fabulous stories that are profitable for nobody and which nobody of sense will read?" Saying this, he cast the book contemptuously upon the floor.

Mr. Fisk assured him that the books we sold were the Law, the Psalms of David and the Gospels, the same books which Christians in all ages have received and acknowledged as their holy Scriptures, and to satisfy himself of the truth of this statement his Honor need do nothing more than just to send and have brought to him the Christian Scriptures from any of the convents of the city and let the comparison be made before him. He was not, however, disposed to take this trouble, but contented himself with saying, "*The Latins say these are not Christian books.*" Accordingly, as if this testimony had decided the case, he gave in Turkish, as our dragoman afterwards interpreted it to us, the following order to Moosa Beg:

"Take these men to the governor, and with my compliments tell him to put them in confinement and send them neither pipes nor coffee nor anything else for their comfort."

But notwithstanding this charge, the governor received us with much more decency than the moollah, first allowing us to be seated and then inquiring after our nationality and demanding our firman. We went through with much the same examination here as before the judge, the governor remarking, as the judge had done, that the *Latins* had declared that our books were not Christian books. While the process of examination was going on, the sheriff, who was sitting by, proposed to his Excellency to have the sale of the books prohibited, and then immediately called a crier, and handing him one of our books ordered him to go to the Armenian convent and proclaim that all books of this sort were prohibited. The man went forth, and, as it afterwards appeared, gave orders not only that these books should not be bought nor sold, but also that all those that had been bought should be given up.

The governor, finding that we were under English protection and carried with us a regular firman from Constantinople, was not disposed to send us to the common prison, but gave command that we be taken to the Latin convent and held in custody till a decision on our case could come from the pasha of Damascus. Our enemies at the Latin convent, it was thought, would take excellent care that we should not escape. But being met on our way to the convent by a messenger who said they refused us admittance at the convent, our guard took us for the moment to our own rooms. Here we found men busily occupied in taking an inventory of all our effects, searching closets and chests and making a memorandum of everything, as if the proprietors were defunct and all was to be immediately *sold for the benefit of the creditors.* It was but a short time before we were remanded back to the governor's, where, we were told, we must spend the night. Our quarters were in a large, dark basement room occupied by the governor's guards. These men, having finished their work for the day, were busying themselves, some in preparing coffee and food for their supper, others in smoking their pipes or playing chess, bestowing on us not the slightest attention. The night shut in; the cold wind blew through the open grated windows, the little flickering lamp scarcely prevailed against the darkness, and as we sat upon the bare stone floor and gazed upon the surrounding objects, the guards and the smoked walls profusely hung round with guns, cutlasses and similar instruments of death, we felt that we were at least within one step of a felon's prison.

About ten in the evening our young dragoman, whom we still kept with us, was sent for by the governor to come up to his audience-room. As he went in he found there, as he informed us, Omar Effendi, a man of great influence in Jerusalem, being the head of the *clan of the green turban*, who claim to be the lineal descendants of the prophet. He had been acquainted with Mr. Fisk and other Englishmen, having received their calls and welcomed them with politeness. The Effendi, Yoosef said, advised the governor to use cautious measures lest severity should cause unpleasant consequences. In reply the governor, as if to palliate his conduct hitherto, inveighed against the books as being mischievous because they presumed to call "Saidna Esa" (our Lord Jesus) the Son of God, whereas he was the *slave* of God (Abd Allah). He said he did not find the men guilty of any high misdemeanor, but that their enemies had given currency to evil reports. Yoosef was told, therefore, to go down to us and say that we should not be retained in confinement, and that to-morrow all would be amicably settled, but possibly we might, after being dismissed, be required to take lodgings in some other convent.

We presented ourselves once more in the reception-room. The governor's manner was visibly softened. He begged us to be seated and ordered coffee for our refreshment. A few inquiries followed similar to those of the afternoon, and of course the same answers were repeated. In regard to Muslims' taking our books Mr.

Fisk explained, saying that when they came and wanted them we did not refuse them, but that we always let them know that they were Christian books and intended especially for circulation among Christians. The governor then made apologies and assigned us a chamber for the night with his nephew, Ho-sein Beg. The young man treated us with all possible honor and made apologies till they became quite tiresome.

In the morning Ho-sein was seen in his bed-room adjoining performing devotions with his door wide open, kneeling and standing by turns, often on his knees bending forward with his forehead on the floor, muttering words in a low tone, and sometimes faintly chanting. His prayers must have cost him half an hour's time, while the governor's brother, who slept near us, despatched his in five minutes.* The governor provided us with a warm breakfast of bread and eggs, but the keys of our rooms were not given us. Ho-sein Beg had assumed a studied reserve, and the governor was inaccessible, being thronged with company the whole forenoon. After long hours of suspense and after a great deal of palaver, we rightly guessed they were playing their card for what they call a *baksheesh*, for whether guilty or innocent, an *accused* man was expected to pay his present. But we had had more done for us than usual. We had not only been *accused*, but a governor's guard had received us at our very door and marched us back and

---

* Perhaps the beg's devotions may have received an inspiration from the circumstance that his window opened directly upon the court of the sacred Mosque of Omar, and that that venerated temple was scarcely a stone's throw distant, and also from another circumstance which he had mentioned to us the evening before, viz., that this was the same house in which our Lord Esa (Jesus) was tried and condemned.

forth in dignified procession through the crowded streets, and, after admitting us to a public examination, had lodged us under the very roof of the chief magistrate of the city. A native could not have received such honor without full pay. The man must pay when his irons are put on, and pay when they are taken off. But we did not see the matter just in that light. What honor we had received we did not seek and would not pay for.

To conclude, two or three men went with us to our rooms, two of which they unlocked for us, and two others—one of them being our large dépôt of scriptures —they left locked, and put on the government seal. This sealing, however, they said, was to be for *a few days only*, and simply to please the moollah. After this they took their seats, as if they were waiting to receive something, but they were plainly told they could expect nothing so long as our doors were closed.

Thus ended our first skirmish with the united forces of the beast and the false prophet. They had imagined a vain thing, and He that sitteth in the heavens had them in derision. It was only a skirmish, but its issue was a good omen of future victory whenever the decisive battle should come.

Those few natives who had been our friends came forth on this occasion with manifestations of sympathy and courage. Even while we were yet in custody our lad Constantine, whom, for his *own* benefit chiefly, Mr. Fisk had given some little employment, had come, notwithstanding his excessive natural timidity, urging his way through the crowd and the military array around the palace, to discover what was about to be done to us. Georgis, a papist, came at the same time, proffering his service, and saying he was ready, if we wished, to go right off to Jaffa and inform the consul of our case. Deacon Cesar, the young Greek pupil of Mr. Fisk, wrote him a line, as follows:

"Your absence, my dear master, brings to my soul much affliction and melancholy, and as I cannot come personally to see you, according to my wish, I pray you, from a distance, be of good courage and fear not, for God is with you and will soon deliver you from the hands of your enemies. Much salutation to Mr. Bird.

"Your afflicted pupil,   CESAR.

"P. S.—Remember the saying of the apostle: 'All that will live godly in Christ Jesus shall suffer persecution.'"

After our liberation came Papas Esa to call on us. In a solemn and feeling manner he began, saying, "I have slept not a wink all night. I could not imagine why honest men, sitting peacefully in their house, should be seized and carried off in such a manner, like criminals, and I thought of nothing but that war might have broken out between England and Turkey. My little boy, in the night, began to speak of you and to ask where you could now say your prayers. I said, 'My son, you must pray for them,' and he immediately rose from his couch and prayed."

After this came in the good Deacon Cesar, and in a half ecstasy of joy seized and squeezed our hands for some time, saying, "You suffer for the love of Christ; our hearts have been with you. Nothing since the death of Procopius has produced such a sensation in our convent, for we are sure that you are spending your lives for our good." Esa, a blunt, frank-hearted Catholic carpenter, entered the room, and first of all, looking upward, he exclaimed, "Nishkur Allah! nishkhur Allah! (thank God!) my wife and children and myself have been praying to Jesus for you all night and have had no sleep; thank God, you are safe again!" Then coming up and kissing our hands, he repeated, time after time, "Nishkur Allah!" The Syrian priest Isaac, also, who had previously brought from his patriarch in Mesopotamia a letter of introduction to Mr. Fisk, called to offer his congratulations, and the venerable Greek metropolitans, who seldom made calls, sent their expressions of joy at our safety, accompanied by a substantial present, such as Melchizedec brought to Abraham.

In all this demonstration of regard some allowance, no doubt, was due to Eastern hyperbole and compliment, but, as a whole, it was made with an air of truth and sincerity which we could not but respect.

We were sorry to learn that in this annoying bluster of "pope and pagan" united the poor Jews had to suffer with us. No mischief could be stirring but a part of it must light on their shoulders. At the same time that we were arrested the governor sent also to the college, as it was called, of the Polish Jews, and turned out all that were in it, listening to no remonstrance, and sealed up the doors. The plea was, "You have English books here." The doors remained closed, of course, till they were opened by the silver key that fits all locks and breaks all seals in Turkey.

In the evening of the day of our liberation we prepared statements of what had happened for the use of our friends and for the consuls at Jaffa and Beirut. Next day we called on Omar Effendi, who assured us of his sympathy, protested by the prophet and by his faith that he knew nothing of our case till the evening of our detention, when he immediately called on his Excellency the mutsellim to inquire into it, and as soon as he understood the matter he told his Excellency that it would not do to treat Englishmen so. The books he knew to be Christian books, for he had copies of them presented him two or three years ago. We informed him that some of our papers had been taken to the governor and not restored. He promised to see to it.

Next day a servant of the effendi called, bringing us several papers which he had obtained at the palace, among which were two documents that had been entrusted to our care, directed to the reverendissimo of the convents of the Terra Santa, whose arrival at Jerusalem was daily expected. The same day a Jew came, and said if we had any more Hebrew Bibles a friend of his would be glad to purchase a quantity. Toward evening also came an Armenian who, after assuring us of the great grief their convent had experienced on our behalf, proposed to purchase seven or eight Armenian Bibles. But our books were under lock and seal, and no crier had yet appeared to countermand the proclamation against their sale.

Our notice sent to Mr. Damiani, consul at Jaffa, brought us his son Yoosef, bearing his father's consular firman. We attended him at once on a visit to the governor. Mr. Damiani handed him his father's consular credentials, the *khut esh shereef* of the sultan. His Excellency, as was due from a servant of the sultan, rose at once from his sitting posture, unrolled the large sheet, put it reverently to his forehead as an acknowledgment of its authority, then resuming his seat and glancing his eye over the document, he commenced again to make his apologies to the young consul. He protested that it was an affair of the moollah, who sent these two men unto him to be put in prison and in chains. But he would not do it, and appealed to us to say if he had not treated us well.

The judge, when we called with the consul, was a little more civil than before, furnishing sweetmeats, pipes and coffee, as to other decent people. But he still carried a high look and spoke in a haughty tone. The sultan's khut shereef did not raise him from his seat nor receive his kiss of homage. After casting his eye over it he began to say that when the complaint was first brought to him it appeared that the books in question were being sold in the markets to Muslims as well as Christians, and that the books were bad books. But he had now to say that the books and all things taken from us should be restored and the sealed doors opened, but on condition that we should sell no books to Muslims, for they contained things that would make Muslims angry. He then took up the Book of Genesis and began reading aloud, as if to give us a specimen of how it would enrage Muslims. When he came to "the Spirit of God *moved* upon the face of the waters," he a second time tossed the book upon the floor, saying, "That is infidelity," as if it must not be said of God that he *moves*. After this he softened down, gave us all of our books that were in his possession and sent a man to go with us and open our rooms.

Immediately after the opening of our depository Yoosef again commenced his book operations, and in four days brought us about fifty dollars from the sale of one hundred and ninety copies of the New Testament, chiefly among the Armenian pilgrims.

CHAPTER VII.

Visit to Bethlehem and Hebron—Cave of Machpelah—Jews—Sheikh Mohammed—Frank Mountain—Cave of David and Saul—Governor of Jerusalem removed—At Jaffa—Beirut.

WHILE Mr. Damiani was with us we thought it a favorable opportunity to visit with him Hebron, the ancient city of Abraham. Our way was through Bethlehem. As we came near the walls of that place there was plainly a great fermentation going on within them. Men, women and children were seen staring

BETHLEHEM.

from every terrace, window and loophole of their houses, not knowing but our little cavalcade might be a band of officers sent on some threatening embassy for their annoyance. They could not have feared from our number that we were approaching with any such order as that of Herod against their young children, but the miseries of a military siege which they had lately passed through were fresh in their memory, and the white turban coupled with arms which Mr. Damiani and some others carried were objects of their execration and dread. Those who were near at hand were soon relieved from whatever panic they might have felt, and some of them gayly fell in with our train and made part of our escort to the convent of the Nativity. As we came near the convent, however, there issued from it in threatening array a force of twelve or fifteen armed guards. They hailed us tumultuously, wishing to know our character, whether friends or foes, and were answered by their own people, "Inglees, Inglees." They then, though rather timidly, unbarred the gates. The Greeks in their part of the convent (for the Latins shared with them in the great building) received us gladly, and Mr. Fisk enjoyed with them some entertaining conversation in their own language. In speaking of their broken state of society Mr. Fisk asked,

"Have you no judge residing in your village to decide your causes?"

"No," said they, "none except the '*unjust judge.*'"

"How, then, do you get your difficulties settled?"

"By brute force—by stones and clubs and daggers."

We saw the place where some suppose the infant Jesus was born, and in immediate connection with it the grotto where St. Jerome dwelt many years and wrote many books.

On the following morning, near Bethlehem, we passed three large pools or reservoirs for water, having walls of mason work, and so placed that the water, after filling the upper one, might descend successively into the two others. They are called "Solomon's pools." Perhaps Solomon alludes to these, Eccl. ii. 6.

We must have passed through or near the Plain of Mamre, and, without having perceived a single village or habitable dwelling, we came to the narrow, stony, muddy streets of Hebron. For three hours the rain had been drenching us, and we entered the city traversing the bed of a running brook which was at the same time the main street of the town. The German Jews were the first friends who received us. The house we entered was intolerably filthy, and the people who came flocking in around us corresponded sadly in this respect with the habitation. It was difficult, from their ignorance of Arabic, to hold intelligible conversation with them, but one of their number understood a little French, and with him Mr. Fisk made shift to get on tolerably well. Two fine-looking lads particularly attracted our attention. They were of the age of ten or twelve years, and must, we thought, be the sons of some rich Jewish rabbi. We found, on inquiry, that they had made advances far beyond ordinary boyhood; they were not even bachelors, but both *married men*.

Among the number present were a few of the Sefartim or Spanish Jews, who are proverbially of neater habits than these Germans, who are called by the distinctive name of Ashkenazim Jews. These Spaniards must have been conscious that we were uncomfortably situated, and invited us to better quarters, where we had good reason to be satisfied.

The evening wore away without eliciting anything important of a religious nature. No man of information appeared among them to enlighten or entertain us, and we were too much exhausted to provoke much conversation.

Late in the evening a sudden bustle was created in our little company, some saying, "Rise! rise! here comes the sheikh!" They generally obeyed the summons, but for ourselves, suspecting what was probably his errand, we did not feel like hailing his arrival with any pretended joy or respect. We were barely civil to the man, and

MODERN HEBRON.

as for the family, it was hardly five minutes before every one of them had disappeared, and the brawny-limbed Sheikh Mohammed was left sitting in the midst. He inquired whether we had brought any letter from the governor of Jerusalem, and some other questions which Mr. Fisk answered after their tenor, and when he had counted his beads and whisked them about his hand sufficiently, and sipped his coffee which our Yoosef prepared for him, he rather coolly departed.

11

Early in the morning, though the rain was still falling, we went out to the farther limit of the city to see the Mosque of Abraham, supposed to be built over the cave of Machpelah. The doors were not open to strangers. As we stepped into the open court there came forth a gruff voice from a little distance, indicating that our advance would be contested, and we withdrew, hoping and believing that the time would come when all who are Israel as well as all who are *of* Israel shall here be permitted, if they wish, to behold with their own eyes the body, embalmed and preserved, of their venerated forefather of long ages past.

Returning toward our lodgings, whom should we meet but our old friend Sheikh Mohammed, walking out to look after our welfare. He passed a hasty salutation, and then, turning on his heel, marched on before us upon the narrow sidewalk, as if to be our escort homeward. But our path happened not to lead that way. We were going to visit another locality which took us away by a side alley, and so our unsuspecting escort was left to proceed like a locomotive broken loose from its train. The Jew who was our conductor was afraid of consequences, but Mr. Fisk pushed him on. We were led to the supposed tomb of Abner, the son of Ner, whom Joab slew, then to the cistern of David, to the sepulchre of Jesse his father, to the monument of witness between Ephron and Abraham, to the wells of Isaac and Jacob, etc.

Having finished our survey we gave orders to Yoosef to have our horses immediately got in readiness for returning to Bethlehem. Entering our lodging-place we found the inevitable Sheikh Mohammed duly arrived and patiently waiting. He had had his pipe and coffee once, and perhaps again, and when we came in was amusing himself by turning over the leaves of an Arabic Psalter which we had left on our carpet, though an intelligent Jew of the family told us he was unable to read a syllable. Scarcely were we seated when it was told us by some one that his sheikhship was expecting a present. The sheikh had offered to send his son to point out to us the place where it was said Abraham entertained the angels, and Mr. Fisk was quite willing to give him something under the name of compensation, but nothing that should wear the appearance of a government exaction. He handed him, therefore, a Spanish dollar. The haughty lord tossed it back in disdain and went muttering from the room. The Jews were agitated, as if the sheikh might in some way make them answer for our delinquency. Mr. Fisk meanwhile picked up his dollar and went on adjusting his baggage as if nothing had happened. But his sheikhship did not mean to let even a dollar slip through his hands when it could be secured so easily, so he soon reappeared and took his seat in a chair that happened to be found in the room, and began to say that all Europeans, when they visited Hebron, paid the sum of two hundred piastres. Mr. Fisk immediately replied that he knew better, and then handed him the pasha's *buyordí*, or passport, to look at, securing the bearer from all demands or annoyances whatever from the local rulers, whether in Hebron or anywhere else. The man, if he could not *read*, could at least recognize the seal of the pasha, and as he returned the paper he remarked that he cared little about receiving anything, but to be offered a *single dollar* he took to be an indignity. We were at liberty, he said, to go when and where we pleased, and if we had need of horses or guards he would readily furnish them. Mr. Fisk handed him a gold piece worth a trifle more than a dollar, and he condescended to accept of it.

Our animals were not yet at the door, and just at this juncture a messenger came from another sheikh, calling himself Abd-er-Rahhman, who wished to do himself the honor of calling upon us (*i. e.*, of receiving his share of the "200"). Our answer was returned to him that we could not wait, and immediately we took up our packages and left the house. As we threaded our way toward the stables the Jew who guided us turned and said, "There comes a soldier from the sheikh. We must go back." Mr. Fisk put his hand firmly on his shoulder and pushed him along before him. We were soon mounted, and Mr. Fisk started to pass from the yard into the open street; but suddenly a man caught his animal by the bits. Yoosef saw it and was there in a moment, and there was something of a struggle between them. Other men were moving about the yard, and we feared a wrangle and perhaps a mob; but Yoosef seemed to understand the matter and soon set all right, and catching up his white turban, which had been knocked off, and twisting it rapidly about his head, he straddled his animal and set us all off with an impulse.

Sheikh Abd-er-Rahhman was left in high dudgeon. Abd Allah, a man whom we had taken from Bethlehem, was afraid to proceed with us, and we left him, expecting to see no more of him till we arrived again at the city of David. Sheikh Mohammed's man, however, held on his way boldly. When we came near the place of Abraham and the angels, which this man was to show us, Mr. Damiani and Yoosef chose to wait for us at the road while the rest of us went aside to examine the locality. The place shown was marked by a foundation wall of some large building, probably a church of Constantine or the Crusaders. The stones were large, and we observed this peculiarity in them, that great masses of sea shells entered into their composition. Before we had fully satisfied our curiosity at this place we heard the voices of our companions calling long and loud after us. Abd Allah the Bethlehemite had arrived from Hebron, and brought intelligence that the sheikh who failed to see us, having come to our lodging and found that we had escaped him, vented his rage furiously upon poor Maallem Hai-eem, our friendly host, for not having sooner informed him of our arrival, and declared he would send after us a band of horsemen and take by force that which we were bound to have given him in courtesy. Abd Allah had fled from the inhospitable city and come on as fast as his donkey could be urged to come that he might apprise us of what had occurred. Our consular friend looked very fierce, drew forth his long blade, examined its edge, brandished it high in air, as if to prove the strength of his arm, or to show the company how much he could do for them, "come to case in hand." But the case did not come, and in the good providence of God we reached Bethlehem in safety without the taking or the losing of any blood.

Next day we visited Frank Mountain and the reputed cave of David, where he cut off the skirt of Saul's robe. 1 Sam. xxiv. 4. Both these places are situated in a south-east direction from Bethlehem at the distance of three or four miles. The former is a steep, isolated hill, in form like a sugar loaf, and is a very attractive object in the landscape as viewed from Olivet, and especially from the convent of Mar Elec-as, between Jerusalem and Bethlehem. Its top, which was at the height of a few hundred feet, was composed of gravelly earth, and was evidently brought up to its present elevation artificially. It presented a concave area of two hundred and seventy paces in circumference, and from the firm wall foundations that remain we may infer that it was once strongly fortified.*

The cave that was shown us was considerably spacious, being thirty-three paces by fifteen, and having several passages leading to other apartments which were said to be numerous and extensive, but we did not explore them.

During this excursion to Hebron we sold sixteen copies of the Scripture and distributed eighteen. We also disposed of sixty religious tracts.

Some ten days passed, and we received a request from the governor to make him a call. He had received a communication from the pasha of Damascus, who, he said, wished to see a copy of our firmans and a specimen of our books. On returning to our rooms we sent Yoosef with Mr. Fisk's firman to be copied, and also four different books, Scripture portions, for the pasha's examination. The governor took the books, as Yoosef

* Doctor Edward Robinson believes, from Josephus, that this was the Acropolis of a large town called *Herodium*, which was built by Herod the Great, and whither Herod's dead body was brought from Jericho for burial. (Josephus says: "The body was carried two hundred furlongs to Herodium, where he had given order to be buried.) Doctor Edward Clarke, from observing this mountain at a distance and seeing its top to be hollow like a crater, pronounced the mountain to be a volcano, and thought it to be situated on the borders of the Dead Sea, thus suggesting that Sodom and Gomorrah were overwhelmed by fire from this mountain.

informed us, and opening one of them and reading a moment, he spit upon the book, exclaiming in their common phrase, "Istogfr Allah."

It was scarcely two hours after this when our ears were saluted by the rapid discharges of musketry in different parts of the city, and the roaring of cannon from the walls and the castles. What was the announcement by this sudden public demonstration? It was no other than that His Excellency, successor of Pontius Pilate as governor of Jerusalem, and who spits contempt upon God's holy word, is driven, like Nebuchadnezzar, from his office and his palace, and another man is sent to occupy his place. The same day was also signalized by the sale of about twenty dollars' worth of books.

When Padre Bastiani, the new reverendissimo whom we had been expecting, arrived at Jaffa, some one or more of the priests in his train happened to fall in with Mr. King in that city, and began to dispute and rail very passionately against the Protestants, denouncing them and their measures with a great deal of bitterness. Mr. King, believing the reverendissimo and all his company to be of the same spirit, wrote immediately to forewarn us of coming evil, beginning his letter with the quotation, "The devil is come down to us, having great wrath because he knoweth that he hath but a short time." Some one had intimated to him that the superior in particular was meditating violence against him. But we at Jerusalem had become somewhat assured, in regard to the approach of this company, by a consular letter, just come from Beirut, in which Mr. Abbott says:

"I am obliged to you for the details of the occurrences

which have taken place with the governor and kadi (judge), who seem to have got so deep into the mud prepared for them by the Terra Santa priests that they do not know how to get out without one or the other's being suffocated in it.

"But the Lord will not suffer his cause to be overthrown by such vile means. I calculate that about this time you will have received the buyordi (order) of the pasha of Damascus, which I transmitted to Mr. Fisk by express to Jaffa, and that it will have had the desired effect of settling all matters with the governor, cadi and other authorities quite to your satisfaction.

"With respect to the instigators of all this mischief and scandal to Christianity (the monks), we will, with divine assistance, devise some other means of bringing them to their right senses."

But, beside this encouraging communication, we had had by us for some weeks a sort of peace offering in the shape of two large sealed packages of documents which had the appearance of being of considerable value to the reverendissimo. These, of course, we were bound to transfer to his hands on his first arrival. They might be a commission or instructions from the pope himself, and we were curious to know what effect it might have upon his spirit to see that these documents had been faithfully kept and safely delivered to him by supposed enemies.

Accordingly, on the first announcement of his reverence being in the city, we handed the papers to Yoosef, charging him to deliver them with our respectful salutations. When he returned he said the reverendissimo had received him very politely, had made inquiries in particular about the signori who sent him, and, learning that one of them had lately been suffering from illness, he expressed his condolence.

While in doubt in what estimation we should hold our new neighbor the reverendissimo, it was with a happy surprise that, almost immediately after the occurrence above mentioned, we received another letter from Consul Abbott, in which he says:

"It may be satisfactory and perhaps not useless that you and Mr. Fisk should be personally acquainted with the reverendissimo. He is just returned from examining the state of all the dependencies of the Terra Santa in Egypt, Tripoli, etc. We have had a good deal of communication together on various subjects, and you may well think I did not omit to acquaint him with the occurrences that have befallen you through the machinations of the members of his community at Jerusalem. So far from attempting to discredit the fact, he related to me many recent acts of iniquity committed by them, deeply lamenting the unprincipled system that had taken such deep root in the administration of the temporal as well as spiritual interests of that establishment. He has agreed to communicate with me from Jerusalem, on this and other subjects, confidentially, which intercourse may be of use to us."

Mr. Abbott's opinion of Father Bastiani, that his principles did not harmonize with those of the monks, was afterward confirmed by the circumstance that the man did not survive one year after coming within the walls of their convent and forming a part of their household.*

* That the death of Father Bastiani was brought about by the Spanish monks was the opinion unhesitatingly avowed by his immediate successor, who occupied his place for a time under the title of president.

Had the reverendissimo reached Jerusalem a little sooner we might have been saved from a good deal of the annoyance that came to us from the direction of his convent, and in many ways we might have profited by his acquaintance, but our stay at Jerusalem was drawing to a close. The disgraceful farce of the Greek fire, which came off this year on Saturday, April 17, was nigh at hand, when the pilgrims immediately prepare for their homes; and Jerusalem, without pilgrims, offered at that time few advantages for evangelical labor.

As soon, therefore, as that day of desecration was past, we set our faces toward our place of rendezvous at Beirut.

In parting from the convent, Mr. Fisk called the head priest, Papas Joel, to his room to pay him his rent. After giving him the money, he, in a frank, downright manner, but in perfect good nature, administered to him the following reproof. Looking him full in the face, he said, "Now, Papas Joel, you must not go to the bishops and tell them another such lie as you told them last year. Don't say that the howadji paid you but *one* hundred piastres when I have paid you *two hundred*." The papas laughed sheepishly, like an unlucky boy when found out and reproved for his mischief, and, putting up his money, turned and went his way. The lie which he told, he probably thought to be only a clever device, lawful, as "it was not malicious and did not deny the Christian faith."

At Jaffa we found our brother King, who had here spent the winter very agreeably in his favorite study. His teacher being a Muslim, he read with him the Koran and engaged him in many religious discussions. At the commencement of their reading together the learned sheikh showed himself very confident and fixed in his own religious sentiments, arguing strongly and boldly, as if he intended and hoped to make a convert of his pupil. But as he went on it was observable that his opinions and feelings became considerably modified. He said one day, "I am willing you should love our Lord Jesus. You ought to love him. I love him myself. I love him more than all things in this world—more than my own life. But I wish you to call him the *Servant of God* (Abd Allah), and not say, 'God was in him and he in God, and that they are one.'"

The next day, continuing the same subject, he said, "I love you very much, and how sorry I am that so good a man should be an infidel and doomed to everlasting fire because he *would* believe that our Lord Jesus is God!" He cautioned Mr. King, in the discussion, to be careful about his words, "lest," said he, "I should be obliged to bear witness of them against you at the day of judgment." Of late, however, his creed was so far changed that he believed that Christians whose works were good might be saved, but that the Muslims of this land were *so debased that God must destroy them.*

We spent a Sabbath at Jaffa and had public services at the consul's. Mr. Fisk discoursed in Italian to a company of fifteen from the words, "Who was delivered for our offences and raised again for our justification."

During the ensuing ten days, under the care of our heavenly Father (a part of us by sea and a part of us by land), we made our way to Beirut, where we exchanged hearty congratulations and mingled our thanks and praises to Him by whose good providence we had been kept during these months of our separation.

CHAPTER VIII.

Mr. Goodell alone at Beirut—First patriarchal denunciation—Letters from Rome—Mr. B. Barker, Bible agent, and Lady Stanhope—Mr. King revisits Deir el Kommer—Conversations with priests—Journey to Damascus, Hums, Hamah and Aleppo — Firman against the Scriptures—Three months in Aleppo—Eventful journey through Antioch and Tripoli to Beirut.

MR. GOODELL, during our winter's absence, had been occupying the stand at Beirut, wrestling alone against principalities, against powers and against spiritual wickedness in high places, but still efficiently protected from personal violence by the official influence of our warm friend Consul Abbott. He had maintained a regular preaching service at the consul's on the Sabbath, had held small meetings for reading the Scriptures and for discussion with the natives, and had done what was feasible in the way of schools.

He had no sooner been left thus alone in his station than he was obliged to bear the brunt of the first papal fulminations against the Bible enterprise. The patriarch of the Maronites had seen some men and had heard of others who had come into the land to introduce into it the sunlight of God's word. Herod the king and all Jerusalem with him were not more troubled at the visit of the wise men than was this vigilant prelaté of Lebanon at the sudden appearing of these Bible men. Without waiting for instructions from Rome and without consultation with his bishops, he lifted up his warning voice to his people after this fashion:

"May the apostolic benediction and heavenly grace descend abundantly and abide continually upon the souls and bodies of our people and of our flock, the children of our community, the Maronites who inhabit the towns and villages in every direction and of every rank and condition; the Lord God bless them. Amen. . . . We inform your love that the artful deceiver and enemy of goodness and enemy of the human race never ceases to infuse his deadly poison into the members of the mystical body, *i.e.*, into the faithful sons of the holy Church, and diligently and laboriously and with all his might to sow the tares of corrupt doctrine in the field of the Lord of hosts. This he does sometimes by himself and sometimes by means of his followers the heretics, the impious enemies of the Roman Church, the mother and mistress of all churches and their guide, that he may thus, by deceits of various kinds, turn Christians astray and lead the simple into error. And now (may God confound him!) he has instigated in these days some persons of the English nation, called Bible men—*i.e., followers of the Bible*—who have arrived lately in the country, and they have come to the village of Antoora under the character of disseminators of their corrupt faith, clad in sheep's clothing, but inwardly they are ravening wolves. And they have begun to travel among our community, the Maronites, pretending that they wish to amuse themselves and see the country, but their heart is full of evil and treachery. They bring with them books of the Old Testament and the New, printed in various languages—Syriac, Arabic and others. These also are of different sorts, some of them replete with errors and some of them correct in regard to the parts that are printed, but they have omitted seven holy and divine books [the Apocrypha], although these books omitted by them are received by the Roman Church, and those who do not receive them as holy and divine are anathematized by the holy general Council of Trent in its fourth session, and their object is to distribute these books of theirs among the children of our community of Maronites, whose faith is sound, established on the rock of Peter, and who have never bowed the knee to the image of Baal. . . . A thing stranger than all this is that they are engaged in purchasing the holy Scriptures of the Old and New Testaments printed in Rome the Magnificent (a thing past endurance), and instead thereof distributing their own books, above mentioned, *gratis*, in order that in the course of time the true books of Scripture may no longer be found, and that *their* books, full of errors, may remain in their stead.

"And, not content with all this, they are continually endeavoring to obtain, if possible, some of the children of our people, and send them to their country that they may there drink in the poison of their pernicious doctrines and return to disseminate it in this country among our people the Maronites. Other things we do not mention for fear of being tedious.

"Now, when we heard of the arts and the blasphemous innovations of these deceivers, by which they degrade the Christian faith and bring ruin to the Catholic religion and perdition to the souls of men, we have been excited, by our paternal zeal, to meet this malady with an effectual remedy. . . . We therefore order and command, in accordance with the holy Council of Mount Lebanon, all the children of our community of Maronites . . . that from this time forward no one possess the books of these above-mentioned persons, and we order that all these books be either burnt in the fire by those who possess them or that they bring them to us at the convent of Canobeen.

"Moreover, we do not allow any one, whoever he may be, of the children of our community, in any case, to associate with the individuals above mentioned in spiritual things or in whatever concerns the Christian religion. . . . Nor do we allow any one to study in their schools or peruse their compositions. And whoever shall audaciously act contrary to this our order ten days after its publication, or shall hesitate to comply with or shall prevent the execution of it, . . . if he be an ecclesiastic he is prohibited, *ipso facto*, from the exercise of his office, and if he be a layman he falls under the penalty of excommunication, the absolution from which is reserved to ourself."

The above document, as compared with the original, has been considerably abridged. His Holiness professes to have made an effort not to be tedious, but in this he failed altogether. In the original he enlarges much on various points, such as the holiness of the Church, especially the Maronite Church, his fatherly affection for his people, his care for their interests, the sly cunning of the adversary, the greatness of the impending danger, the warnings he is obliged to utter and the terrible penalties he will be obliged to impose on the disobedient. Perhaps among his own people his epithets and repetitions added force to his proclamation. That it had an effect for a time was sufficiently evident. The solitary missionary at Beirut suddenly became an object of odium and suspicion. All the children of the Maronite community were especially shy of him. He became an object of public gaze to all. The aged and venerable priest Simeon ceased his friendly evening visits, and many, as they met the Bible man in the streets, refused to return his social salaam.

The good priest above mentioned, seeing the storm-cloud rising, had, the evening before the anathema was read in church, though with evident reluctance, returned his Bible, not consenting either to burn it in the fire or to make a three days' journey with it to Canobeen. Few followed the priest's example by returning their books, but there was no good reason to believe that any copies of the Scriptures were either destroyed or given up to the priests.

The Bible man meantime went on quietly in his vocation, working at the language, preaching in English at the consul's, distributing the Scriptures with increased encouragement among the Greeks and reading and conversing about the great salvation with all who were accessible.

In the midst of these occupations he writes: "I am happy to say that a desire to become acquainted with the sacred word has apparently increased in consequence of there being no small stir about this way. Almost every day a greater or less number of Arabs call upon us to read the holy Scriptures. Some of them read several hours in the course of the day; some of them spend the whole evening thus, and some not unfrequently ask permission to carry the sacred treasure home with them for the night, promising to return it the next morning. The desire for instruction appears also to increase. Several adult females come occasionally to be taught by Mrs. Bird or Mrs. Goodell, although their attendance is very irregular and their disadvantages very great, they being without Arabic books and their friends deriding their efforts, yet it is evident they are making improvement. While we pray that a blessing may attend these very feeble efforts, which we are grateful that we are able to make, we have much confidence that, as we acquire a knowledge of the language, the great Head of the Church will open to us among this people a wide door of usefulness."

But the danger arising from the light of God's word among the papal flock was not felt alone in Lebanon. Rome herself was startled. An ancient and still venerated college establishment of the Jesuits had fallen into the hands of the Bible men and had become a radiating point for all the untold evils which the word of God in the vulgar tongue is known by experience to produce.* Something must be done. The fearful ruin which the Bible threatened to bring upon the Christian religion † must by all means be prevented. To this end three several documents, all of the same date and nearly of the same tenor, were issued from the "eternal city" to the following three several ecclesiastics: the new Maronite patriarch, Bishop Hanna Maroni and Monsignor Bishop Gandolfi, pope's legate for Syria; all were officially signed, "Cardinal Somaglia, Dean of the Sacred College, Proprefect," etc. Of these three epistles the second one only will here be given:

"MOST ILLUSTRIOUS AND REV. SIR: We have received the unwelcome intelligence that a certain man by the name of Wolff, of Bamberga, together with other Bible men, has rented of you, for five years, an old college situated on Mount Lebanon, in Antoora. This sacred society holds it for certain that your Excellency

---

* Doctrine of the Council of Trent.   † Patriarch's proclamation.

has not thought how great spiritual mischief this new enterprise of the Bible men would produce among the Catholics of that region. Under the cloak of pretended zeal they are the heralds (banditti) of error and corruption. They distribute Bibles gratuitously, in the vulgar tongue, but Bibles corrupted and depraved. It ought not therefore to be permitted that such men should have in Mount Lebanon an asylum from which they can with impunity scatter abroad their poison, to the injury of a nation, too, that has ever shown itself constant in maintaining unsullied the deposit of the faith," etc., etc.

Consequent upon the receipt of these letters the patriarch had immediate recourse, for the recovery of the college, to the Emeer Besheer, who consented, as many other rulers before him have found it convenient to do, "to give his power and strength unto the beast." He sent his soldiers to quarter in the house of Bishop Maroni, and vexed him until, for his relief, Mr. Lewis, whom no law could have forced to do it, consented to give up the papers of the contract and quit the premises.

Soon after our arrival at Beirut, Mr. Abbott received information, through one of the Capuchin friars, that about the time we left Jerusalem a general meeting of the Terra Santa establishments was held in that city, at which it was resolved that no Bible man should from that time be received as a guest into any of their convents or be granted any favor of hospitality whatever. A friar had arrived at Beirut with a huge packet of circulars to distribute, cautioning all people against the Bible men. The same man was just embarking for Rome, where he was going to make a full exposition of all our proceedings.

In the midst of this imposing manifestation of hostility to the Bible there came to Beirut a salaried agent of the British and Foreign Bible Society, Benjamin Barker, Esq., of Smyrna, a brother of John Barker, Esq., British consul at Aleppo. He was not intimidated by the prevailing opposition to his work, but made a full offer of his "pearls of great price" to the people, and not without success. In spite of patriarchal fulminations, copies of the Scriptures were sold in considerable numbers at Beirut. One man living near us said to Mr. Barker, "They have forbidden our reading these books, but there are twenty of my neighbors as well as myself who are determined to read them, for our priests have been deceiving us. They have taught us to be idolaters, contrary to the word of God."

Mr. Barker, as he was passing on southward toward Jerusalem, had intended to make a call of civility on Lady Stanhope, between whom and the Barkers there had long been an intimacy, but he was doubtful how he would be received. Her ladyship had courteously treated the Rev. Messrs. Way and King, to the latter of whom she had even furnished letters of introduction to her native friends—letters which Mr. King at the time esteemed to be of more influence than those of a pasha. But on the other hand she had manifested toward Mr. Wolff an uncommon rudeness. Mr. Barker, therefore, without writing her a formal note, had taken care that his intended visit should be intimated to her beforehand, so that at least his appearance should not take her by surprise. However, during his business detention at Beirut, the matter of his visit to her ladyship was definitely settled by a letter written by her own hand in the following courteous terms:

"Dear Sir: I have not forgotten you, as you seem to suspect by what you said to my servant whom you saw at Tripoli. He, as well as your brother, Mr. John Barker, has acquainted me that it is your intention to pay me a visit. I should be delighted to see you (as I should any branch of Mr. Barker's family, for the friendship I bear toward him has not diminished by a long absence), but your professional duties will deprive me of that pleasure.

"I have made a determination to have no communication with persons who interfere with religion. I should never have seen Mr. Way had I known what was the object of his visit here, and Mr. Barker may recollect, as far back as eleven years ago, there was a report of two Mr. —— I do not know who (considerable men, however, and warmly protected by my cousin, Lord Grenville) coming to Antioch to sell Bibles or rebuild churches; in short, I have forgot what, but Mr. Barker may perhaps recollect that, even at that time, I declared that if they came near me I should shut the door in their faces. Therefore I hope you will not take unkindly a refusal dependent on a general line which I have pursued for many years.

"You may make this letter as public as you please, in order that it may not be imagined that I can slight any part of Mr. Barker's family. I hope, however, we shall meet when the rage of Bibles and misguided zeal is at an end; till then believe me," etc.

Till when? Till zeal for the Bible shall cease? The Christian religion has stood upon the Bible eighteen hundred years. Will it now come to an end in good season for you to enjoy a pleasant visit from your friend?

Since this communication passed between the two friends both have gone beyond these mortal shores; but had they lived they would have seen that from that time to the present their chance of meeting according to appointment has been rapidly growing more and more distant.

Mr. King's residence of some months at the capital of Lebanon had produced a deep impression on the people. It had imparted to them the first reliable information they had recevied of Protestantism. He had succeeded in gaining the confidence of many friends, and ensuring for evangelical truth a respectful hearing. It was worth while for him now, after a six months absence, to revisit the people and see whether any fruit of his labors for them remained. On his way up the mountain he met with individuals to the number of forty or more with whom he spoke, letting fall a few words to direct their thoughts to the concerns of another life. His friends of the house of Domani, whither he again directed his steps, gave him a cordial greeting, and many called to salute him on both the first and second evenings after his arrival. Four priests of the papal Greek Church were among the callers, and religion was the subject of their conversation. The next day was the Sabbath, nearly the whole of which was spent in receiving calls. Among those who came in the evening were three priests with whom he conversed two or three hours.

The next morning Aboona Girgius called, a papal Greek priest from Barook, three miles distant toward Damascus. In conversation they came upon the expression "thou art Peter," when the priest ventured to affirm that the Bible declared Peter to be the head of the church. Mr. King handed him his Bible, and begged him to show him where that was said. He searched a long time and finally closed the book and retired. The same day came Aboona Germanus, superior of the Maronite priests of the city. He received Mr. King with all the kindness and attention which he manifested last year, introducing him to his friends with flattering compliments.

Aboona Saba from Deir Mokhollis, one of the two superiors of the convents of the papal Greek Church, called at the house of Mr. Domani. He was often mentioned to Mr. King the previous summer as being one of the most learned priests on Mt. Lebanon. "Go," said the people, "and dispute with Aboona Saba. Convince him and we will follow you." He spoke Italian, having spent ten years at Rome. He was very polite and entered freely into conversation. He said the discovery of America had been an injury to religion. Infidels have made people believe that the natives of that land could not be the descendants of Adam. He asked of what sect the Americans were.

Mr. King said, "We are Protestants."

"You have protested, then, against the true church."

"No, sir; against the errors of the church."

"Errors in the church! No, no; that cannot be. Old things are better than new."

"Very true. Therefore it was that we protested. The Roman Church was full of new things, and so we left it and returned to the old church of Christ and the apostles."

The next day Priest Yoosef came in, and spoke of the order that had come from the patriarch to destroy all the books that had been distributed by the English, but saying that neither he nor the people here would obey the order.

Soon after Priest Yoosef had gone, Saad-ibu-Bas a Maronite of Mr. King's former acquaintance, came in. He said, "I suppose you have heard of the patriarch's order?"

"Yes—that all the Bibles distributed by the English should be burned. Why is that? Are they not the word of God?"

"Yes; I told one of our bishops that I had read your Bible, and found it, word for word, like the one printed in Rome, and asked him whether it made any difference where the book was printed provided it was the word of God; and he said no. And suppose the book were printed by a bad man, by a Muslim, where would be the harm for me to receive it and read it? He replied, 'You might receive it from the hand of a Muslim, but not from the English.'"

The man inquired of Mr. King what motives the English had in printing the Bibles and sending them here.

Mr. King replied, "What motives had the Apostles in going abroad and publishing the gospel? It was the command of Christ that they should make the gospel known to all people. This command is binding on us. What could have been our motive in doing what we did for the Syrian patriarch Jarwi? He came to England and the English gave him money, a large sum of money, and told him to go and print the word of God on Mt. Lebanon. An American gave him a printing-press which was worth some hundreds of dollars. Had they, think you, any bad motives in doing this?"

"No; but did the English really do this?"

"Surely, and for the express purpose that you might have the Bible. It is now five years since the patriarch was in England. I called on him last summer, and asked him why he did not print the word of God. He said he had a right to do as he pleased. So your Maronite patriarch takes the same course. He neither gives you the Bible nor will he suffer us to do it."

"Oh yes—we have Bibles printed at Rome."

"But what is the price of that Bible? At least a hundred piasters. Such Bibles are useless. They are not Bibles for the people. The truth is, the Romish Church does not wish you to have the Scriptures."

"But the Church is of authority. 'Thou art Peter, and on this rock will I build my church.'"

"Yes. You profess to be built upon St. Peter. Why do you not obey St. Peter? He says you would do well to go to the Scriptures as to 'a light shining in a dark place.'"

"St. Augustine said that if the Church should say the Scriptures were not good, he should say so too."

"By no means. He said this—that if the Church *had not received* the Scriptures at first, he would not receive them. He did not mean your *Roman* Church, but that of the apostles and their followers."

"I hear that the English have purchased in Kesruân some copies of the Scriptures printed in Rome and burned them."

"That is a lie of some son of the father of lies. Any Englishman who should burn the Bible would be accounted a miscreant—a madman. The English do not even burn the Koran."

The man parted with Mr. King as with a friend, and seemed to carry away with him the impression that his patriarch had taken a wrong step in issuing his late order.

One day Mr. King called in to see the superior, Germanus. He found Priest Aioob (Job) with him. As soon as he entered, the superior said to the priest, "This man is my friend. The first time I saw him I loved him. Go tell Father Paul to come and talk with him." When Father Paul came the conversation turned upon the apocryphal books that were left out of the English Bibles. While this was under discussion four or five other priests came and as many more of the common people. The American was on all sides surrounded. The superior himself sat in a chair outside of the ring, as if to act as judge in the contest, and said but little. After dismissing the Apocrypha, Father Paul said, "When did the schism take place between the Church of Rome and the English?"

"About three hundred years ago."

The superior asked, "What was the name of that king of England who took the girl? The schism began with him."

"His name was Henry. He was a persecutor of Protestants, lived and died a Roman Catholic, I believe."

Father Paul then repeated, "It is about three hundred years since you left the Church?"

"We never left the Church; we only left the *errors* of the Church."

"*Errors* of the Church!" said they all together; "the Church in error!"

"To be sure. So we believe; so *I* believe."

Father Paul continued: "What is the difference between you and the Church? What occasioned the division?"

"If you will listen a little while I will tell you what occasioned the division."

Here Mr. King entered into a detail of some of the abominable practices of the Church of Rome about the time of the Reformation, and on his remarking that the Church at that time had become very corrupt, both priests and people, Father Paul and all present exclaimed, "The Church corrupt! the Church corrupt! *Impossible! Impossible!*"

"Not at all impossible. The Jewish Church was once the only Church of God, and did it not fall into error and wickedness?"

"But the Christian Church cannot wander, for Christ said, 'Lo, I am with you alway.'"

"Yes, with his Church to prevent it from destruction, but not from wandering, for St. Paul says that in the last time there shall come in errors—many shall depart from the faith, giving heed to doctrines of devils" (Father Paul interrupting, "Yes, yes, that is very true"), "forbidding to marry, and commanding to abstain from meats which God hath created to be received with thanksgiving."

This word among so many priests and monks was like fire to powder, and there was at once an explosion from the whole body of them. So great was the tumult that for some time it was impossible to speak. At length Father Paul's voice was heard above the rest, saying,

"There's no such thing in the Bible. What you refer to is a passage about keeping holy days."

"I mean what I said. It is the word of God. It is in Paul's Epistle to Timothy."

"There is no such passage."

"Are you a priest and do you not know your Bible better than this? Bring me your Bible and I will show you the passage."

All now became very noisy, every one wishing to speak to Mr. King at the same time. So he said, very gently, "Brethren, listen." At this gentle request they were all still, and he proceeded, repeating mildly what he had before said, and bringing to a conclusion the history which he had begun to give them of the separation between the Protestant and Roman Churches. The discussion had hardly reached its legitimate close when it was announced that the hour of prayer had arrived. All immediately arose and took their leave.

In the latter part of June, after a three weeks' visit at the mountain capital, Mr. King, being joined by Mr. Fisk from Beirut, set off on a visit to Damascus and Aleppo. They had also in company the Rev. Charles Cook, an English Wesleyan. Passing a night at Jib Jeneen and another at Demas, they reached, in twenty-two traveling hours, the gates of the very celebrated city of antiquity, Damascus. Here Messrs. Fisk and Cook alighted from their beasts, because the Muslims dwelling in Damascus consider their city to be so holy that it would be polluted, desecrated, or some foul thing, if a Christian should happen to be seen in it on horseback. But Mr. King was disposed to try somewhat the mettle of these fanatical followers of a false prophet. He would ride at any rate till he was stopped. He had not proceeded many rods when a Muslim came up, and finding he was a Frank and consequently a Christian, ordered him down.

"For what reason?"

"Come down!—come down!"

"But I am an Englishman. I have a firman from the grand signor giving me leave to walk or ride where I please."

"Dismount, I say, dismount!"

"What! an Englishman dismount?"

"No matter who he is, he must dismount."

So the Englishman (for the English-speaking American was so accounted), with his firman, having tried his

DAMASCUS.

experiment, yielded to the force of circumstances and consented to walk the rest of the way. They were informed that not long before that time a French gentleman, a consul from Bagdad, attempted to maintain his right to ride in the city, and was cruelly maltreated. A firman from Constantinople was obtained for the punishment of the offenders, but, like other laws and orders from Constantinople, it fell dead.

Our travelers found it difficult, in all this great commercial city, to obtain a place to lodge in for the night, and were obliged at last to accept very uncomfortable quarters with a private family. A friendly priest, however, Aboonah Michael, and he a Maronite, learning their situation, obtained for them very decent lodgings in the house of a brother Maronite of his.

They made here a visit of only twenty days, in which time they conversed extensively with Maronites, Latins, Greeks, Syrians, Jews and Muslims, and distributed a few Scriptures. After this, Messrs. Fisk and King set off in company with a large caravan northward for Aleppo, Mr. Cook leaving them to return to Beirut.

At Kara they found about thirty Christian families, half orthodox and half papal Greeks. Some of them received the Scriptures. At Khaseeah also were about the same number of Christian families and a Greek priest. They asked for Scriptures, but the travelers had none to give them. Hums (Emesa of the Fathers), with twenty thousand inhabitants, had five hundred Greek families and two churches. One of the deacons was very friendly, and begged that if any fellow-laborers of theirs should come to reside in Hums they would come directly to his house. Thirty miles farther on they arrived at Hamah, probably the Hamath of Scripture (Josh. xiii. 5), a large city like Hums. Here were a thousand Greek Christians. The priest was friendly to the distribution of the Scriptures. From this place their caravan was increased to three or four hundred souls, and, having been reconnoitered on their march by Bedawin robbers and suffered excessively from the driving sand and heat of the sun and want of accommodations, in four days they arrived at Aleppo.

They had on their journey some valuable opportunities to preach the gospel to Muslims. When they were encamped at Kara several Muslims came around and began to talk about religion. One asked Mr. King, "Do you believe the Koran?" He answered, flatly, "No." Another said that the sun, moon and stars were all made for the pleasure of Mohammed. Another asked, "What do you think of Christ?" He answered, "He was the Son of God. God was in him. He created all things. He will judge the world at the last day. There is no salvation but by his blood." The Muslims said, "God forbid! God forbid!" One of them asked Mr. King, "Why do you not become a Muslim and embrace the true faith?" He answered, "Give me reasons. Show me proof that yours is the true faith and I will turn Muslim. I am not a Christian because my father was. Our father Ibrahim (Abraham) left his father's religion because it was not the true religion. So ought I and so ought you to do in like case."

One day Mr. King had a good deal of conversation with his man Haji Ahmed, telling him it was his duty to examine for himself, etc. Ahmed listened very attentively while the way of salvation was pointed out to him. Soon after this, Sheikh Taw-ha, who was esteemed the greatest sheikh in the caravan, rode up to Mr. King and began to talk in a most violent manner, pouring out a torrent of words and repeating with great rapidity a multitude of verses from the Koran. After a while he said, "You want reasons. Here are the reasons, and yet you will not believe: 'There is no God but God.'" This he said very loud, and many Muslims gathered around. Mr. King was apprehensive that they were planning to pick a quarrel with him, and that they were watching to catch something out of his mouth as a pretext to insult or do him some violence. He thought it, nevertheless, his duty to vindicate, before them all, the cause of Christ, and as soon as he had opportunity to say a word he said, "That there is no God but God is one of the first articles of my belief, and Jesus Christ is God."

At this Taw-ha began again in a most violent manner, saying, "You are an idolater; you worship images; I have seen them in your churches in Damascus and at Jerusalem. You ask the priests to pardon your sins."

Mr. King denied, saying, "We do not—we do not."

"But I have seen them *with my own eyes—with my own eyes.*"

After hearing the man rail a long time, Mr. King said, with a loud voice, "You do not know my faith. The Meta-wallies call themselves Muslims. Would you not be offended if I should call you a Meta-walli?"

"Yes."

"I am an Englishman, and my faith is no more like the faith of the Christians in this country than yours is like that of the Meta-wallies. What signifies all your talk till you know what I believe? I do not worship images; they are not in our churches. We do not pray to saints: that would be a sin. We do not ask the priest to forgive us: God alone can pardon sins, and to him is our worship due."

On hearing this the sheikh lowered his voice a little and said, "But you believe that Jesus Christ is the Son of God?"

"Yes, because he was not begotten by man, but was miraculously conceived by the power of the Holy Ghost."

The conversation continued for some time longer, and was brought to a close in much good humor.

When they were encamped near Er Rasta, on the banks of the A-see-ah (Orontes), they could procure neither milk nor *leben*. There was an encampment of Bedawin half an hour distant, where they might have procured milk, but the Arabs of the company were afraid to go to them for it. "Toward night," says Mr. King, "seeing a Béda-wy leading his flocks on the other side of the river, I passed over by a bridge, and going up to him bade him *salaam* (peace). He returned my salutation, but fixed his eye steadily upon me with all the starings of an old warrior. His face was dark, his eyes were sunk deep in his head, and his whole appearance was that of one inured to want and accustomed to suffer. I said to him, 'I am a stranger. I am come to ask you if you can furnish me with a little milk, for which I will pay you.' 'Bo,' said he, a word which I did not understand, and asked an explanation. Turning to his flock he said,

"'Here I wander about daily with my flock, but I eat not of their flesh and have no profit. Government takes all.'

"'There is a better world than this,' replied I, 'which we shall soon enter if we are prepared for it. The world we are in is fast passing away. In a few years we shall return to the earth from whence we were taken. I am a Christian. I believe in Christ. If we are in him, and believe in him, and love him, we shall be happy in the world to come. He died to redeem us. We are all sinners. There is no salvation but through the blood of Christ.'

"While I thus addressed him, his stern countenance

softened, and I said to myself, 'Who can tell but these few words may be the means of leading his mind to God, and saving his soul?' He offered me a pipe of tobacco as a mark of friendship, and as I turned from him I said, 'I shall probably never see you again in this world, but I hope we may meet there (pointing upward) and be happy.'"

At Aleppo the brethren were kindly received by the English consul, John Barker, Esq., and were entertained for some days in his family. The very day after they came, the pasha, who was a surly Turk, sent word to the consul that a firman against the Christian Scriptures, printed in England, had come to hand, and that all such books as had been distributed must be called in and placed in a sealed dépôt till they could be sent back.

This firman, however, on examination, was found not to specify Scriptures from *England*, but made use of the general expression "The Frank country"—Europe. It also ordered that the books "be taken and cast into the fire," at the same time that, in another place, it orders them to be "sent back." It was a document most bunglingly patched up, full of absurdities, repetitions, and contradictions. Moreover, it required a violation of articles of treaty. No Turk was at liberty to take and destroy property belonging to Franks.

There seemed to be good reason to believe that the document was purchased by Roman gold, and came forth through unofficial and unpracticed hands. It, however, procured for the whole anti-scriptural party a temporary advantage. Even some of the Greek ecclesiastics, who had begun to fear the influence of the Scriptures, took occasion to oppose their distribution by pleading this firman as an excuse. The Turks themselves never showed any zeal in carrying out the order, except as they were set on by anti-Bible men among the nominal Christians.

The Protestant consuls, with Mr. Turner, the British chargé at Constantinople, at their head, resisted the order from the beginning, and from the difficulty of executing it the matter in a few months passed into oblivion.

The most of the three months spent by the two brethren in Aleppo was occupied in study. They, with Mr. Lewis, who had joined them from Beirut, maintained a regular preaching service at the English consulate, and they had occasional opportunities, which they improved, of conversation with the people; but the threatening firman had for a time the effect of preventing the usual efforts for Scripture distribution.

On leaving Aleppo, Mr. King gave the only Arabic Bible he had left to the man with whom he lived, and Mr. Fisk gave his to a Greek priest from Killis.* This priest reported that the Turks had been to Killis, taken all the books they found in the churches (Greek and Armenian) and put the priests under keeping; but after examining the books, they restored both them and the priests. They found no Bible Society books in the churches, and the private houses they did not search. The priest urged the plea of poverty to Mr. Fisk, and assured him that there was not in all Killis among the Greeks an Arabic Bible.

In the latter part of October the missionaries, including Mr. Lewis, accompanied by an English traveler, Mr. Maddox, set out from Aleppo for Beirut. The third day they came to Antákia, the village remnant

* A town a day or two north of Aleppo.

of the ancient Antioch, where the believers in Christ were first called Christians. This once famous city among the cities of the world, "third in rank for beauty, extent and population," was supposed in 1824 to contain only five thousand inhabitants, five hundred of whom were Christians, chiefly of the Greek rite. And these Christians had no place of worship better than a grotto, or hole in the rock, which the natives were afraid to have the travelers visit lest it should attract the attention of their Mohammedan masters and bring upon them some act of oppression.

The missionaries found here the Greek patriarch who had lately come on a visit and whom they had seen at Damascus, where he resided. He informed them that soon after they left Damascus the firman about the Scriptures was made public in that city, and the governor immediately sent after the Bible men by way of Jerusalem, supposing they had gone in that direction; that the Greeks were afraid of some injury in consequence of the firman, but they had suffered none, nor had any books been taken from them.

Leaving Antioch, the travelers passed a night at Suadia (Swa-deey), near the mouth of the A-see-ah (Orontes), and the next day, under torrents of rain, they came to Casáb (or Kessáb), a village of one thousand Armenians. They were well treated in the hovel of the sheikh, with whom they left an Armenian New Testament, and also a second copy for his father, the priest of the village.*

---

* Since this visit the village of Kessáb has received attention from the mission, and has, to a large extent, become Protestant, having an evangelical church, with its own native pastor, and a new house of worship.

Another day brought them to Ladikia (Laodicea), where they remained three days on account of the disturbed state of the country. For fear of the Nuseireeyies no muleteers could be obtained by the company to carry them on. They therefore felt obliged to undertake a passage to Tripoli by sea. From stress of weather, however, they were forced to take shelter in a harbor near the river Banias and the town and castle of Merkab.

They obtained animals here and again commenced their journey by land. It was past noon when they got under way.

The storm which had been long threatening soon broke upon them furiously, and they rode under pouring water till night. A very friendly Turk with whom they fell in at the khan, and who offered to be their guide, took them up the mountain, steep and rocky, to a little village of six or seven hovels, where they might lodge for the night. At one of the doors they knocked, and an old man with a white beard came and opened it. Could they remain in his house for the night? "No," said he, talking loudly and boisterously. He had no room for them. After a while, however, he gave way and consented to admit them. They found one half the room filled with cotton seeds and cotton; a lamb was lying by the fire, and two cows stood in one corner. One other corner only remained for the old man's family of seven or eight persons. These stepped aside to make room for the strangers and took their stand among the bags of cotton. The fire had no outlet for the smoke, but right glad to find any shelter from the raging storm without, the travelers sat down, soaked with rain, and had the few articles of baggage they had brought from the boat, which also were wet as themselves, placed under and around them. They called for wood. The fire was increased and so was the smoke. With streaming eyes they ate a fowl, a bit of bread and a little fruit which they had brought. All except Mr. Maddox had left their beds in the boat to go by water; but had they brought them they would have been wet and useless for want of space. So each one endeavored to sleep as best he could in the place he happened to take on first entering, for there was no lying down without incommoding each other. Mr. King, who could not sleep, contrived to beguile the time by conversing with the family. The old man's name was Abraham, and they were glad to find that he was of the Greek Church and not one of the Nuseireeyies.

They were glad when they found that the morning had dawned and the rain abated. At their leaving the village they gave the old patriarch a few piasters, at which he and all the rest of the family expressed themselves highly gratified. The neighbors also flocked out to see them and wished them blessings and a happy journey.

At **Tartoos** (Tortosa) they were treated with great respect by the governor of the little village, who procured for them a room, invited them to dine at his house and waited on them as they ate.

Off against Tartoos is the small island of Irwad, once the site of a considerable city, the evidence of whose existence still remains in various architectural ruins. It has a name in the Scriptures, as the home of the Arvadites (2 Kings xviii. 34; Ezek. xxvii. 8, 11), and a present population of some thousands, chiefly Muslims.

At the river Abrash their very obliging guide, Hadji

Ahmed, left them. He was passing from Ladikia to Tartoos, when he found our travelers at the khan of Merkab, and offered them his services as a guide. He delayed his own journey for their sakes, found for them the village in the mountains, sleeping himself in the stable; he introduced them favorably to the governor of Tartoos, and there again lodged among the horses, asking in no case for money, or food either for himself or his horse. Instead of going directly from Tartoos to his house in the mountains, he went with the company several hours out of his way till they came in sight of Tripoli, and then, without asking for anything, accepted thankfully a small reward and rode off. When thanked for his generous services to men who were strangers in the land he replied, "I, too, am a stranger from the land of Egypt."

Tripoli was reached at eight in the evening, where they were hospitably entertained by the consular agent, Mr. Catziflis, until their boat from Banias arrived with their baggage. Meantime a Sabbath was passed, and Mr. Fisk preached in Italian to a small audience consisting of the consuls and persons belonging to their families. From Tripoli the travelers proceeded by land, lodging the first night in Batroon (ancient Botrus), at the house of the Maronite priest Stephen, and reached Beirut the next day, weary and worn after a ride of fifteen hours. Nineteen days had they been journeying from Aleppo in circumstances of exposure, and at times of extreme discomfort, and they were not now slow to express their gratitude for being found once more under the same roof with those that cordially sympathized with them in all their labors and privations.

THE MARONITE PATRIARCH.

CHAPTER IX.

Reply to the Patriarch's Bull—Mr. Fisk robbed—Patriarch Jarwi roused—Mr. King with Mr. Fisk at Jaffa and Jerusalem—Pasha collecting taxes at Jerusalem—His cruelties—Journey to Beirut—Robbers—Assad Shidiak—His casting a lot about the Pope—Mr. King leaves Syria.

BEING now fully represented at Beirut, that is, both missions, American and English, we held consultations together on the interests of our common Protestantism. Among other objects to be accomplished, we decided in favor of a public reply to the slanderous proclamation of the Maronite patriarch.

Of this reply the following is an epitome:

1. You accuse us of distributing the word of God under the influence of Satan. *Ans.* You think then the work of publishing God's own truth is a *Satanic* work. Did not the apostles and Christ himself perform this kind of work? Paul recommends taking God's word as a sword to *fight* the devil with. St. Cyprian says the word of God brings the heretics out to the light and refutes them.

2. You accuse us of distributing Bibles full of errors. Our Bibles are a faithful reprint of your own Propaganda Bible. Is that Bible full of errors?

3. You say we have omitted seven holy books. The Jews, from whom we had them, never said they were holy. The early Fathers said they were not so. Jerome, Gregory Theologus, Athanasius and the Council of Laodicea reject them.

4. You glorify your Church as being founded on Peter. *Ans.* Paul says there is no other foundation but Jesus Christ. Chrysostom and others of the Fathers say that the Rock on which the Church was founded (Matt. xvi.) was *not* Peter, but Christ. Jerome, the author of your own Vulgate Bible, expressly says that *"the bishop of Rome can claim no divine authority for his Church above that of any other bishop."*

5. You accuse us of preaching false doctrine. *Ans.* We challenge you to the proof by the only true standard, which is the word of God.

6. You assert that we buy up the Bibles printed in Rome that we may eradicate them from the land. *Ans.* The accusation is utterly unfounded. A few years ago

it is well known that the English contributed a considerable sum of money to enable the Syrian Catholic Patriarch to print the Scriptures correctly, *according to the Roman Church*. Could they do this and wish to root out Roman Bibles from the land?

7. You warn the people against receiving the Scriptures, *although accurately printed* after the approved Romish edition. *Ans.* No wonder, since the Council of Trent declares that "the Scriptures in the vulgar tongue do more harm than good." But Jesus Christ said, "Search the Scriptures," and "Ye do err, not knowing the Scriptures," that is, *because* ye know not the Scriptures. And the apostles exhort men to *take heed to the Scriptures* as to "a light shining in a dark place," and affirm that "all Scripture is profitable for instruction, that the man of God may be perfect."

When this document was ready to be delivered over to the hands of the translator* at Antoora, Mr. Fisk was appointed to be the carrier. While on his way he experienced one of those serio-comic adventures for which Syria is somewhat remarkable. It was a time of anarchy in Lebanon on account of the pending contest for power between the reigning prince and the Druze Sheikh Besheer. Mr. Fisk had finished more than half his journey, having reached the foot of the mountains, when a man suddenly showed himself by his side and demanded of him a *pinch of snuff*. He soon caught Mr. Fisk's beast by the halter to prevent his proceeding, but, after a little expostulation from the rider, loosed his hold and let him go on, keeping, however, near by and repeating his demand with increasing emphasis. Mr. Fisk, to put him off and gain time, affected to understand

---

* Bishop Hanna Marone.

him literally, assuring him that he did not use the article he wanted, at the same time spurring up his beast to get out of his way. But he was not to be put off so. He was sure that the man had some of the snuff that he wanted, and quickening his pace, was again at the head of the animal and had brought him to a halt. The mule-driver then came up and compelled him to loose his hold. He then immediately drew forth a pistol, cocked it, opened the pan, and removed the paper put there to keep his powder dry, all the while having his eye sternly fixed on his threatened victim. At this moment the latter, without giving the villain time to shut the pan, caught hold of the weapon with both his hands, and a struggle ensued in which the rider was unhorsed. The struggle continued, but neither was able to wrest the pistol from the grasp of the other, when a stout lad came up with an open knife and was about to try its edge on Mr. Fisk's hands. The latter, not knowing how many more men of like occupation there might be in the vicinity, gave up the contest for that time and walked on. The man for the moment was quieted, but soon began again to renew his clamor, and became so furious and threatening that his antagonist felt impelled to try again to gain possession of the pistol. He was again unsuccessful; but finally the man came to terms so far as to accept the offer of a few piasters and not insist that the *snuff* should be paid in kind.

He had now become all at once a different man, and told Mr. Fisk of the dangers of the road he was traveling, but said, "If you choose to go on, I will be your guide and protector, and if fifty men meet you, never fear—it shall be all upon *me*." Mr. Fisk believed him to be sincere and trustworthy, but did not care to expose the generous robber or himself to the possible harm that might happen to them, and so turned his face backward toward Beirut.

The reply to the patriarch, however, was in due time translated, copied and sent, in manuscript form (for we had then no press), in various directions in the mountains, and, strange to say, it was received, even by ecclesiastics in some cases, with approbation. Bishop Stefano, of the Mar Moosa convent near Brummana, recommended it to be read to his people. Khoori Anton, chief priest of the Greeks in Beirut, extolled it highly, and called the patriarch hard names for having said against us what he had in his manshoor.

But there was one among the ecclesiastics of Mount Lebanon that did not like it. This was the notorious Peter Jarwi, Roman Catholic patriarch of the papal Syrians of the East, once Bishop of Jerusalem and solicitor in England for help to print the Scriptures which he never printed.

Two or three months after the publication of the reply to the Maronite patriarch's proclamation, we received a sealed document headed thus: "A manifesto in the name of the Lord. To all to whom these presents may come, greeting."

It proceeded: "Whereas, we have lately seen an address of the Bibliani (Bible men), dated January 1, which they are pleased to call a reply to the manshoor of our Right Rev. brother Joseph, Maronite patriarch of Antioch, and we have seen it full of statements and opinions reprobated by the holy Catholic Apostolic Roman Church, mother and instructress of all churches, having one visible head on earth, the pontiff, successor of St. Peter the apostle, whom Jesus Christ constituted vicar in his stead, entrusted to him the keys of heaven, to loose and bind, and set him as a rock on which he built his Church, and after his resurrection submitted to his care his flock of sheep—that is, all Christians with their governors and teachers; that consequently all Catholic believers of every condition, rank and office should glorify God in their subjection as members united to their head, who is the father of all believers, and that they should receive no other doctrines than those of their only mother the Roman Church, to whom it pertains not only to give them the holy Scriptures and to declare what books are canonical, but to give their interpretation also."

After this brief sentence for a preface, the prelate says that the Bibliani insinuate that he is an accomplice with them in the dissemination of the Scriptures. The crime of such a thing would be so great that he cannot bear even its *insinuation*. "Be it known, then, to all men," he says, "that when we first thought of obtaining a press, we sought permission from the holy Society for Propagating the Faith, who gave a written recommendation of our design when as yet we were in the office of Archbishop of Jerusalem. When we went to London to obtain assistance it was with reference solely to the Roman Catholics of that city, but the Protestant English, *of their own accord*, chose to make collections for our benefit. We made known to them and to others, in word, in writing and in print, that we, by the grace of God, were Roman Catholic, yielding subjection to the pontiff, and acknowledging him to be not merely Bishop of Rome, but GENERAL DIRECTOR AND HEAD OF THE WHOLE HABITABLE WORLD.* And when

---
* The dogma of infallibility anticipated.

they had collected their charities and were about to present them to us, we then, a second time, declared to them all that if they consented to make this gift on the ground of a mere charity, without any restriction whatever, we would receive it; otherwise, not. . . . We therefore disclaim all shadow of confederacy and all semblance of communion with these Bibliani in the business of printing and disseminating the Scriptures, and we hereby declare, affirm and publish to *all men*, individually and collectively, of every rank, condition and office, that we, by the grace of God, have never been united with these men in their object, and, by the grace of God, never will be. . . .

"IGNATIUS PETER,
"Ignoble Syrian Patriarch of Antioch.

"Given in the Convent of Mar Efram, Mount Lebanon, on the 9th day of the month Adar (March 20), 1825."

The Bible men had declared that they did not buy up Roman Bibles to get them out of circulation, but, on the contrary, had given money to the Syrian patriarch to *increase* their circulation. To refute the assertion of the Bible men he should have shown, either that the English gave him *no money*, or that it was not to be applied to the printing of Bibles. But he shows neither. How the two parties (the English and the bishop) understood each other the two following epistolary extracts sufficiently explain. Professor Yates, of Oxford University, writes to the bishop thus: "O thou good shepherd of the Eastern flock, . . . you have come from the land of Syria to England, to the city of London, to help us in the good work of the Lord, even to accomplish the printing of the word of God in the language of your country. . . . You see, sir, how many thousands of Christians there are in this land, sincere believers in the Lord Jesus Christ, who are zealous for the gospel and are engaged in discipling all men by the doctrines of Christ, for so our Lord commanded," etc.

The archbishop replies: "I have received your letter written in Syriac, and was gratified by it with gratification unspeakable. . . . I have come hither to receive the donations of the Christian people dwelling in this noble city and its neighborhood, and that I may procure type to print the holy Scriptures, the doctrine of the truth, that it may the more easily be acquired by all. Now, I perceive here very many of every sect, not only rejoicing, but associating together, in this work so necessary to my flock.

"And I pray that our Lord Jesus Christ will grant me to know and teach that knowledge of life which is found in the divine Scriptures.

"THE LOWLY GREGORY PETER JARWI,
"Syrian Archbishop of Jerusalem.

"City of London, 1819."

Comparing these two letters with each other and with the preceding strange "manifesto," we see two things— not only that Protestants are not to be accused of buying up Romish Bibles to destroy them, but also that the "Archbishop of Jerusalem" of 1819 and the "Ignoble Patriarch of Antioch" of 1825 were two very different men.

On the 1st of July we forwarded one of our joint letters to Boston, of which the following abstract will show the state of the work at that time:

"Notwithstanding all that has been attempted to frustrate our purposes and to throw a cloud over our mission, we believe that we can say with truth, and we would say it with the most devout thankfulness, that, so far as Beirut is concerned, our prospects for usefulness never wore a brighter aspect than at present.

"The menacing circulars of native ecclesiastics and the denunciations from Rome were comparatively powerless, but the imperial firman, for a time, spread consternation throughout all Syria. Still, in the face of all that is formidable in the whole combined, we have, during the last six months, given away, lent and sold in our neighborhood two hundred of our sacred books.

"The school that we established a year ago has prospered beyond our most sanguine expectations. It contains between eighty and ninety pupils, all Arabs and all boys but two. One of the exceptions is the teacher's wife, who is about fifteen years of age, the other a little girl about ten. Three of the boys are of the Mohammedan faith, two are Maronites, two papal Greeks and the remainder of the original or orthodox Greek Church. From the increased number of the pupils we have found it necessary, for the last two months, to employ a writing-master as an assistant.

"About four months ago we succeeded in establishing a second school in a village several hours distant from our city, which has twenty pupils. This, of course, cannot enjoy so much of our supervision as the other, but it is subject to the same regulations. The cost of it will be about forty dollars annually.

"Four times a week through a part of the winter, and twice a week the rest of the time, we addressed a company of beggars, consisting frequently of a hundred and fifty persons, at the same time administering to them a pittance for their bodily wants.

"Two or three ecclesiastics of high standing in the Armenian Church have been, by the good providence of God, brought into close connection with us—brought to an intimate acquaintance with whatever we may exhibit of correctness in Christian example or the simplicity and purity in Christian worship, and to an open renunciation of their former errors. They have already written to their brethren in various parts, exposing the errors of their Church and the wickedness of the priests, and we cannot but hope that it is the design of Providence to make them, in their limited circle, reformers of the age.

"In our own families we have daily opportunities for reading and expounding the Scriptures and speaking of the things of God to a greater or less number of persons, and the voice of Providence, unless we misinterpret it, is, 'Be not afraid, but speak, and hold not your peace, for I have much people in this city.'"

Messrs. Fisk and King, who had passed the winter chiefly at Jaffa and Jerusalem, after a tedious detention at the latter place, reappeared with us at Beirut in May, 1825. The history of their labors and adventures during their absence was of considerable interest.

At Jaffa began the first regular stated Protestant preaching in the native language in Palestine. Mr. King on nine successive Sabbaths delivered nine Arabic discourses to an audience of six or eight to twenty hearers, in the house of the English consulate. The house stood by the sea-side, and its foundations may have belonged, for aught we know, to "Simon the tanner." The inclination of the people was such as would evidently have led them to assemble in greater numbers had not priestly jealousy laid the meetings under the ban of excommunication.

At the close of March the brethren went on to Ramla and Jerusalem. At the former place they were glad to be assured by the Greek superior that none of the books sold there the year before had been taken away, nor had the people suffered any annoyance from the sultan's firman. In going on to Jerusalem they fully expected, on account of the influence of the Latin friars in the city, to be received with more than usual reserve. But these men had found themselves unable to make the anti-Bible edict accomplish all that was intended by it. The Greeks, instead of being shy, were more friendly than ever. Some of them, hearing of their approach, came out with lanterns to meet them. At the convent they were received by the inmates with open arms, and it was told them that when it was announced in the city that they were expected prayers were offered up for them by the priests.

They had just become quietly settled in their convent-home when the pasha of Damascus, in his annual visitation for his "tribute money," appeared with his army of three thousand men and encamped near the western gate of Jerusalem. His arrival had always been, to some extent, the harbinger of desolation and woe, since no law but his own will limits his demands upon the people, but this year it might be said of his visit, with special emphasis, "These be the days of vengeance."

The brethren, in their present visit, could do but little in the way of preaching. Amid the suffering and terror that pervaded the city the people were intensely occupied with the question how they should save their persons and their property. The soul was little thought of. Yet some few persons (on two or three occasions, twenty) came together of a Sabbath to hear a discourse from Mr. King in Arabic, or from his colleague in Greek, English, or Italian. At Mr. Fisk's last discourse he had eighteen hearers, a majority of whom were Greek priests.

The pasha's measures in making his collections were perfectly tyrannical. Says Mr. King, "The Greeks at this time were in great affliction. Terror and distress were spread through the city. Last night the pasha took the superior of the convent of Mar Elee-as, a Greek, and gave him five hundred blows on his feet, in order to make him confess that he had concealed in his convent the treasures of the people of Bethlehem, who have all fled to Hebron. He also threatened to raze the convent to the ground, and to send his soldiers to the great Greek convent in Jerusalem and take away whatever was pleasant to his eyes in case the priests should not deliver to him such a sum of money before the end of the day.

"The soldiers have been about the city breaking open houses, taking men into custody, binding them, beating them and putting them in prison. This they do to Greeks, Armenians, Roman Catholics, and even Muslims, as well as Jews, so that the whole city is filled with consternation. The Greek Metropolitans are under guard, and soldiers are stationed in the principal convents. Of all the inhabitants none have so much reason to fear as the Greeks. They are poor. No pilgrims come now to bring them relief, and their country is at war with the Porte. Their countenances are pale with terror, and I may say that with very few exceptions they are literally in tears. Our hearts sicken with the cry of grief all around us. Jerusalem now weepeth sore in the night and her tears are on her cheeks; among all her lovers she hath none to comfort her.

"The soldiers are stationed around upon the wall, and we hear at times, or fancy we hear, the cries of those who are suffering under the hands of Turkish cruelty. The severities suffered by Flavinus, the superior of the convent of Mar Elee-as,* which were almost incredible, with attending circumstances, were thus told by himself: 'Two days after the arrival of the pasha, one of his soldiers came with a Greek monk to the convent, and told me that the pasha wished to see me to inquire what treasures I had received from the peasants of Bethlehem. I showed the soldier seven trunks, and told him those were the things of the peasants. I then showed him my own things, and told him those were mine. He then brought me to the pasha, who immediately asked me what things I had belonging to the peasants, and I told him the same that I had told the soldier. The pasha replied, "You infidel, confess. The staff is ready! Tell what else you've got." I answered, "There is nothing." As often as he asked me what else I had, I made him the same answer, and when he threatened me with the bastinado, I replied, "Use the staff or the sword; my head is at your disposal." The pasha then ordered them to lay me down, and they fastened my ankles between a pole and a cord twisted round it; two men then lifted up the pole on their shoulders, and ten others, five to each foot, laid on the blows. After a little while the pasha ordered them to stop, and said to me, "Is there no

* This convent is midway between Jerusalem and Bethlehem.

more?" I answered, "There is none." Then he ordered the blows to be applied again. This was done three times successively. Chains were then brought and put on my neck and legs, and my arms were bound behind me. After remaining a while in this state, I gave my keeper fifteen piasters to take the chains off.

"'Afterward came the Tefenkgi Bashi, and tried to make me promise to pay eighty purses, but I told him I had none to pay. He then brought a cord and tied it about my neck, as if to strangle me, and tightened it till my eyes seemed starting out of my head; the cord was then removed, and the officer asked me again if I would pay, and I again replied, "I have nothing." "Are you not afraid of death?" said he. "Why should I be afraid of it?" said I. "I must die once, and whether it be to-day or to-morrow it makes no difference." The cord was applied and tightened a second time, and afterward again just above my eyes and upon my temples. After this I remained there on the open ground, without food and without sleep, for three days and nights, when I was taken up and brought into the convent.'"

The chief Greek convent was accustomed to pay yearly one hundred and twenty purses, and against all demands above this it was protected by a high-sounding firman from Constantinople; but in spite of sultans and firmans the convent had to pay two hundred purses, beside endless presents to the pasha's officers and servants, as well as to members of the city government. The bishop affirmed that the pasha's visit had cost them in all not less than about twenty-five thousand dollars.

The share that fell to the Latins was very nearly the same. The Armenians fled from their convent to Hebron, but the governor of Jerusalem sent a force to bring them back, and so they were compelled to bear, like the rest, the chastisement of which all were partakers. Rabbi Mendel, chief among the Jews of the city, was seized and thrown into prison, under a demand of thirty thousand piasters. But the rabbi happened to be a European subject, and at the order of the Spanish consul of Aleppo, Mr. Durighello, who was then at Jerusalem, he was released. This, however, did not release his people from their share of the inevitable exaction.

Omar Effendi, chief of the green-turbaned Muslims, and Moosa Beg (the same who carried the missionaries to prison the year before), were both called upon for large contributions. The former was taken with the pasha to Damascus, the latter was left in Jerusalem in prison till he should pay the debt.

To secure a contribution from Aboo Goosh, the powerful sheikh of the mountains between Jerusalem and Jaffa, the pasha obtained possession of his brother, Abder Rahh-mán, and sent him in custody to Nablus till the sum of thirty-five purses should be forthcoming for his ransom. The sheikh was in a rage, and declared that he *would not pay five paras, though the whole country should be sunk.* He wrote to the three great convents insisting that they should take this matter off his hands and settle the account with the pasha, or otherwise not another pilgrim should pass through his mountains, either to or from the Holy City. So here was a new and unavoidable item of expense for these convents, already so heavily drawn upon.

The four missionaries (including Messrs. Lewis and Dalton) had made up their minds to leave Jerusalem on Saturday, the 30th of April, in company with the Spanish consul and three English travelers, but they were providentially detained by the failure of their muleteers to bring their animals in season. The proposed arrangement between Aboo Goosh and the convents had not been fully completed, and the metropolitan bishops sent in to the detained ones a congratulatory message, saying, "Every hindrance to your going to-day is for good." They remained, therefore, over the Sabbath, and the two Americans preached on that day their last sermons in the holy city.

By Monday morning everything had been settled by the convents; the roads were pronounced free. Aboo Goosh himself appeared at Jerusalem and gave the missionaries a recommendatory letter to his brother, at his mountain village. They set off accordingly, and at evening found the other travelers waiting for them at Ramleh. These, by commencing their journey a day too soon, had found themselves subject to new impositions on their way, costing them about twenty dollars each.

The next day they all started again on their journey, but instead of passing on to Jaffa, as is common, they, with the exception of the consul, took a direction northward, passing by Lydda, the city of Æneas the paralytic, and making for Nazareth through the interior. The second evening they encamped at Ain Lejjoon, a place which, like "the way which goeth down to Jericho," had been somewhat noted for its inhospitalities. The adventures of the night and of the following day are thus described by Mr. King:

"After pitching our tents in the centre of the khan an old Egyptian Arab came and sat down by us, and told us that we were in a bad neighborhood and that we must be on our guard through the night if we wished to keep our things from being stolen. This caution he repeated two or three times. Before retiring to rest I proposed that a watch should be kept by some of our servants, as I supposed, not only from what the old Egyptian had told us, but from what I had heard previously, that the place was rather dangerous. A servant of Mr. Lewis was one of the first appointed to keep watch, and when we lay down to sleep he took his station in an old tower which rose a little above the wall of the khan.

"Being much fatigued I soon fell into a sound sleep, but about one o'clock we were all suddenly awakened by a terrible outcry and the firing of guns. From the noise I supposed we were attacked by a band of robbers, and that they and our servants and the muleteers were perhaps actually killing each other.

"Some sprang up in a fright, crying out that we were attacked. One, as he started out of his sleep, not knowing what he did, got hold of his pillow instead of his pistol under it; others seized their arms; all were in confusion. When the noise had a little abated we learned that a trunk of Mr. Lewis had been stolen by a couple of Arabs. The alarm had been given by a mule. Ali, one of our muleteers, had tied the mule to his leg, so that he might be awakened in case any one should attempt to steal his animal. The mule, being disturbed by the thieves, gave a sudden jerk, which awakened his master just in time to catch a glimpse of them as they left the khan. He set up the cry of 'Robbers!' but could not follow them, being tied to his mule. When the morning came we agreed to go in search of the trunk. Presently three Arabs came to look at us, and some of our party seized upon them and bound them with cords. I remonstrated and said, 'I can have nothing to do with such proceedings.' These men were afterward released, and two others who were suspected were seized at a neighboring mill and brought in with their hands tied behind them. They were fastened to each other by ropes about their necks and led off before the caravan.

"As we left the khan and passed over the stream, which I call a branch of the river Kishon, the two Arabs who walked bound before us made signs and called out to three or four men that were sitting down near the village, and in a minute or two after I heard those other men calling as if to some person or persons at a distance. In the land of the Philistines, as we came from Egypt, I had seen the Arabs spring up like grasshoppers, where at first only two or three were visible, and I felt very sensibly that our present situation was dangerous. So I hastened forward to speak to our friends who were in the foremost part of the *kofila*, near the two prisoners, for the company was at this time stretched along in Indian file, with muleteers and baggage in the rear. Our path lay down the gentle declivity of one of those hills which skirt the borders of the plain of Jezreel, and on either side of us were high weeds and grass, so that we naturally fell into the position above mentioned. On coming up to the prisoners I said to our leader, 'You had better let these men go; you will be in difficulty; the safest way is to let them go.' To this I had no reply. But the words were scarcely out of my mouth when an Arab came furiously riding along by the side of the kofila, then stopped suddenly, turned and set up a loud cry. I then said, 'They are coming,' and again requested that the two Arabs should be liberated. No answer was given, but in a moment we saw a large company of Arabs pouring down upon us, and I then ordered a Muslim who was near to me to untie the prisoners and let them go.

"At this instant the dragoman of Dr. B——, an English traveler, leveled his piece to shoot the Arab who first came on horseback. I presumed that if he fired we should, in all probability, be cut down by the infuriated mob that was coming, and I cried to him not to fire, and so did Dr. B——. But he did not seem to hear, and a Muslim, one of our company, ran up and caught hold of his gun. The Muslim had no sooner done this than one of the Arabs who was pursuing us came up in a most determined manner, and, running up to the prisoners, with one blow of his sword severed the rope that bound them together, then cut the cords that tied their hands and set them at liberty, giving one of them a heavy blow upon the shoulder, for what reason I could not understand.

"While this was passing every part of our kofila was attacked by the Arabs, who poured down upon us like a torrent, some on horses, some on foot, with drawn swords, guns and heavy clubs, at the same time setting up a tremendous yell like the war-whoop of the American savage. It was no time for parley; all was confusion. No one knew what to expect, whether life or death. The latter, however, seemed to stare us full in the face. Some of our men I saw falling from their animals, and all of us were put in motion and driven like a flock of sheep before a band of wolves. I was unarmed, and if I had had arms I should not have used them.

"The cry was 'Flee!' and we fled, or rather we were

forced on by the Arabs. They were among us and around us, beating us with their heavy clubs and guns, brandishing their swords, riding by us on their swift horses and screaming like so many furies. One of them aimed a deadly blow at Mr. Fisk, which providentially did but just graze his forehead, knocked off his turban and slightly touched his arm. Flight from the assailants was impossible. We were, for the most part, badly mounted; their horses were fleet as the wind; we had twelve miles to go over the plain; we were unacquainted with the road; our pursuers knew every turn.

"Our baggage was at length cut off. There seemed now to be a little cessation of fury on the part of the enemy, and I hoped that, being content with the possession of our baggage, they would let us go in peace. But in a moment I saw them coming on again, and thought that probably all was lost, and that having got possession of our baggage and yet were not satisfied, they now intended to take our lives. It was an awful moment. I could only say, 'Heaven defend us!' I was in front of the kofila and a little distance ahead when an Arab sheikh came flying up to me on his steed, with a large club in his hand. Making a halt, I addressed him, calling him, 'Brother,' and said, 'Do me no harm. I have not injured you.' I spoke to him words of peace and gentleness. Upon this he let down his club which he had been brandishing, halted, listened and presently turned away. Soon after I saw him driving back some of our pursuers, and the cry of 'Ah-mán!' (safety) was heard by us. The baggage, too, to my surprise, was permitted to come on. No life was lost, and I now presume it was not the intention of the Arabs to kill us, for if this had been their design there was nothing to hinder it.

"The attack was a gallant one, and was made by them as if they were fully resolved to carry their point through life or death, and I have no doubt that, had any one of their party fallen by our hands, it would have been the signal for the slaughter of us all. I will now say, 'The Lord is my rock and my fortress and my deliverer, my God, my strength, in whom I will trust.'"

At Nazareth the four Bible men, being forbidden entertainment at the Latin convent, lodged at the house of the Greek priest, and the next day went on a visit to Tiberias. "The morning was fine," writes Mr. King; "all around me was peace and stillness, and I could not but feel in my bosom emotions of gratitude and joy. I had been for about two months at Jerusalem in the midst of sorrow and sighing. I had seen the tear of oppression and heard the groans of the bruised, the wounded and the dying; our journey from thence was through a troubled country, and we had just escaped, as it were, from the jaws of death. This, I might say, was the first day of peace I had enjoyed since the day of my arrival at Jerusalem." They visited Cana of Galilee, with which Mr. King expressed himself charmed. It is called by the natives Kfer Kenni. "It is situated on the slope of a hill overlooking a most lovely plain, beyond which the prospect is limited by lofty mountains. Its beautiful situation, its vicinity to the mountains, its excellent water, the character of its inhabitants, one-half of them being Christians, and its vicinity to Acca, Tiberias, Safet and Nazareth, conspire to render it an inviting place for a missionary station.

They spent a Sabbath at Safet, where they made some

visits among the Jews, and on the subsequent day, passing through one of the finest parts of the country they had yet seen, they reached the little city of Tyre, from which two more days brought them to Beirut.

Their "journeyings often," so far as this land was concerned, had now come to an end. Mr. King, however, after recruiting a little, went to spend a short season with his old acquaintances at Deir el Kommer.

CANA.

He took with him as teacher a very intelligent young Maronite named Assad Shidiak, who had received a finished education at the patriarch's college of Ain Waraka. His theological knowledge was considerable—far beyond what was claimed by the great majority even of Maronite priests. Mr. King found him a most interesting companion. They were together from morning till night, and spent hours, almost every day, in discussing religious subjects. The candor of Shidiak was uncommon, as well as his patience in listening to the arguments of his antagonist. It was seen that in his composition he had nothing of the bigot or the fanatic, and their disputations always ended in good nature. After many earnest discussions in which Popery and Protestantism were set hand to hand in hopeless contest, he said, in a rather pleasant mood, "Now I am going to have this question decided by lot, which is to be preferred, the pope or the Bible men—the Protestants. I take my Testament, and, as I open it at random, the first passage I set my eye upon shall be for the Protestants." He opened the book and his eye fell upon Luke i. 2, last phrase, "*ministers of the word.*" He was struck with its appropriateness. The Protestants make everything of the WORD. They print it, they spread it in all languages, they preach from it, they appeal to it to prove all their doctrines; they are called, therefore, *Bible* men—men of the word of God.

"Now," said he, "I shall open for the pope." He opened, and directing his eye, just as before, on the first corner of the page, he caught the word "*unclean,*" "the unclean spirit." Luke xi. 24. "When he goes out of a man," he returns with "seven others more wicked than himself." He was struck as with an electric shock. He closed the book, rose from his seat and walked the room in silence. The subject was not again broached that day.

It cannot be denied that under the circumstances the lots fell on two very remarkable passages, and the effect on the young man's mind was not to be wondered at. It was enough to have impressed a mind trained among a people even less superstitious than his. He remembered cases in Scripture where divine decisions had been received by means of a lot (Acts i. 26, etc.). The appeal he had made was virtually an appeal to God, and it seemed as if God had so received it and given answers too intelligent and apposite to be the work of chance. But, however clearly it might have appeared to the mind of Shidiak that God himself had spoken in that room and decided the great question between pope and Protestant, yet it soon appeared that the impression he received was not enduring. He was neither a converted man nor an antagonist of the pope. He still continued, however, with Mr. King in the capacity of instructor, and was very useful in assisting him to prepare his farewell address to his Syrian friends.

Though the letter might be read with profit by *other* religious denominations, yet it was composed *particularly* for such acquaintances of his as belonged to the *Papal* church. They, as was natural, had urged him to acknowledge the pope, and so to become a member of the *holy Catholic apostolic Roman* Church. He, in this address, gives his reasons why he cannot do this, quoting various doctrinal passages from the Scriptures and setting in their immediate connection the doctrines of the pope contradicting them. This composition was put into a neat style of Arabic by Shidiak, who then transcribed numerous copies to be sealed and forwarded to individuals designated by Mr. King. The letter was afterward put into general circulation as a tract, at first in manuscript and then in print. It has since appeared also in other languages.

Just before the setting out of Mr. King for America we visited, by invitation, the Shidiak family at Hadet. While there we had also the opportunity of calling on the two emeers of this village who had the last winter joined in the rebellion against the Emeer Besheer, who had punished them with the loss of their eyes and of their tongues.

The Emeer Phares described the process of punishment in his case. He said his eyes were pierced to the depth of half a finger with a red-hot iron, and his tongue was sliced off twice, being held out with a hook. After the first cutting he had cried out "*Yaakhi!*" (O my brother!), words which he could easily pronounce without a tongue; but they said, "The rebel can talk yet; we must slice him again." And so they did. Nevertheless both the princes spoke still quite intelligibly.

The Emeer Phares professed to be a Christian, and of the Maronite church, yet he conversed with freedom on the subject of religion, confessed some of the errors of Popery and begged us to call again. He even sent the next day to Beirut to invite Messrs. Fisk and King to come out again and spend the day with him. The brother of this man was called Sulmán, and was a Muslim. As Mr. King addressed him, he asked, "Are you that Mr. King, of Beirut, who lately wrote the letter on Popery?" He said the letter had been read to him, and he thought it was unanswerable. This led to much interesting conversation about the gospel way of salvation. He showed by his talk that he was a Muslim, but he listened attentively, as did also his son, to all that was said in behalf of Christianity.

CHAPTER X.

Shidiak and the Patriarch—Sickness and death of Mr. Fisk—Shidiak in custody of the Patriarch—Escapes by night—Describes in writing his sojourn with his Holiness—Is visited by his acquaintances and relatives—Priest Girgis mocks at him—He is recaptured by the Patriarch—Plot against the Bible men—The Lord of Hosts breaks it up—Attack of Greeks on the city—Mr. Goodell's house plundered before his eyes.

SHIDIAK, who had been engaged with Mr. King, soon came into our employ at Beirut. He produced a letter which he had quite lately received from his patriarch, in which that "faithful pastor of the Lord's flock," as he styled himself, felt in duty bound to warn him against giving to us or receiving from us any instruction whatever, and said that he had received frequent letters from Rome urging him "by *all means* and in *every way* to persecute those individuals so long as one of them should remain in the country." Still the young sheikh ventured on coming, and commenced, under our direction, a small school for the instruction of Arab boys in Nah-hoo—Arabic grammar. But soon this bold step of his was made known at head quarters, and drew forth a letter from Patriarch Joseph Peter so threatening and violent that he thought proper, for a time at least, to show it deference, and so returned once more to his home in Hadet. His brother Tannoos also, who had been engaged for some weeks instructing Mr. Fisk and copying tracts, went with him.

But in less than a month the former was again at his post. This bold defiance of the patriarch's authority produced quite a sensation at Beirut. One evening there came in eight or ten of his neighboring acquaintances, and among them the active priest Girgis, a former fellow-student of Assad's at Ain Waraka, and now a spy, doubtless, of the bishop and patriarch. They were standing around him engaging him in animated conversation. One of them, by way of expostulation, inquired of their heretical friend what great plan he had in his mind—what he proposed to accomplish by his present extraordinary course. A short pause ensuing, Priest Girgis felt constrained to make answer to the question. Like Elihu, he was "full of the matter and ready to burst like a new bottle of wine."* Speaking in a loud voice, he said, "I can tell you what he means to do. He means to introduce among us a new gospel dispensation. He will bring us a new holy Bible, accompanied with his own learned notes and commentaries. We shall have no more need of the holy fathers. Gregory, Chrysostom, Augustine and the rest will all be old-fashioned; they'll stand for nothing before this new angelic doctor. He'll raise up many that will trumpet his praise and cry, 'Who is like unto this great *maallem?* Who is able to dispute with him? Hosanna to the incomparable Assad ibn esh Shidiak, the holy prophet of Hádet!'"

All this, accompanied with due emphasis and gesture, brought forth a burst of laughter. Assad himself joined mildly in the laugh, sensible, evidently, that the best argument the priest knew how to use in the premises was ridicule.

* Job xxxii. 18, 19.

In his late short absence he had had various conversations with the princes and others of his village respecting the sentiments advanced in Mr. King's letter. The Emeer Phares had previously had it in mind to write something by way of reply to it. "But," says the emeer, "when King affirms that the gospel says thus and so, I cannot contradict him, for I do not know what the gospel *does* say. Pray, can you lend me a copy of the Bible? And yet I fear the priests. What will they say to it? Will they not excommunicate me?"

On hearing this report respecting the prince, that he wanted a Bible to aid him in refuting the Bible (for Mr. King's arguments were all Bible), we took pains to remove his embarrassment as soon as possible by sending him one, hoping that the priests, in consideration of his worthy object, would consent to make an exception in his case, and hoping also that the book, being read to him, would prove a light not only to the blind prince himself, but also to his reader. How far the emeer proceeded in his pious undertaking we never learned. The probability is that, either from the prohibition of the priests or from the inherent difficulties of the task itself, he did not succeed.

At this point in our work it pleased God to throw us into deep affliction. We had just lost one of our two elder brethren, to whom we had been wont to look up for counsel, instruction and social sympathy, and now it was so ordained that we should be deprived of the other. Our endeared and venerated brother Fisk, our earthly stay and staff, just at the moment of entering on his course as an efficient preacher in the native tongue, was suddenly cut down by a malignant fever, leaving the rest of us, in our inexperience and conscious unfitness, to pursue our way alone.*

The patriarch had abundant time to get word of the return of Shidiak to our employ, and we were every day expecting from his hand a paper of excommunication. But instead of this there arrived a letter of *benediction* by a special messenger, and he no less a personage than the patriarch's own brother. His Holiness, two or three years ago, was chief instructor in the patriarchal college of Ain Waraka, and the brightest scholar he had was Assad Shidiak. He, therefore, knew the young man well, and how much trouble he might cause him if he made him his enemy. He thought it expedient, evidently, before resorting to the extreme measure of excommunication, to try the use of gentle means still longer. Accordingly, the letter now sent by him contained not only a paternal blessing on the head of the "dear son Assad," but also the promise of a lucrative employment. Moreover, the messenger himself had brought a verbal promise of forty purses in money, if, as was understood, that was the amount which the Bible men had given to purchase his adhesion to them. Assad at once assured Priest Nicolas that he had received nothing whatever on such an account, and that his wages as instructor were far from being extravagant. If Assad had been disposed to play the villain at this time, he might have acknowledged the report to be true, accepted the patriarch's two thousand dollars and gone back into quiet security in the bosom of his

* Mr. Fisk was born in Shelburne, Massachusetts, June 24, 1792, graduated at Middlebury College, Vermont, in 1814, and at Andover in 1818. He and his associate, Parsons, were college classmates. A memoir of Mr. Fisk has been published by Rev. Dr. Alvan Bond, of Norwich, Connecticut, and one of Mr. Parsons by Rev. D. O. Morton.

"Mother Church." But he preferred the truth to the money. Perhaps it was because the Lord had given him a new heart. Perhaps it was this which gave him such an entire equanimity while in hourly expectation of the patriarch's curse. Possibly it was this which moved him to go with Priest Nicolas and put himself in the patriarch's power. He believed that he could do the patriarch good. He had before this expressed a desire to have an interview with his Holiness, that he might repel some of the slanders he (the patriarch) had heard and remove the suspicions he had conceived against him, solemnly assuring him that in what he did he was acting not from love of publicity or love of gain, but from honest conviction of the truth. Moreover, he hoped even to conciliate the patriarch's good-will toward the dissemination of the Scriptures and the enlightenment of his nation. The rest of us did not share with him in his expectations of the good to come from his accepting the patriarch's invitation, and strongly advised him to refuse going. But, like Paul on his last visit to Jerusalem, he would not be persuaded, and we ceased, saying, "The will of the Lord be done."

The first news we had of him after his departure was by the following letter, which was quite corroborative of the best hopes we had formed of him: "I am now at the convent of Alma, and, thanks to God! I arrived in good health. But as yet I have not seen the patriarch. I pray God the Father and his only Son Jesus Christ our Lord that he will establish me in his love, that I may never exchange it for any created thing, that neither death nor life, nor things present nor things to come, nor height nor depth, nor riches nor honor, nor dignity nor office, nor anything in creation, shall separate me from this love. I hope you will pray to God for me, and I beg this not only from yourself, but from all the brethren and sisters, after giving them—especially Mr. Goodell—abundant salutations."

After this, weeks having passed with no word of additional intelligence, we sent a trusty messenger with a line to him. Happily the messenger found him alone, and, after a short conversation, received from him the following billet:

"Your note has reached me, and has added another proof to the many I have received of your kind regard for me. I now beseech you once more to pray for me that I may be delivered from the dark devices of men. I find myself reduced quite to an extremity. One or more of three things are before me—either to be thought mad, or to commit sin, or to offer up my life. I call upon God for deliverance. I cannot now write fully, but the bearer will tell you all."

The messenger informed us that the emeer of that district had threatened to send him to Bteddeen to be put in prison. Assad had replied to him that he was ready to go to prison and to death. He was engaged in daily disputations with the patriarch and others. His countenance wore a shade of melancholy and his eyes were red apparently with weeping.

He was not literally in prison, but was under constant surveillance, was denied the privilege of society and the use of books, was accused of being possessed of the devil and threatened with death by his own bishop if he did not repent. He endured this kind of treatment for two months and then made his escape in the night. He rose at twelve o'clock, and, leaving on his couch a paper with the Scripture quotation, "Come out of her, my people," etc., he set off for Beirut on foot, committing himself to God for protection and strength. The darkness was such that he often found himself astray from his path, sometimes stumbling over rocks and hedges, sometimes wading in water or miring in mud. After some hours of weariness and anxiety he arrived at a place on the sea-shore where he found a large boat thrown up, under cover of which he threw himself and gained a little rest; then addressing himself again to his task, at about the rising of the sun, he was joyfully received at one of the mission-houses at Beirut.

Toward evening a Maronite youth of our acquaintance arrived, who was present in the morning at Deir Alma when it was first discovered that Assad had fled. The startling intelligence was communicated to the patriarch and his train when they were chanting their matins in the chapel. Immediately they were all in a quandary, looking very blank at each other, inquiring what was to be done. One man among them who was friendly to Assad and had spoken encouragingly to him, telling him he was right, now came out boldly in Assad's defence. "This," said he, "is just what you had reason to expect. Why should not the man leave you? What had he here to do? What had he here to enjoy? Books he had none, friendly society none, conversation against religion abundant, insults upon his opinions and feelings abundant. Why should he not leave you?" Others—especially the great ones—were full of pity for the "poor maniac," and sent in quest of him in every direction, lest, peradventure, he might be found starving in some cavern, or floating in the sea, or dashed in pieces at the bottom of some precipice.*

* At our request Sheikh Assad, soon after his return, gave us a

This successful escape of Shidiak from custody excited a strong commotion in the neighborhood. Yoosef el Khoori, a burly old constable, sent for him to come and see him, and afterward came himself for an interview at his lodgings. In the latter case the English consul happened to be present, so that if he had any designs against the fugitive his purpose was thwarted. He, doubtless, immediately made known his failure to the patriarch, who had employed him, and who next sent for help to his family in Hadet. Two of his elder brothers and a furious uncle came, and were closeted with him for half an hour. Their talk was loud and imperious. They were three against one, and seemed bent on gaining their point by dint of superior noise and numbers. They assailed him with rebukes and sneers in so harsh and unfeeling a manner that it made one tremble to hear them. To use a phrase of the brother Tannoos on a subsequent occasion, their "hearts were *iron* against him." They contradicted, scoffed at him, threatened him, called him mad, under the power of Satan, and so on. Assad was not intimidated nor was he vanquished,

narrative of this visit of his to the patriarch, in writing. The document is too long to be inserted here, but the following incident, among many, is worthy of special record: "The bishop and priest" (Bishop Blabul and Priest Bernandus, of Gazeer) "then begged me, in presence of the patriarch, to say that my faith was like that of the Roman Catholic Church. I replied that I feared to tell a falsehood by declaring that I believe a thing while in my reason I actually do *not* believe it. 'But,' said they, 'the patriarch here will absolve you from the sin of the falsehood.' I turned to the patriarch and put the question to him whether he would so absolve me. He answered that *he would*. I replied, 'What the law of nature itself condemns it is not within the power of any man to make lawful.'" Priest Bernandus himself, before this document was published, borrowed a copy in manuscript at Beirut, read it and testified to its truth. Papal priests, then, claim the power to forgive sins *in advance*.

but he finally told them he would leave the English and go home as they wished, on one condition, namely, that they would obtain from the patriarch a written assurance, on the faith of a Christian, that he would not molest him—not abridge his liberty of speech. This they would not attempt to do. No man, they said, could approach the patriarch with such a proposal. But Assad was firm, and they had to return without their prey. The brother Mansoor, however, could not go without calling him to the door and quietly but threateningly telling him that his life would not be safe if he did not submit.

After they were gone Assad walked the room in deep thought for some time, and then betook himself to the loft at the end of the room, where he usually slept, and threw himself upon his couch, evidently in prayer. Just then a knock was heard at the door. It proved to be Galeb, one of the younger brothers. He had probably come to the neighborhood with the rest, but chose not to appear till now. Assad was called, but making no answer, his brother was conducted to the reception-room, where Assad, with a full and heavy heart, not long after made his appearance. The two brothers saluted each other with considerable embarrassment, and sat together for some time not unlike the manner of Job and his comforters, when "none spake a word unto him, because they saw that his grief was exceeding great." Assad had had trial enough for one day, and evidently wished to be alone, and Galeb, sympathizing with his sadness, after a few unmeaning remarks, went his way. He appeared again, however, the following day, and spoke freely, and the next day came the youngest brother, Phares, accompanied by the mother. All united in urging Assad to come home with them to Hadet. But to no purpose. He answered all their arguments and remained steadfast. To his mother he said, "Of what use would it be that I should go home with you? You wish me to go, you say, that I may show people that I am not mad. But you, who come here and see and converse with me, still say I am mad. How shall I convince others that I am not mad when my own mother, who is with me, believes that I *am* so? Or do you imagine that when I get out among you the air of Hadet will change my opinions, or induce me to be silent? These are vain expectations. I see nothing to be gained. If I should go forth among you and tell people what I believe, that you are all going astray—that you are worshiping idols instead of the living God—that I could wish to tear down every picture in your churches—that the bread and wine of the mass are not Jesus Christ—that the pope is the Beast of the Revelation, whose business it is to deceive the people and destroy their souls—by all this I should injure your feelings, enrage the people, stir up the persecuting spirit of the emeers, bishops, and patriarchs, and then come back here just as I am now."

Finally, to silence his mother's importunities and put an end to the interview, he sat down and wrote a paper for her to show to her friends, and to whomsoever it might concern, in which he declared his belief in the Holy Trinity—that Christ was God—that Mary was his mother—that he was not a follower of the English—that his religion was not from them, etc., all which she was right glad to know, and, taking and carefully folding the paper, went home evidently much pacified.

Yoosef el Khoori, the burly old sheikh, having

failed to intimidate the refugee, now, through the medium of one of the priests, offers him his daughter in marriage.

In concert with the rest the bishop of Beirut, whose ordinary dwelling is high in the mountains, is now walking about the suburbs of Beirut. Meeting a young friend of ours one day he took the opportunity to inquire about his spiritual son, Assad Shidiak, asking why he did not go home to his mother's house, and saying he had nothing to fear there any more than in Beirut.

Many other proofs existed of commotion in the enemy's camp about these days. There were plots concocting and measures preparing to put, if possible, an effectual stop to the spread of this leaven of heresy—to cut off these "false apostles" from all residence in the country—to unite all sects, including even the Jews and Muslims, in a conspiracy not to rent them any of their houses, so that the vagabonds should be compelled either to leave the country, or, like Jeremiah's outcast sons of Zion, become desolate in the streets and die embracing dunghills.

Besides the hostile measures of the Maronites, a new battery was opened upon us by the Syrian Catholic bishop at Deir Sharfi. One of our cooks who belonged to his fold received from him a peremptory order to leave his situation at once or be excommunicated. It was a great trial to the poor man, but he could not stay.

To complete the combination of influences for the recovery of Assad, the patriarch himself sends him, by a special messenger, as before, a letter couched in the softest terms, expressing his continued paternal regard, gently reproving his distrustful son for leaving Deir Alma so abruptly, as if he had thought himself in danger, assuring him that there was no real ground for his apprehensions, whatever he might have thought, and finally urging him to put an end to the prevailing scandal by retiring from Beirut to his own home in Hadet. There he might remain in quiet, and no violence or harm should be offered him.

To this plausible and, as it proved, thoroughly deceitful epistle the patriarch had set his own hand and seal. Such a written assurance of safety was nearly or quite all that Assad had demanded in his interview with his uncle and brothers, and for which they had pretended that no one would dare apply to his Holiness. It assured Assad's safety even without the condition of his silence. It seems as if the three delegates, in reporting to the patriarch the result of their abortive mission, had informed him of the terms on which alone he would consent to leave his present asylum, and his Holiness now accepts the terms.

Assad was sensibly moved and encouraged by this insidious letter, and wrote, as we suppose, a favorable reply. It was one of his weaknesses that he was too artless and confiding. He had not yet known the depths of Satan, as they speak. He had indeed read in the Appendix of the Romish Bible the declaration, *"It is our duty to destroy heretics,"* and had been astounded by it, and had called it a doctrine of Nero; but he had probably never read, in so many words, the standing Romish maxim, that for the good of the Church *"It is our duty to break promises made to heretics,"* though the former of these "duties" seems to involve the latter, for to *deceive* a heretic is surely not worse than *killing* him.

We supposed that the patriarch, as soon as he received this yielding letter of Assad, sent it directly to the family at Hadet, enjoining upon them to hasten and bring him to their house; for, on the very next day after the letter was written, a deputation of four came for him, among whom was the youngest brother, in whom the others knew that Assad much confided, and whose presence they rightly judged would increase the probability of their success. Suffice it to say they succeeded.

A majority of us opposed his going. One of our number spoke against it most earnestly, and as he was departing took him by the hand and said solemnly, "Assad, I expect never again to see your face on earth." He smiled incredulously at these fears, made some brief reply, gave us his last spoken salaam, made us his last bow, and we saw his face no more. All of us knew there was danger before him. He knew this himself. But neither he nor we imagined such a complication of perils and sufferings as that through which he was destined to make his way during the rest of his short life.

The patriarch and bishop, with their combined forces, had now, in their warfare against the gospel, obtained a signal advantage. By one of those stratagems, or rather by a *series* of those stratagems, which are reckoned justifiable in war, they had succeeded in capturing one of the most formidable champions of their foe. But God had determined that their plan of operations for the remaining part of the campaign should become like the counsel of Ahithophel. He gave them other things to think of beside turning Bible men out of doors and banishing them from the land. The bishop, who had come down on this business, suddenly had to betake himself to a precipitate flight, and was glad to regain in safety his mountain fastnesses, while the Bible men and their families, instead of being houseless, found themselves the only families that had houses in all the suburbs of Beirut.

These sudden and unlooked-for events were brought about by no human skill or foresight. To us who were on the ground they seemed to be the acts of a special divine interposition.

The very day after the departure of our persecuted friend, and, as we loved to think, Christian brother, there sailed into our harbor, late in the evening, three or four Greek vessels of war. A considerable number of other ships, whose approach had been descried off at sea, were evidently bearing toward the same destination. The whole city was panic-struck. Muslims were in dread of the enemy from without, and Christians of the enemy from within, the city. Among the Christians, every man—especially every *prominent* man, bishop, priest, wealthy merchant or scribe—felt himself exposed to violence or insult, and if he could flee he fled.

At the earliest dawn in the morning an irregular discharge of musketry announced that the expected attack upon the town had begun. Some scores of Greeks had been landed from the ships, and having taken a position on the eastern side of the city, where the cannon of the castles could not harm them, seemed bent on making a breach in the walls with musket bullets. The attack was perfectly harmless except to the assailants, who received a few scattering but damaging shots through the loopholes in the city walls. As the day drew on the Greeks gradually retired toward their ships, leaving some fifteen of their comrades dead upon the field. During the whole of this mock attack the fleet remained quietly at anchor some miles distant. But, presently after, the sails were unfurled, and thirteen vessels were seen coming forward in threatening array against the city. Three or four of the largest led the van. These few alone seemed to reach their appointed station for the attack, and, without waiting for the rest to come up, immediately began pouring forth their broadsides. The firing of the men-of-war was most inaccurate in its range and feeble in its effects. Some of the balls passed whizzing over our heads nearly half a mile off. Two were lodged in the empty house of the consul at a similar distance, and others fell scatteringly around us in the mulberry gardens. In the city a few house-walls were pierced, one poor Christian boy had both his legs shot off, and half a dozen other persons were either killed or wounded.

What *might* have been the result of this attempt upon the city in ordinary circumstances it is impossible to say. The assailants might have been willing to accept a heavy contribution from the citizens, and so leave the city without actually entering it, or they might have taken possession and given it over to indiscriminate plunder and slaughter. But we were saved from these possible calamities by another interposition signally providential. He who "hath his way in the whirlwind and in the storm" came and stood in the gap, and said to the Greek, "Hitherto shalt thou come, but no farther." A thick black cloud which had been gathering in the west swept terribly over the place, borne by a furious wind. The whole Turkish navy could not have better defended our city. The ships became suddenly unmanageable and were seen scudding before the tempest back to their anchorage ground. The cloud was "big with mercy." Who can tell how many lives it saved, how much ruin and misery it prevented? "The Lord looked through the cloud and troubled" the Greeks, "and they said, Let us flee from the face of this people, for the Lord fighteth for them against" us.

As the land forces were loitering along back toward their vessels we improved the occasion to distribute among them all the Greek tracts we could muster, which were received with all civility.

At our houses, during the day of the attack, all was panic and confusion. Besides attending to the personal wants of the people who fled to us for protection, the day was mostly spent in receiving and storing goods brought by our neighbors, preparatory to a general flight to the mountains.

In a day or two it was proclaimed that an army from Abdallah Pasha was in rapid march toward Beirut for its protection. The army was composed of Muslims of the coast and Bedawin Arabs of the desert. Through fear of this "protection" the whole vicinity outside of the city was at once cleared of its inhabitants. As soon as the army made its appearance it was announced by the usual military signals of the rattle of drums and the booming of cannon. At the same moment the large flag-ship of the Greek admiral was seen spreading her white sails to the wind and slowly moving from the harbor, while the others, in bustling activity, were preparing to follow. The whole fleet soon disappeared in the direction of Cyprus.

The army saw the departing enemy; they found the hundreds of houses around the city unoccupied; what better opportunity for pillage could be presented to a Bedawin Arab horde whose trade was robbery and whose military reward was plunder? At once, like the Nile on arriving at the Delta, the army of pillagers spread themselves to the right and left and began their work. Strokes of violence, with club and stone dashing through doors and windows, were heard on every side. Closets and chests were smashed in pieces and their contents taken into possession or strewed upon the floors. Even our own houses, though the natives generally feared the Franks, were not wholly secure. The house of Mr. Goodell was broken into and pillaged before his eyes. His own account of this bold transaction is here given in his own words:

"Several parties of the Bedawin came in the course of the day to our house, but I told them we were English and they went away. At last some of their more resolute and reckless ones came, and in their strong, guttural voices called upon me to 'iftah el bab' (open the door). I told them I should not *iftah el bab;* that they saw from my dress I was not a native; that the house was English, and if they broke it open they did it at their peril, for the sultan would soon hear of it, etc. They said they knew neither English nor sultan, and they fell to work in good earnest. Fine-looking, noble fellows, those Arabs!—choice, independent spirits, the very lords of the desert, with a voice like thunder, were those Bedawin Arabs.

"I had barricaded the door very strongly with stones and wood, and they must have been half an hour in cutting their way through. During this time I was reasoning with them from a narrow window above, showing them how they were violating the most solemn treaties, and calling upon them to desist. Sometimes they would stop a few moments and listen to what I had to say, and then return with redoubled ardor to their work. One man leveled his gun and threatened to shoot me, and I stepped aside a moment from the win-

ROBBING THE HOUSE OF DR. GOODELL, AT BEIRUT.

dow. At last they cut and split that door to pieces, and then rushed up like so many tigers for their prey. Several Turks from the city who knew us came along at this time, and they hastened up after them and stood at the door of Mrs. Goodell's room and did not permit one of them to enter there.

"They seized hold of boxes, trunks, kitchen utensils, everything that came in their way, and carried them off, and I in the mean time threw as many articles as I could into Mrs. Goodell's room, and some of my things I even snatched out of their hands and threw in there, when any one had laid hold of more than he could well defend or carry away at once. On this account one of them came very coolly the next day to claim some tobacco which he said I stole from him while he was engaged in the lawful work of plundering my house. But really it was a false charge. He could not prove it and I refused to pay him.

"Three times I sent to the city to the English consul, informing him of my situation, and three times he sent to the leader of these troops, and three times the old sheikh sent horsemen to protect me. But no sooner had these horsemen left the city than they galloped off to plunder for themselves.

"At last, what with my own remonstrances and those of the Turks that were present, together with the assurance that complaints had already been lodged against them, they ceased operations, begged pardon for what they had done, hoped I had not been very much frightened nor very much injured, took what they had got and went off."

At this time, with the exception of our own two families, we knew not of one that was left in all the vicinity outside the walls of the city. We had, however, a single neighbor, a French merchant, who, perhaps unfortunately, had sent away his family and was keeping house alone. The Arabs entered his dwelling, broke in pieces most of his trunks and furniture, his piano among the rest, and took from his person some few hundred piasters.

Monsieur P—— had worked hard for his money, and was very sensibly touched by his losses. He wept while he related to us the story of the robbery—how the *canaille* ruffians insulted him, took him by the throat, drew their daggers upon him and threatened to take his life.

Having had a rather discreditable exhibition of what kind of protection the pasha's troops were affording to the citizens of Beirut, we concluded to have Mr. Goodell's residence vacated for the present and unite the two families into one. But our increased numbers did not avail entirely to save us from the rapacity of burglars. Twice our store-room below was dug through by night and spoils taken from it, and at another time we were roused at midnight by robbers at our very chamber-doors. These last, however, finding themselves discovered, fled with the greatest precipitation, and neither they nor any of their kin gave us any further molestation.

In fine, through all this upheaving, collision and panic of the people, we were enabled gratefully to say, with the exception of Mr. Goodell's temporary privation, that we had suffered neither harm nor loss. As for the bishop of Beirut, his visions had suddenly exploded; he had early made his exit to the mountains, and his fellow-conspirators were now intent upon their own affairs. The people favored us as their safe-guard, and we might probably, for a moderate compensation, have had our choice among all the houses of the suburbs.

The pasha was liable for the spoliations of his soldiers in the houses of Franks. Monsieur P—— made application for reimbursement, and the pasha put him off, declaring that the guilty men were not his, but soldiers from the mountains. Mr. Goodell, therefore, provided himself with a drawing of his house and of the men who violated it, and our friend, Yacob Aga, was despatched by the consul to claim remuneration for the spoiling of an Englishman's house by his soldiers.

Yacob was ushered into the presence of the pasha and his courtiers, with all the ceremony due to a messenger on important business from the chief consul of the pashalic. There he stood, a tall, upright figure, comely in countenance and dignified in manner, for it was not the first time that he had stood before kings. The demand was made in the name of his Honor the English consul. The inventory of lost articles, with their values annexed, was handed in and examined. But his Highness and those about him began, as was expected, to demur and quibble, saying it was the work of men of the neighborhood, and not by their trusty Arab soldiers. Yacob assured them there could be no mistake about it, for there were plenty of witnesses that could testify who the men were. But when he saw them still disposed to cavil and prolong the talk, he drew the picture from his bosom and said,

"Dukhl-kom, Effendom (I pray your Excellency), and all you here present, let me call your attention. Just look! here is the very house just as it was; you see the men at the door beating and saying, '*Iftah!*

iftah!' (open! open!); you see their striped beneeshes, their loose yellow turbans, their blue sherivals and their dark faces. Look at them. That's the sort of people that did this mischief. Judge ye. Are they Beirut men? Are they mountain men? And there you see the Frank himself standing above and saying to them, ' Dukhl-kom, don't break open my house. Allah ye-tów-wil aa-mar-kom! (may God prolong your days!) this house is English; you're breaking the laws; your pasha will punish you.' "

The pasha gazed at the picture with astonishment. He could not dispute what kind of men they were that were represented on the paper, and, without stopping to reflect that the drawing might be a mere work of fancy, he at once yielded his point, and, in his mortification, fell to railing against the man who drew the picture, wishing to know by what satanic art he could have put the exact likeness of those men on paper—"how could he have caught their features in the midst of such a bustle?" He next turned his tirade against the consul who had sent to get away his money. "Perhaps the Englishman has never seen money. Let him come here and look at my strong boxes, that he may know what money is. "Go, give him a little of it," said he to his *surráf*. "Let him have a little specimen to keep by him, that he may know what kind of a thing is money." The command was obeyed. The money was soon counted out, the bag was brought forth, carefully sealed up, and delivered to the messenger, and on opening it at Beirut it was found to contain the exact amount of the bill, including five separate paras (fifth parts of a cent), to make it very precise.

CHAPTER XI.

Phares Shidiak driven from home—Letters from Assad—He is taken to the clutches of the patriarch, never again to be free—Additions to our communion—A second Papal bull—Excommunications—Sheikh Naameh Lattoof—Two youths of the Trodd family—Imprisonment and trial of Tannoos el Haddâd—Mr. Smith's arrival—Priest Girgis—Bishop Zachariah friendly—Bishop Gerasimus and the schools.

THE day after the plundering of the suburbs Phares Shidiak came to us with the following account of himself: "Yesterday morning, as I was in my room reading the New Testament, my brother Mansoor entered, and, drawing a sword that he had, struck me on the neck. I continued with the book in my hand till some one snatched it from me. Mansoor afterward drew up his musket, threatening to shoot me, but my mother interposed and prevented him. My brother Tannoos, hearing a bustle, came in with a cane, and, without stopping to inquire, began cudgeling me, calling out, 'Will you leave off your heresy and go to church like other people, or not?' Mansoor, not finding Assad in the house, as he expected, went to Assad's chest which stood near me, seized all the books he had received from you—Hebrew, Syriac, Italian and Arabic—tore them one after another in pieces and strewed them on the floor. I left the house and came down near to where the soldiers of the emeer are encamped, and passed the night there in company with my brother Galeb; this morning he returned home, and I, without his knowledge, came here, fully determined never to go home again. And now I will go to some place, either in this country or some other, where I can enjoy my liberty."

Phares seemed resolute in his determination to withstand the pressure put upon him, but his family friends called repeatedly to see him, and, partly by flattery and partly by force, took him home again.

We waited three days more without hearing anything additional from Hadet, and, being solicitous to know what further might have happened to Assad, we sent a special messenger to inquire, who brought us this letter from his own hands:

"You ask respecting my health. I answer, I am in a state of anxiety, but not like that in which I was some days ago. On Thursday last, on returning from a visit to the Emeer Sulmân, I found upon the floor the remnants of the holy Scriptures, torn in pieces, as there is reason to believe, by order of the bishop. When I was told that my brother Mansoor had done this, I returned to the emeer and informed him of the affair. He sent to call Mansoor, while I returned to the house. I now learned that my brother Phares had gone off. After searching for him for some time I went down to the inn in quest of him, but he was not to be found. As I was on my way returning from the inn I prayed to God that he would take everything from me if necessary, only letting faith and love to him remain in my heart. As I went on a man came up and gave me information that all the consuls at Beirut were slain and that you also were slain with them. The report came from a man who said he had deposited goods with you for safety. I asked the man if it was really true, and he reaffirmed that it was. Ask me not what was the state of my feelings at that moment.

"On reaching home I heard this terrible news confirmed, and at the same time looking out and seeing the heap of ashes near the house, all that remained of the eleven copies of the Holy Scriptures that had been destroyed, I burst into tears and committed all my concerns into the hands of God, saying, 'The Lord gave, and the Lord hath taken away; blessed be the name of the Lord,' and so I prayed on with tears and groanings which I cannot describe. I afterward heard that Phares was probably in the neighborhood, and I set off again in search of him, by night, but found him not. When I heard the news of your death confirmed I sent off a messenger for him, that wherever he might be found, he might be induced to return, and when I received his letter informing me that he had gone to your house I yet could not believe that the former report concerning you was false.

"But when the truth on this subject began to appear, then I heard, by a person who came to me yesterday evening, that the patriarch and the Emeer Besheer had made an agreement to put me to death, and that they had sent a man to lie in wait for me for that purpose. I was afterward told, by another person, that some of the servants of the emeer were appointed to accomplish this end.

"Here I am, then, in a sort of custody, enemies within and enemies without. One of my brothers, the other day, advised me to surrender myself unconditionally to the mercy of the bishop, whereupon I wrote the bishop a letter (a copy of which I here enclose) and gave it to my brother Tannoos, begging him to take it to the bishop and bring me his reply. Tannoos read the letter, and without saying a word threw it down in contempt. I then gave it to my uncle with the same request, but as yet I have had no reply.*

"All my concerns I commit into the hands of God who created me. Through the blood of our Lord Jesus Christ I hope that all my distresses will be for the best."

Thus closed the life of liberty for this persecuted disciple. On the day that the above letter was written, or the day after, he was seized by his relatives and conducted to the patriarch. One week after, Phares appeared at Beirut direct from Deir Alma, whither he had accompanied the convoy having his brother Assad in charge. On arriving, Phares delivered us the few following words, written in Assad's well-known hand: "If you can find a vessel setting off for Malta in the course of four or five days, send me word; if not, pray for your brother Assad."

This letter was replied to by Phares, but the messenger was seized and robbed. The victim had been effectually secured and all access to him prevented. He was soon taken to Canobeen, a convent built in the side of a high cliff of Lebanon, most difficult of access, and surrounded on all sides by an unmingled Maronite population. He made attempts to escape, but was always discovered, brought back, beaten, and in every way abused, till finally he was walled up in a narrow cell, where, in utter filth and neglect and obloquy, he languished three years, and whether crushed by these accumulated sufferings, or whether by starvation or by poison, he at length died.

---

* The letter contained a strong argument against all image-worship.

A solemn and joyful day was the first of January, 1827. It was the day of the general concert of prayer for the spread of the gospel. It was the day of our communion season at Beirut, and what was more, it was the day of the *ingathering of the first fruits* of our Syrian labors.

MT. LEBANON, WITH THE CANOBEEN CONVENT IN THE MIDDLE FOREGROUND.

We held our meeting in one of our largest upper rooms. The number of the names together was fifteen; five missionaries, including Mr. Nicolayson, six Armenians (including two wives), Mrs. Abbott and daughter, and two young men, sons of a mountain sheikh. Two of the Armenians were our Sidon friends, Yacob Aga and priest Stefan, the latter in Mr. Goodell's employ.

Before this little assembly Mrs. Abbott and the two hopefully converted Armenian ecclesiastics presented themselves and made a public profession of their faith in Christ, and entered into covenant with God and with the little company of missionary believers.

Mrs. Abbott was born and educated in Italy, and came to Beirut a member, of course, of the prevailing church of her country. After the consul, on our arrival at Beirut, had kindly consented that we should have weekly preaching at his house, she favored the meetings with her regular attendance, and listened with evident interest to the discourses. Her interest was seen to increase apace, and she not only exhibited a marked pleasure in our Sabbath-day exercises, but also began to make one of our number at our week-day meetings for prayer and conference. Without any impulsive excitement, and before we were prepared to recognize the happy event, it became evident that she had fully embraced the truth as it is in Christ, and had decided to cast in her lot with the Lord's people.*

Bishop Dionysius Carabet, who entered the service of the mission, was born at Constantinople, spent thirty-six years of his life in the Armenian convent at Jerusalem, during the last nine of which he enjoyed the office of bishop or archbishop, and for a long time was chief secretary of the establishment. In the year 1824, becoming sick of the superstitions of his church and skeptical as to its doctrines, he left the convent and what property he possessed (which the convent refused to deliver up to him), and came to Sidon, intending to proceed to Constantinople and end his days in his native city. At Sidon, however, he obtained a consular agency for the kingdom of Naples, but after a short time was transferred to the employ of Mr. Goodell, at Beirut.

---

* Mrs. Abbott became a widow in 1834, and was afterward adopted into the mission as the wife of the Rev. Dr. Thomson.

Archbishop as he was, he used profane language freely, and at first appeared quite unconscious that it was wrong, but on being admonished for it, he abandoned the practice. He invariably attended our divine service on the Sabbath, though it was generally in English, and appeared greatly pleased with the serious manner in which it was conducted, the like of which he was pleased to say was nowhere else to be found in Syria.

Being harassed with letters from his convent, inviting, beseeching and commanding him to return, he renounced his monastic vows, and to cut off all hope and possibility of reconciliation with his Church he entered into the married state.

So bold a step, which, in fact, set at naught the whole monastic system of his Church, became matter of surprise and discussion throughout all Syria. His case came up for consideration in an Armenian council held at Bagdad, but it was concluded there that nothing could be done against him. It is true, however, that a firman for his arrest was afterward obtained at Constantinople, as well as for the arrest of his two brethren who had offended in the same manner, but the order was never put in execution.*

Gregory Wortabet, another of our helpers, was born in Boloo, a town in Bithynia, in 1798. He early became an orphan by the loss of both his parents, and, looking upon the world as full of vanity and vexation of spirit,

* When the mission in 1828 retired for a time to Malta, Bishop Carabet accompanied it, and was very useful in aiding Mr. Goodell in the printing of his translations. He had hoped that after the Russian war was over he might continue in Mr. Goodell's connection at Constantinople, but meeting at Smyrna with a deadly persecution, he fled and came once more to Beirut, where, in 1850, he died at the age of about seventy-five years.

he was for many years a very serious-minded and, in his way, prayerful youth, and profited in his own religion above many his equals in his own nation. Being of this turn of mind, he was noticed by the priesthood, was furnished with the means of a tolerable education, was sent to Jerusalem and occupied for a time the office of secretary to Bishop Gabriel, of that city. Here also he was ordained a *wortabet* or priest. By the wickedness of two of the bishops in the convent, who hated him for his integrity and for the partiality of the patriarch and others toward him, his life in Jerusalem was made wretched, and he accepted the appointment of *navirag*, or collector of funds among the churches of Cappadocia and Bithynia. He was so well received by the people, so successful in his occupation and so much flattered and caressed, that his brain was turned. He became proud and vain, ceased all devotional habits, and, seeing corruption everywhere prevalent among the priesthood, he joined in their abominations and became an infidel.

"I sought," he says, "only worldly ease and pleasure and honor and profit. Of what is called the soul I had not one thought. I looked upon man as the grass of the field that springs up and flourishes and then dies for ever. I violated my monastic vow October 30, 1825, and, agreeably to the instructions of Paul, took to myself a wife. After the lapse of several months, having obtained a residence near the missionaries and being intimate with them morning and evening, and indeed at all times, I became by degrees more inclined to read the gospel, and began to compare the missionaries' works and all that was done in their families with their preaching and with the precepts of the gospel. From day to day I read and examined the word of God, and I found that their actions were in perfect accordance with it, and that even the most minute part of their conduct was regulated by it. I read the word of God with them every day and every night for three months. We went through the whole New Testament from beginning to end. A light began to dawn upon me. I endeavored to commit my soul to the divine teaching. I became fully satisfied of the authenticity and inspiration of the Scriptures. I acknowledged with my whole heart the living God to be the Creator of the world and to be my God."*

The influence of the Bible was extending around Beirut; the members of the Shidiak family were displeased with the patriarch's treatment of Assad, and some clamored for his liberation; two sons of Sheikh Lattoof, of Eh-heden, having business with the English consul, naturally accepted, meantime, of an invitation to board with us; all these things were a vexation of spirit to the prelate of Canobeen, who thereupon favored the public with another manshoor, of which the following is the substance: "To all our beloved sons of the Maronite nation: We wish to inform you that, as we before issued a *manshoor* against certain Bible men, in which we condemned their books and commanded them to be burned, and prohibited all persons from all sorts of intercourse of a *religious* nature with them, these impostors,

---

* Wortabet accompanied the other members of the mission company to Malta and continued a short time to render service in the printing of the New Testament translation, after which he returned and resided at Sidon, where he exhibited a remarkable zeal for the gospel. When our hopes of his future usefulness were highest he was suddenly taken from us. He died of cholera in Sidon, September 10, 1832.

enemies of the Roman Catholic Church, instructed by their master, that hellish dragon, who never—not even for one moment—desists from waging war with the faithful, are still unwearied in sowing the tares of their heretical doctrine. . . . And now, since we cannot restrain ourselves from opposing this evil, which grows upon us every day, . . . we command and ordain, by the word of the Lord, which is almighty, that all our people separate themselves from these Bible men, followers of the Scriptures, with a perfect separation as to all connection or commerce whatever, *religious* or *worldly*," etc., etc., closing with the usual threats of degradation to priests and of excommunication to laymen if they disobey.

The petty princes and sheikhs of the mountains were now excited by the priests to break up our schools. The ruling druze sheikh at Shoo-air began the work by violently threatening the teacher and compelling him to resign.

Next followed the school at Mhait-ty and that of Kfer Akkáb, these being in the Maronite district. But other schools out of their sphere of influence—as at Tripoli, Tripoli-port, and those in Merj Aioon, Hasbei-ya, Rashei-ya, Deir Meemas and Jedeideh—were spared a while.

Priest Girgis, of Beirut, zealously co-operated with the measures of his patriarchal master. He sent for our Maronite servant-woman and ordered her to leave our service that very week, under pain of the greater excommunication. Her remonstrances against such hard usage were earnest but unavailing. "I am a poor woman," she said, "with a blind husband and three small children on my neck, and the times are hard;

how am I to get along?" "I know nothing about that," said the priest. "Such are the orders of his Blessedness, and so it must be." He finally offered to give her a letter stating her case if she would carry it to the patriarch; peradventure he might excuse her. But a journey of fifty or sixty miles across mountains and valleys seemed for her too great a task, and she did not accept his offer. Mrs. Dalton's servant-woman was laid under the same interdict, and both these needy women were thus forced from their situations.

In connection with these events it was given out *in terrorem* that, on the coming Sabbath, the Maronite church would be hung around with black, and that the priest by the light of a solitary candle would read, in a tremendous voice, an excommunication against all those, by *name*, who still continued to have intercourse with the Protestants. The two Maronite daughters spoken of above would doubtless have shown still more reluctance in leaving their places, with which they had professed themselves to be so well satisfied, but in view of such a storm rising up, so lowering and so black, they would rather flee at a sacrifice than to face it. Something like what was threatened did actually come to pass, but in no such imposing form. Peter Te-én, teacher of Mr. Nicolayson, in Safet, Anton Adam, our translator, and two or three others were looking for a share in the tempest, but when it came it burst alone on the head of poor Peter. The youth, however, bore it right manfully. All the harm it did him was that of detaining him one day longer at Beirut than he had intended, for the Maronite muleteer who had agreed to set out with him the next day for Safet broke his engagement, because faith with heretics was not to be kept. But Peter found some Druze or Jew who had conscience enough to keep his word, and though he was additionally threatened with an arrest from the Emeer Besheer, yet he went off unmolested in the face of all his enemies.

Even our guest, Sheikh Naameh Lattoof, thought it not impossible that *his* name might be with others on the black list, for on the day preceding the Sabbath of the curse he was invited by the ever vigilant priest, Girgis, to an interview in which he was closely catechised.

Like many others in the land, Sheikh Naameh seems never to have been a papist from *conviction*, but only by birth and tradition. Sheikh Lattoof, the father, was strongly inclined to the latitudinarianism of the French, with which people he had had much to do. The son, on having his attention directed to the Scriptural arguments of Protestants, could not contradict them, but was almost persuaded to be a Protestant. It was this half-persuasion which made him ready to give short answers to the priest's catechetical questions. Not long after these events the two young sheikhs returned to their home in Zgarta, near Tripoli.

Among the subjects of special persecution at this time in Beirut were a lad named Assad Kheiât and two cousins of the family of Trodd. They were all of the Greek denomination. The first had been our pupil for years, and had become so much attached to us that his friends became alarmed lest he should leave his church. He also became alarmed at the threats uttered against him, and ceased to visit us. Of the other two, Ferj Allah Trodd was a young man of more than twenty years, thoughtful and quiet, not specially gifted in intellect, but respectable for his candor and independence.

We were, however, most interested in his cousin Michael. He was considerably younger, and much more sprightly, social and communicative. Their chief foe was Nicola Trodd, one of their own household, as the Saviour had taught them to expect. This uncle held the office of secular agent of the Greek church of the city. He managed the church funds, and assumed, even in spiritual matters, a sort of associate authority with the bishop. Uniting himself with his Maronite associates in fulfilling their "bounden duty to destroy heretics," he procured and read in the church an address, as if from the bishop, denouncing and threatening to punish all such as should continue to hold intercourse with the Protestants. Again, on the succeeding Sabbath, the same ceremony was enacted, only with increased emphasis and acrimony, and in concert with a similar one in the church of the Maronites. Even previous to this second denunciation, Michael's father had been so much opposed to his course that he had threatened to disinherit him if he did not cease to come to us; but now, after this new, emphatic tirade, his feelings of paternal responsibility for his son were kindled with new ardor, and he was determined on more compulsory measures.

Michael went home that evening from one of his accustomed visits, and took his usual seat at the supper-table. While he was in that posture his father came in, accompanied by his brother, the notorious Nicola. Anger shot forth from both their countenances. As they approached toward Michael he fled from the table, and, gaining an outer terrace of the house, he leaped to the earth and ran from the city. He came back to us weary, hungry and naked (that is, in his undress), and we ministered to his wants.

By all these hostile demonstrations the whole vicinity was in commotion. It was in some of its features like a general revival of religion. Our houses were thronged with inquirers, and we could do little else but converse with the people on the great subject of salvation from morning till night.

In spite of all efforts to intimidate our friend Ferj Allah, he continued with us for a whole week, night and day, near the close of which time a communication was sent him by his furious uncle. He comes right to the point thus:

"What a base, abominable and filthy name have you gotten to yourself! Time will never remove the stain. You rest under the power of our excommunication. You have put yourself on the ground of disobedience to the ecclesiastical authorities as well as to the orders of our lord the sultan (the most high and most merciful God assist him!), and have made yourself the common talk of the whole town. David in his time said, 'Deliver me from disgrace,' but you have gone abroad to seek and buy it, and you shall soon see the fruits of your folly at the hand of the government.

"If you return this day we will receive you, as says the apostle, 'Receive him who forsakes his infamy,' and we will take off the tax laid upon you. But if you do not return, prepare for consequences. The hand of the wazeer (pasha) is powerful. If you think to be protected by the Franks, remember what happened to Ibn Khlât and Ibn Zreek.

"Moreover, if God has seen fit to open the way to you to take so corrupt a course, what have you to do with my son Yacob that you should take him with you as a waiter? If Yacob connects himself with you in your evil way, *kes-met Allah!* [a great oath] my anger shall know no bounds. I'll *annihilate* you with an utter destruction, and no repentance shall avail you. You know who I am."

An immediate answer was requested by the messenger. "Tell the writer," said Ferj Allah, "he may expect an answer *within three days.*"

The messenger informed Ferj Allah that his uncle had obtained authority from the governor to hold all his property in custody until he should return to his good standing in the church, and that Michael also had been heavily taxed.

Tannoos el Hadâd, our honest, Christian-hearted schoolmaster, was arrested and taken before the governor, who asked him why he was attempting to change the religion of the country, and without further ceremony sent him to the common prison. We informed the consul of the case, who immediately sent his dragoman with us to see the prisoner. He was in a narrow, dirty dungeon, without air or light, and fit only for the worst of criminals. As they had accused him of no crime but that of corrupting religion, he felt that he was suffering for Christ's sake and was happy to enjoy the honor. He prayed for his persecutors, and begged us to quiet all the apprehensions his wife and mother might feel respecting him. As we were coming away we asked the dragoman, who was a papist, what he thought of the imprisonment of a man so irreproachable. His reply was,

"Are not those books forbidden?"

By this it seemed that he as well as the governor knew the real crime was the teaching of the children to read the New Testament and the Psalms in the school.

As this accusation was not likely to injure the teacher much, a new one was afterward invented which it was believed would answer the purpose better, and when Wortabet was deputed by the consul to demand the prisoner's release as keeper of the English cemetery, the governor said nothing about religion nor books, but the man had committed a heinous crime against morality. Wortabet still demanded, in the consul's name, the liberation of the accused and the production of the lad who was said to be the accuser. The former demand was granted, and an official was despatched with Wortabet to open the prison door, but about the lad the governor could not answer. In the way as they went whom should they meet but Nicola Trodd, whom the official immediately hailed and asked, earnestly, "Where is that boy? We want the boy." The wakeel of the bishop was greatly embarrassed. The demand was repeated. Nicola wished to know what was the matter; he was very ignorant. A few more words passed between them, and it was proposed to look into the subject "to-morrow."

On hearing all this account the consul was greatly exasperated, the more so as he said the same Trodd had only the day before brought an accusation to him against his own nephew, Ferj Allah Trodd, which turned out to be totally false.

The morning came, and Mr. Abbott invited Nicola to an interview. He sent his brother in his stead. The consul would not see him, but sent another message to the wakeel demanding that he produce the "*boy*." But the boy is gone to the mountains, and Nicola shakes his cloak and is in utter ignorance of this whole matter. Messengers are next sent to the governor to say that a man under English protection having been seized and imprisoned under accusation of a crime, and the examination of the case having been appointed for to-day, the consul begs leave to say that all on *his* side are ready for the trial. "*Bring on the witnesses!*"

The governor, after giving a few silly excuses and seeing that he was compromised in an affair of which he was utterly ashamed, rose and cried out to his scribes and constables,

"Up! Go about your business! Clear away this muddle forthwith! You that have thrown us into this swamp and mire, get us out of it! Produce the *boy*, whether above ground or below ground! Find him! bring him!"

The chief secretary spoke, and said the whole matter had better be dropped and have no further trouble about it, but he was told that such a course would not satisfy the consul. However, under the circumstances, the main witness being in the mountains twenty miles off, no trial could be had till another "to-morrow," and so Nicola had one more lease to live and breathe for twenty-four hours, unconvicted and uncondemned before any tribunal but that of his own conscience.

The morrow came, and the governor quite unexpectedly sent word that the said boy was at hand and the trial might go on. Four of our Protestant company were appointed to attend the trial. The lad proved to be one that had formerly attended our Italian school. He came forward, took a respectful posture before the judge, and, without any oath or ceremony, commenced recounting his story of the crime. When he had finished, any one was allowed to make such remarks as he chose, the judge meantime sitting a silent spectator and listener. Being cross-questioned, the lad soon found himself involved in puzzling contradictions, and in a short time began to refuse to answer questions at all. The judge looked steadfastly at him, as if wondering at his bold wickedness, and was heard to say, in a low voice, "Ah, he's a sad fellow! he's an accursed rogue! it's a plot of the devil."

When the boy had thoroughly finished his testimony the mother, who had previously sought the privilege of bearing testimony to corroborate that of her son, was sent for. While waiting for the mother's arrival some words were addressed to the witness that might work upon his conscience, particularly the words of the commandment about bearing false witness against one's neighbor. He sat uneasily. His eyes wandered about hurriedly, and he finally rose, and, kneeling by the ear of the judge, confessed to him in a whisper the whole truth. His whole testimony had been a tissue of lies. But a certain man had offered him a reward if he would go to the governor and enter such an accusation, and so he did. The man in question was Nicola Trodd, and the reward was to be a paper of recommendation *testifying to the good character* and poverty of the bearer and requesting alms from all good people. So ended this attack!

On the 18th of February, 1827, we were favored by the arrival of the Rev. Eli Smith, accompanied by the English missionaries, Gobat, Kugler and Muller, and a colored man from Abyssinia. The four last named were destined for the gospel work in Egypt. Mr. Gobat has since become bishop of Jerusalem. Mr. Smith, our American brother, afterward so eminent for his high scholarship and labors, had come to cast in his lot with us, to aid us in sowing the good seed, and to share with us in the prospective harvest. This new missionary, desirous of obtaining a knowledge of the Arabic in the most rapid way possible, engaged our schoolmaster, Tannoos, to go with him and board in a neighboring village where he would be obliged to speak the language and hear no other spoken. With this friendly man and, as we believed, Christian brother at his side for sympathy and instruction, and having no interruptions, his studies were very successful. It was well for the missionary and well for the schoolmaster that his school was broken up; for though Nicola could not do this by false accusation, he succeeded in doing it by opening a free school in the name of the church and persuading his neighbors to patronize it. These neighbors, for his zeal in behalf of the church, overlooked his iniquity. Moreover, the school went on without expense to us, and was taught by an acquaintance of ours and a friend of the Bible cause.

Our Maronite woman returned to our employ, declaring that the priests had broken their engagement to find her work. Priest Girgis of course loaded her with his curse and excommunication from society. After some time she chanced one day to spy the priest near the house, and accosted him, as it appeared, in no very civil language, and there succeeded a war of words such as seldom happens between a pastor and one of his flock. To conclude the affray the priest hurried round to our door and wished to see the man of the house. He was invited to come up and see him at his leisure. But this he probably would not have done even though a vision like that of Peter should have taught him that we were neither "common nor unclean." Finally, an opportunity was given him for an interview just at the middle of our out-door stairway. He stood waiting at the bottom in company with some of the Maronite neighbors. He seemed afraid to set foot on our polluted stone steps, though they were outside the house and copiously washed every few days by the pure rain of heaven and bleached in the sun. But when he saw that further *condescension* was not to be had, he wrapped his priestly robes tight about himself, and, summoning all his resolution to the task, he mounted up his half way, and there we sat nearly side by side. Scanning his new colloquist up and down a moment, he said,

"I am not inferior to you, sir, Ana kod-dak" (I am your equal).

"Very well, sir; please proceed."

He then spread out his complaints against the woman as being one that had no principle and no religion, going about uttering insufferable slanders against him, and would we harbor such a woman in our family?

"But we have never heard of these slanders. We must have more evidence before turning the woman out of doors."

He then called upon the bystanders to testify, which they did, saying they had heard the woman *curse his beard* and call him hard names. He was then assured that cursing and calling hard names were not approved in our house nor agreeable to us in any shape, but that such talk was hardly to be called *slander*, and that, moreover, it was not a sin peculiar to the woman. Cursing and calling hard names was a very fashionable weakness in the neighborhood in those days.

He began to wax warm and to press his case with vehemence, reproaching us with countenancing wickedness in our house. He finally said that if nothing could be done by persuasion, he would see what could be done by force, and that nothing short of a law-suit would satisfy him. Saying this, he rose and went off with his companions, muttering his resentment.

On inquiring of the woman why she had so spoken against the priest, she said she had been much insulted as she passed people in the streets in consequence of the priest's anathema, and so (as is the custom of the country) she returned evil for evil and cursing for cursing. The priest being the medium and instrument of her degradation before the people, she naturally vented her outraged feelings upon *him*. And, indeed, in this act the woman had a good deal to say for herself. The priest threw the first stone. He began the cursing, she does but follow his example. Besides, he curses in public, she only in private. He curses her soul, she only his *beard*.

Our school agent, Yoosef Lufloofy, and his brother Michael, temporarily with us, were put under excommunication by the patriarch of the papal Greek church. The former having occasion to go into the city saw all his old acquaintances turning their backs upon him, and one, more zealous than the rest, lifted up his voice in the words of the 68th Psalm, "Arise, O God, let thine enemies be scattered; let them also that hate thee flee before thee." Yoosef endeavored to make light of all this, though he evidently felt the insult keenly. He very soon wrote to his patriarch on the subject, and endeavored to draw him into a discussion, but his Holiness refused.

This movement against the gospel, concocted by the Maronite patriarch, was intended to enlist all the papal interests in the land—patriarchs, bishops and priests—and to enlist also, from the Greek community, as many as, by intimidation, flattery or purchase, could be induced to join hands in the enterprise. The papal Syrian bishop at Deir Sharfi had driven away our cook; the papal Greek patriarch had struck at the family of Lufloofy; the bishop Benjamin and his wakeel, Nicola, were subsidized from the Greeks of Beirut, and Bishop Gerasimus from those of Hasbeiya and Merj Aioon. The last mentioned lent his aid in the enterprise by breaking up our schools that remained in the region of Mt. Hermon. The only bishop that stood up boldly against this papal assault was Bishop Zachariah, residing at Tripoli. In visiting the schools at Tripoli, Lufloofy had cultivated a familiarity with him, and on his hearing that Yoosef had been excommunicated, he wrote him a letter, not of condolence, but of congratulation. The bishop also wrote to the mission, enclosing a copy of a letter to "his Blessedness" the Greek patriarch, in which he earnestly deprecated the persecution of the distributors of the Bible and the closing of the schools.

Previous to the arrival of Bishop Zachariah's letter we had sent a request to the patriarch, which he answered thus:

"About the schools, we reply that we had been informed of their establishment and had never forbidden them. But particularly of those at Hasbeiya and Merj Aioon we at first had no knowledge. Afterward, when disputes and divisions about them arose among the people, we, in order to restore harmony, wrote to them, saying, 'Have you lived so many years in the habit of teaching your own children at your own expense, and now do you look to others to instruct them as a charity? What has happened to you to render such a step necessary?—a step which has introduced among you variance and strife.' This, and this only, was the amount of our letter to them."

Here are *two questions* the patriarch asks about the schools, but he gives no *order*.

With regard to Bishop Zachariah's letter, the patriarch replies: "He begs us to write a circular to all our people, exhorting them to receive these schools of yours." [In the bishop's copy to us there is nothing about such a "circular."] "Now we acknowledge the work to be one of the greatest benevolence, and one for which we render you hearty thanks, but to send out a public proclamation to our people to receive them is a thing which, through fear of the late firman forbidding this work, we cannot do." [The firman forbade the *books*, not the *schools*.] "That we should, however, actually *forbid* this work is equally impossible, since the books you bring, the Old and New Testaments and the Psalter, we have examined and pronounce to be such as are universally received among us, and you will, for their distribution, have your reward. . . .

"We shall write hereafter to Bishop Gerasimus, our brother, to see if there is a prospect that the schools can go on among his people without divisions, and if the people generally wish for them, let them be continued; there can be no objection. . . .

"Please God, we shall not be wanting in our compliance with whatever you demand. Let us hear from you often. Inform us in what way we can be serviceable to you, and may the Lord prolong your days. So prays for you,

"METHODIUS,
"Patriarch of Antioch and all the East.
"Damascus, March 27, 1827."

Bishop Gerasimus in announcing to us the breaking up of the schools wrote us in these words: "We have to inform you that there was sent by the elders of the village and others, to his Holiness the patriarch of Antioch, a letter respecting the schools established by you among our people, saying they wished to have them broken up, and there came an answer from his Blessedness *ordering* them to be abolished. Therefore, *according to the order*, we have given instructions that the school in Hasbeiya, as well as those in Merj Aioon, shall be discontinued according to the *universal wish*."

The "*universal wish of the people*" was to abolish the schools, yet the parents somehow would continue, against their will, to send their children to them, and there was no means of enabling them to act according to their universal wish but to obtain an "order" from the patriarch, and this "order" is briefly comprehended in these words, "Why do you look to *strangers* for your schools?" "This, and this only," the patriarch declares, was his "order." One would suppose they might have done according to their "universal wish" without it. Moreover, the "order" was for the village of Hasbeiya only, for *there* was the only quarrel about the school. Yet, upon this "order," Bishop Gerasimus gives us to understand he abolished also the three other schools in Merj Aioon. To the people, however, the bishop, whose letter was shown us, spoke of no "order," nor even of any patriarchal *permission*, to destroy the schools. He spoke in *this* way:

"We have searched into this matter with all diligence and have discovered it to be full of deadly poison, for these men are full of heresy and vile infidelity and monstrous blasphemy against the sacraments, ceremonies and customs of our religion, and the result of this work of theirs will be future vexation and corruption to no small extent, and we fear lest the dragon should corrupt your thoughts and lest the evil serpent should infuse his mortal poison. We are bound, therefore, to put a total and final stop to these schools, for what concord hath Christ with Belial, or what part hath he that believeth with an infidel?"

After all, contrary to "the universal wish" and to patriarchal "orders," and in spite of all the doses of poison, heresy, infidelity and monstrous blasphemy which were attempted to be poured down the throats of these people by the Bible men, they still upheld the schools, until the bishop was forced to come to them in person, and then and there confess to them that he was impelled to this course *by letters which he had received*, not from the patriarch, but *from Mansoor ed Dahh-dahh, Maronite secretary of the Emeer Besheer*, whom he "*dared not disoblige;*" just as Bishop Zachariah said in his letter to the patriarch, "it was done *solely to please* the Romanists of the *West*."

CHAPTER XII.

Sick child taken to the mountains—Excommunications—Removal from Eh-heden to Ba-whyta—Negotiations with the patriarch—Sheikh Girgis, of Besherry, intercedes—Interviews of the sheikhs with his Holiness—Sheikh Naameh exasperated and indomitable; the others pardoned.

WE had a sick infant that was pining away dangerously, and to save its life a skillful foreign physician advised a residence for a time in a higher atmosphere. The young sheikh Naameh Lattoof was with us at the time, and invited us to his father's house in Eh-heden. No place in the mountains could have been offered more favorable for the health of the child. We obtained a paper from the Emeer Besheer to the Emeer Ameen, his son, who had command over the district of the Gibbeh, where Eh-heden was situated. It was an order for our safety and respectful treatment. Armed thus with a safe conduct from the source of all authority in the mountains, we supposed we should be safe anywhere till we should have time to present it to the subordinate prince for his more local orders.

The patriarch was, of course, kept well informed of all our movements, and no sooner had we reached Eh-heden than the people were summoned to the church to hear the patriarchal excommunication against the family of our host. The document had doubtless been made ready beforehand and was waiting our arrival.

After speaking of the "infernal hardihood which the unhappy and wretched Lattoof el Ash-shi and his sons had reached in having dared to associate themselves with the family of a Bible man," and that, too, in spite of many warnings, he proceeds:

"We, therefore, make known to all that those sons of wickedness, Lattoof el Ash-shi and his sons, together with all the rest of the family, both male and female, have fallen under the heavier excommunication, and now we, by the word of the Lord, which is almighty, do confirm this curse upon them. They are therefore *accursed, cut off from all Christian communion; and let the curse envelop them as a robe and spread through all their members like oil, break them in pieces like a potter's vessel and wither them like the fig tree cursed by the mouth of the Lord himself; let the evil angel rule over them by day and by night, asleep and awake, and in whatever circumstances they may be found. We permit no one to visit them, or employ them, or do them a favor, or give them a salutation, or converse with them in any form or manner, but let them be avoided as a putrid member and as hellish dragons.*"

He goes on with a similar warning against all communication with the Bible man and his family, and closes with his patriarchal "blessing on the obedient."

We were furnished with a copy of this proclamation by the good bishop Stephen Dwyhee, of Eh-heden, some ten days after it was read in the church.

A patriarchal document similar to the above, specially intended for Lattoof, was read before his window in his hearing. After copying for our own use the order of the Emeer Besheer to his son to ensure our protection on the mountains, Naameh set off immediately with

20 *

the original to present it to the younger emeer at Gebail.

The darkness of the evening had scarcely begun when our ears were suddenly assailed with loud and continued screams of some females out of doors in distress. The servant-girl came running in, saying they were beating the daughters of Lattoof at the oven. They had gone out with their mother, as usual, to prepare their bread for the Sabbath. The oven being owned in common by the two sheikhs, Bootrus and Lattoof, the former had sent his men to drive these excommunicated females away. Sheikh Lattoof hastened out to see what might be done for the protection of his wife and daughters, and was followed by the sheikh's mother-in-law. He was met by one of the bullies of Bootrus, who brought him to the ground by a blow of his club. When he had recovered himself he was seen standing apart from the crowd that had collected, with a violent man close before him, club in hand, threatening him furiously with death if he did not leave the ground. One of the daughters also came and begged him to go into the house. At the same time, in the midst of the idle crowd of spectators near by, were seen the other daughter and the mother screaming and holding with all their might the club of another bully, who, with his turban knocked off, was wringing and twisting in vain to free the weapon from their hands. These three were the only apparent actors in the exhibition.

The sheikh suffered himself to be led into the house and laid on his bed. He had one deep cut in his scalp and two or three others in the scalp and face. While these wounds were being dressed the tumult without became quieted and the mother and daughters came in.

LATOOF'S WIFE AND DAUGHTER RESISTING THE PERSECUTORS.

The grandmother had been struck and seemed badly hurt. The mother had a bruised arm, about which, however, she made little ado. The young daughters came in gay as larks, complaining of nothing and telling us not to be alarmed, and that this was a small affair compared with some which they had experienced in their intercourse with Sheikh Bootrus. He had sometimes fought against them with *swords* instead of clubs. But the old lady took the matter more seriously. She sat and held her broken hand and wrist, and, recollecting that she was once sole mistress of a great share of the property now held by Sheikh Bootrus and that it had been taken from her illegally, she moaned forth in her agony,

"O thou son of Yem-meen! O thou son of Yem-meen! Is it not enough that you should eat up my property? Must you also beat and bruise my poor body at this rate? O thou son of Yem-meen!"

It was an unlooked-for mercy that the young daughters had escaped so nearly unhurt. They had been in the thickest of the fight, and borne, with their mother, the brunt of the battle. But they told us that the *howalies*, the emeer's tax-gatherers, had been near them and shielded them from the blows of Sheikh Bootrus' men. It is probable, however, that they owed their escape more to their own heroic courage, for, to a spectator, they, as well as the mother, seemed nerved to a boldness and strength quite beyond the capacity of such feeble frames.

The two sheikhs lived in opposite ends of the same house, so that the terraces of both parts were on the same level. During the night heavy steps were heard of men coming from Sheikh Bootrus' part of the house and walking over our heads. They were evidently watchmen, set to prevent any persons passing to or from the house. Once they sent us a stone of considerable size, which came thundering down the chimney into the fireplace. But they were restrained from all further violence by Him who maketh the wrath of man to praise him and restrains the remainder of it, so that they neither broke through our terrace nor assailed us with any more stones, nor with threats or revilings. Moreover, our little invalid boy, whom the mountain air had already begun to revive, slept sweetly.

The following day being Sabbath we rested according to the commandment. On Monday morning early Yoosef Lattoof and the Bible man left the village and went toward Tripoli. On the way we came to Ain Siba-il, where Is-hoc Turbyhh, a friend and relative of Lattoof, dared to send us a breakfast and inquire the news. A daughter of his was affianced to Sheikh Naameh, which added to his interest in our case. At his advice we spent the day under a pear tree in sight of his house. He had sent a messenger to Canobeen to negotiate in behalf of Lattoof and the excommunicants. We waited for the issue. As there came no favorable news from his Holiness we went for the night, at Is-hoc's advice, to the neighboring Greek convent of Hantoora to lodge.

The next evening found us in Tripoli, where Sheikh Naameh, after having visited Beirut as well as the prince at Gebail without succeeding according to his mind, met us and advised that we remove the family from Eh-heden to the neighboring district of Dun-neey, equally favorable for its atmosphere and under Mohammedan government.

We visited the two brothers governing the district, told them our story, and their ready answer was, "Go through all our district, and the village and the house you like best are yours."

We engaged a man to go with us to prepare a house in the village of Ba-whyta, and, moreover, obtained animals and men to remove the family and goods from Eh-heden to Ba-whyta "before to-morrow night." We had intimated to the sheikhs that they might have difficulty in obtaining the goods on account of the patriarch's excommunication. They laughed at the suggestion, and seemed glad to show in what contempt they held the priestly tyranny of such a man. The outlawed families had, in their eleven days' confinement, suffered somewhat from famine, and more, perhaps, from fear and anxiety. But the life of no one had been lost, and our infant had suddenly been relieved of every threatening symptom.

But to return to the patriarch. It was to have been expected that when his Holiness should hear that his chief adversary, the Bible follower, had fled, he would be quieted, but, on the contrary, he seems to have become, if possible, more bellicose and unrelenting than ever, for while the latter and his young fellow-fugitive are hastening out of his way, he follows close at their heels with new thunderbolts. Repeating his curses of "the infernal Lattoof and his whole family," and praising the zeal of those who "drove the prowling wolves" away, he exhorts the Sheikhs Daw-hir to "persecute those devils" from all places under their authority.

Sheikh Solyman Daw-hir, one of the men addressed, happened to be a man in sympathy with the persons thus heartily anathematized. He was at Lattoof's when the Bible family arrived there, and honored us with a short call. He was an eye-witness of the uproar the same evening before the house of the two sheikhs, and knew whether the patriarch had spoken the truth in calling it an uprising of the people against the foreign family, by which the offenders were driven in a moment like prowling wolves from the village. It was from this sheikh's mouth at Gebail that Naameh Lattoof first learned the fact of the uproar, and said to him, "Had you been there, so equally divided were the parties that *blood* as well as water would have flowed down the streets of Eh-heden.*

Our retirement from Eh-heden did little or nothing toward mitigating the severity of the patriarch's quarantine against the family of our host. The wife and daughters of the oppressed sheikh had managed to walk out to the next village, Besherry, and to profit by an interview with their friend Sheikh Girgis, of that place, who was ever ready to lend them all the aid in his power. We also occasionally sent them from Ba-whyta some partial relief.

The patriarch improved the occasion of the first Sabbath of our residence in Ba-whyta to cause to be published against us his stereotyped anathema. But he was now attempting to operate beyond his limits. His system of church discipline was found to be much less adapted to Mohammedan than to *princely* rule. His spiritual weapons of chain and prison and quarantine were wanting. The proclamation instead of setting the whole people off at a speechless distance from us brought them to our door. Scarcely a moment of the day passed

---

* Eh-heden is copiously watered by a mill stream running through the midst of it.

without the presence of some of the villagers immediately about us.

Sheikh Girgis, of the neighboring village of Besherry, looking at the untoward events that had passed, though an undoubted friend of both the persecuted families, considered it a hopeless effort in Lattoof any longer to withstand the power of the patriarch. He thought him to be like the king with ten thousand going to make war with him that cometh against him with twenty thousand. He had better send an embassage and desire conditions of peace. So when Lattoof wrote to him for advice he replied in the inflated style of the country as follows:

"HONORED BROTHER: After saluting you, I have to say that your letters reached us yesterday, and we lost no time in communicating the subject to his Holiness, enclosing your letters in mine. We addressed ourselves in a strain of intercession to the great ocean of his pity, and from the abundance of his compassion his high pleasure was moved to accept our petition whenever you and the sheikhs, your sons, should come and do yourselves the honor to kiss the footsteps of his Holiness, with entire submission, with a firm resolution to quit all connection with the Bible men, and with sincere penitence for the past.

"Our advice to you is, therefore, that now you call together your sons and come, all of you, this very day, that we may go, we and you in company, and *kiss the tracks* of his Holiness. As for ourself, our special desire is, that there be no delay, as we have no time to lose, intending, if God will, to go to-morrow to kiss the hand of his Excellency the Emeer Ameen (may God assist him!), at the convent of Meifook. If you wish for the favor of God and of his Holiness come at once, you and your sons with you, without delay. Tarry not."

This letter Sheikh Lattoof took, and enclosing it in one of his own, sent it to his two sons, who were with us at Ba-whyta, recommending their compliance with the counsel of their worthy Besherry friend. Yoosef at once complied, and set off for Eh-heden; but as for Naameh, he did not at all covet "the honor of *kissing the tracks of his Holiness*," nor could he believe that his father was really in earnest in wishing him to do so. He, therefore, sent by Yoosef a respectful letter to his father, excusing himself from coming, and hoping that he would be willing to go on and enjoy the honor and profit of the proposed interview without him.

The three sheikhs repaired to the patriarch at Deman, a convent across the chasm over against Canobeen. The prison of Assad Shidiak was at Canobeen. His Holiness was doubtless unwilling to summon these new "devils" for trial in so close contiguity with the *old* one.

After the kissing part of the ceremony was over the trial began. "What is this, Lattoof, that you have been doing? How could you send all the way to Beirut to bring us those heretics and place them down here in my very beard? Why did you not bring them direct to Canobeen itself and seat them in the patriarchal chair, and send me off to be a pastor of sheep and goats? What new spirit has possessed you? What new faith have you? Let us know the articles of your creed."

"I wish," said the sheikh, "to be summoned before some man of religion and conscience, and then I shall be ready to declare my faith what it is, but until that is done I shall excuse myself from the duty. With regard to the religion and conscience of your Blessedness, here is the evidence of what sort they are," showing his swollen hand and lifting up with it the bandage from his gashed forehead.

"But what have I to do with all that?"

"All this is the work of your Blessedness, and it is written in the book of God for you to account for."

"I wish you distinctly to understand, Lattoof, that it is not you, but your son *Naameh*, that I have particularly in view in what I am now doing—that wicked youth who unites with the heretics and assists them, and even preaches their doctrines in public harangues."

"Pray, who ever heard my son Naameh preach?"

"I have many witnesses to prove that he preached not only in Eh-heden, but also in Tripoli."

"I tell you it is all an abominable lie."

Sheikh Girgis, to whom this report was no less new and incredible than it was to Lattoof, united in assuring his Blessedness that such a thing could not have taken place, and that it was a slander from some enemy.

"No; it is really true. I know all about this matter, and if that youth Naameh—that miserable *Rabshoon** the second—does not cease from his work of heresy, I'll be the death of him. I am able to accomplish it. I can do what the Emeer Besheer cannot, and wherever that Rabshoon may think to hide himself, in that place I shall be sure to send and *burn him*."

"Had it not been for the emeer you would have put an end to him long ago. The emeer seems to be the man of peace and of conscience, and you the man of blood."

* Lord of hell. Shidiak was Rabshoon the first.

The patriarch then acknowledged that he had written to the Emeer Besheer to instruct the Emeer Ameen not to suffer Naameh to leave Gebail alive.

A long talk was then had about an arrangement for the absolution of the family, but it was all to no purpose, as the main transgressor had not yet presented himself. Nothing would do but that Yoosef should immediately return and inform his brother that his presence was absolutely necessary to a settlement, and that in the mean time the father should remain at Deman waiting Naameh's arrival. Sheikh Girgis left the place, having, as he had before intimated, an appointment to meet the prince at Deir Meifook.

Yoosef appeared in due time at Ba-whyta, bringing a letter from the father expressed in such terms that he was convinced his father was now in earnest. The patriarch had to a certain extent promised to procure the return of their property which the emeer had taken from them. It was added, also, in the letter, that his Blessedness had pledged himself before the sheikhs, bishops and others present that Naameh should be perfectly secure from all personal restraint or harm provided he came.

As his presence might subserve the cause of truth by revealing the false impressions and accusations of the patriarch, and might relieve the sufferings of the family, we did not attempt to dissuade him from going. He accordingly set off, taking with him Arabi, our faithful Muslim, to bring us word again if any mischief should befall him. Yoosef remained with us.

The third day after he left us he reappeared and gave us the following account of his visit. The patriarch received him with remarkable courtesy, ordering sherbet and coffee and handing him even his own pipe to smoke. Soon his Blessedness entered upon the business before them, saying:

"My son Naameh, what is this new religion which you are about setting up among us? You have the honor of being a descendant of one of the most respectable families of our nation—a family who have always lived in quiet spiritual union with our sons of the Maronite Church. Why should you now turn away from their pious example and lend your aid to heretics? You know to what trouble and expense I was put to dislodge those Bible men from Antoora, and now you are renewing the same sort of trouble by giving them a residence in the Gibbeh. Why do you thus take part against your own mother Church, and by your example give occasion of infidelity and offence to the whole Maronite nation?"

"I would answer you," said Naameh, "by asking why your Blessedness issues against those worthy men proclamation after proclamation filled from beginning to end with notorious misstatements and false insinuations, and thus become *yourself* the occasion of infidelity and offence to the whole Maronite nation?"

The dialogue thus spiritedly begun waxed warmer and warmer: "What are those worthy individuals you speak of? Will you call men worthy or even honest who buy men to become of their religion?—who seduce men from their own Church by means of their money?"

"I will tell you," said Naameh, "what I myself have witnessed. At a certain time I was present when one of the sons of the Church came to a Bible man pleading poverty and wanting money, declaring himself ready to become one of his followers, to believe all that he believed and to reject all doctrines that he rejected. The Bible man answered, 'We buy no man's religion here, sir;' then pointing to a New Testament on his table, he added, 'There are my doctrines. Take that book and read it and obey it, and I ask you not to be my follower, nor is it of any consequence whether you ever see my face again.'"

"Those Bible men are but a club of devils."

"Were they as fond as some others of quarrels and other *devilish* work, they would have come, not to Ehheden only, but to Canobeen, and ridden upon your neck, for these men are not in the country by permission of the emeer nor yet of the pasha: they are under the shield of a special firman of the grand signor. But they are men of peace, and retire from contention wherever they find it."

"They are men abiding under the anger of God, incorrigible heretics, and the only proper medicine for them is *lead*."

The patriarch then accused Naameh of having entered his name on our books as one of the Bible company, and of having come to Canobeen in secret three several times to effect the escape of Shidiak.

"These accusations are, the whole of them, perfectly false."

"But my witness is no less a man than Priest Girgis of Beirut.

"And will you receive the testimony of such a man as that? Go to Beirut and hear what the people say of him. See him strut and swagger through the streets, spreading his robes to the wind, stroking and smoothing his beard, and talking big as if he were an aga of the Janisaries. He is a reckless hypocrite, unfit for the priesthood, and unfit to be a witness against any man."

The patriarch became extremely excited, and threatened to put Naameh in confinement by the side of Shidiak.

"I am not one of your Ain Waraka boys," said Naameh, "nourished at your expense and bound to you by oaths, that you should think to do by *me* as you do by *them*. Do not think that I came on this visit through any fear of your excommunication, nor that I came to be frightened by threats. I am not under your authority, and if you order me to be seized, here is my *hanjar*. I shall do my best to defend myself."

Lattoof, whose great aim now was to appease the patriarch, rose in opposition to his son and requested him to be quiet; but at this Naameh, vexed into a fury at seeing his father taking part against him, drew his hanjar and cried out, "Leave me, father, leave me! I shall stab myself with impatience!" The excitement had become intense, and, as it was evident that no progress was making toward peace, the parties separated in mutual dissatisfaction.

Naameh was conducted for retirement to the room of Bishop Simaan, who had been the patriarch's messenger to the emeer at Gebail, who saw Naameh there and treated him rudely, but who was now perfectly changed. He had completely shifted sides. He could not have shown Naameh more marked attention than he did now; he made every apology for what he had said at Gebail, called the patriarch hard names, patted Naameh on the shoulder, saying, "Keep up your courage, man; don't be frightened by the animal, but use with him the stoutest language you are master of." Thus spake a bishop respecting his patriarch in the patriarch's own house.

Naameh continued firm in his position, quite as unyielding as the patriarch himself. Lattoof, on the contrary, was all compliance. Quieting his conscience by the plea of necessity, he made a ready sacrifice of all principle, and whatever his master proposed he received without a moment's hesitation, saying, "Just as you please, my lord—just as you please."

But even this blind submission did not avail him, for his "lord" still kept all his "blessedness" to himself. Not a particle of it could he spare to the sheikh or to any member of the family. The curse must remain, wrapping them round like a robe and spreading through their members like oil, until such times as *"Rabshoon the second"* should also come and tender his submission. It was in vain that the sheikh said, "Naameh is of age; he must act for himself. He is not an inmate of my house; he is not under my authority. If he will remain obstinate or wicked, that is no fault of mine. It is no fault of my family." Two days or more being spent in fruitless attempts to effect an arrangement, Naameh mounted his horse and left the place.

After an interval of a week or two Naameh made a second visit to the patriarch, but with as little success as before. The interview was almost a repetition of the former one. He said to the patriarch, "I have learned one thing in this quarrel, and that is that the Almighty is not under your direction. He does not come and go at your bidding. Once I should have trembled under your excommunication, for fear of the curse of God in this life and the next. But now I see little difference. I neither see my body shivered like a potter's vessel, nor feel the curse like oil in my veins, nor feel the torments of that evil angel whom you have set to belabor me day and night. And as to my spirit, I know if I have done anything to cut me off from communion with God and his people, that God has excommunicated me without your agency, but if not, your curse will not injure me."

At hearing these last words the patriarch raised his fists, and, striking them upon his knees in a rage, said, "That's the doctrine of the accursed Bible man."

Naameh finally left the patriarch abruptly, declaring that unless he lowered his demands he would never submit to them. A week after this Is-hoc Turbyhh received a letter from his Holiness informing him that in consequence of the sincere repentance of Sheikh Lattoof he had blessed him and all his family with the exception of Naameh, who had been deluded and corrupted by the accursed Bible man.

CHAPTER XIII.

Convent of Belmont—Monks afraid of the Bible—Worshipers of Mary—An eclipse of the moon—Famous Greek preacher, Miniati—Battle of Navarino and panic—Account of events at Beirut and vicinity in various letters—Return to Beirut—Retirement to Malta.

THE Irish physician who had recommended a mountain air for the invalid child spoke highly also of the Greek convent of Belmont, near Tripoli, as a place of residence, having himself resided there for a time. To this place, therefore, we next retired, the rains of the mountains and the cool air threatening to become uncomfortable. It was past the middle of October, and we had reaped all the sanitary advantage we could expect from our mountain climate. Nothing had occurred during our stay in Ba-whyta to interrupt our harmony, and as we departed the neighbors gathered around us, and, with every appearance of good-will, gave us their parting salaams.

At the convent of Belmont, which seemed to be well peopled and well kept, we were shown to a set of rooms in a separate wing of the building, where we might live quite aloof from the regular inmates of the establishment. The Greeks received us kindly, as their sect generally had done. The mild-tempered Rey-is called in upon us the first evening to tender to us his welcome. He was a man of gray hairs, gentle and frank-hearted in his demeanor, and came fully up to the favorable representation we had received of him from our friend Dr. Madden.

It was two or three evenings after this, when Sheikh Naameh had come down from Ba-whyta, that we returned the call of the superior in his large reception-room. On this occasion the greater part of the inmates of the Deir were present, and Sheikh Naameh narrated before them the whole account of his late difficulty with the Maronite patriarch. They paid close attention to the recital, sometimes amused and sometimes execrating the patriarch.

Attention was next turned to the operations of the Protestants in this land. An elderly man, a scribe of the Mohammedan prince of the district, ventured to say that the Greeks at first were very ready to receive the Protestants and co-operate with them, but since the sultan's firman came out against them they had chosen to take an entire neutral stand, neither blessing nor cursing them. But after confessing that he never had read the firman, he was told for his better information that there had been no firman at all against Protestants—that the proclamation which he had in mind was not against *men* of any class, but simply against *books*, against the holy books written by Moses and David and Paul. The firman had not a word to say about Protestants any more than about the Greeks, so that cutting off intercourse and friendship for such a firman was hardly justifiable. It was true that the Greeks had fallen away from their first cordiality; the old man had only misstated the true reason, which was that *the Books of Moses discouraged the worship of the "holy pictures."* Probably this thought was the reason which led one of the priests immediately to introduce the subject of worshiping images and pictures. Naameh could not endure the practice, and spoke decidedly against it. The priest fired up in a moment, and declared that whoever refused to worship the sacred pictures was a heretic. Their discussion was a rude assault upon the prevailing friendly feeling of the company. But the blame was the priest's. Naameh challenged him to justify or show the lawfulness of that kind of worship.

"I'll show it," said he, "both from the Old Testament and from the New, referring to chapter and verse."

"I defy you to do it," said Naameh.

A deacon was despatched to bring the boasted proofs. He brought a large folio book. A lamp was set in the middle of the room. The priest took the book, saying, "Here are the Old and New Testaments," and seating himself beside the lamp began to read. It was not scripture that he was reading, but might be a preface to something in point, and so the sheikh listened a while in silence, but soon he began to be impatient, and hurried him on to his " proofs, chapter and verse." The priest said, "*Wait, wait a minute, have patience,*" and read on and on, referring to different authors, but especially to St. John of Damascus. Naameh waited for the finishing of a half a folio page or more, when, discovering that his patience profited him nothing, he would bear it no longer, and expostulated with the priest, saying, "Where are your proofs from the Old and New Testaments?"

"What!" said the priest; "are these no proofs?"

"No," said Naameh; "in all you have read I have not heard a proof that is worth a straw, and, besides, it is not scripture."

The priest shut his great book with a slam, blew out the lamp he had been reading by, and took his former seat. This closed the interview. As we rose to make our bows and salaams the Rey-is spoke to Naameh aside and apologized for his over-zealous priest, saying that he was half mad and not worth minding.

The Maronite patriarch was very sensitive on the subject of purchasing a man's religion. In a *Protestant* it was unpardonable, but it seems that he himself had made use of such an inducement to buy Lattoof back after turning him out of church. It was a consideration of no small importance to Lattoof to repossess his property, and after his restoration he made an early call on his Blessedness to know what he desired to do in regard to it. Respecting this call the sheikh furnished his son Naameh at Deir Belmont with the following account. He says:

"I have just come from a visit to his Holiness to obtain the fulfillment of his word of promise to me. On proposing my business his Blessedness said to me, 'I can do nothing about this matter. Your son Naameh is still with the accursed Bible man, and I have just now been credibly informed that such is his state of corruption in their heresy that he once kneeled down for the miserable heretic to lay his hands upon him and pray over him, and that he afterwards rose and kissed his hands.' I told him it was an abominable lie. He said he could prove it by two substantial witnesses. I assured him the story was a downright lie from beginning to end. He then raised his voice to a very loud pitch, and I raised mine louder than his, till at last he said, 'Leave me, Lattoof; I have once let you out of your difficulty and quitted you, and now all I want of you is to quit me. It is written* that in the year 1845 the people shall rise up against their superiors and throw off their alle-

---

* By Bernardus, a Roman bishop.

giance, and you are now making a beginning of that work. The Lord avenge himself upon you.' I replied, 'The Lord will not avenge himself upon me at your dictation. He is not under your command; if he were so, I would no longer serve him. I have not come here to-day to beg *alms* of your Holiness, that you should wish to drive me from your presence. I have come to demand my *right*, to request you to fulfill a solemn promise, but as you refuse this, I have nothing more to say.' With that I rose, turned my back upon him and left him without a compliment. On reaching Besherry I related the whole occurrence to Sheikh Girgis and Sheikh Zaitar, and when I had finished they both said, '*Well done.*'"

An eclipse of the moon occurred on the 3d of November, and as we were gazing at it Sheikh Naameh remarked that on such occasions the people in the mountains were accustomed to get out all their brass plates and vessels and drum upon them, and make as much noise and clangor as possible until the moon should give back her light. The sister of the superior sitting by, who had had a threescore years' experience in this life, explained to us the nature of this phenomenon and the design and utility of the ringing of bells and kettles. It was the same identical old story of the great dragon attempting to swallow the moon and being frightened away by the tumult. But even Sheikh Naameh himself had never known the cause of the eclipse, and when told he was struck with admiration and delight at the new discovery.

One of the best informed and most influential persons among the men of the convent was Deacon Athanasius. He made us a friendly call soon after we came, and inquired frankly, and apparently without any sinister motive, respecting Protestant doctrines and customs. He saw that we differed in many points from the Greeks, but instead of condemning, he in some things commended us. It was painful to find a man of his ability readily confessing that the great objection of the Greeks to the free circulation of the scriptures was the discredit into which it brought the use of the holy images.

The "mad priest," whose name was Neophytus, was after all the most social, if not the most friendly, of all the inmates of the convent. He was in a bad state of health, and two or three days after the ceremony of his "scripture proofs" he called in at our room for a little medicine and sat and talked a long time with a feeling of the utmost good-nature. He honored us with many calls and friendly talks, but endeavored to profit us most by commending to our admiration the excellences of the blessed Virgin, the queen of heaven.

The superior himself seldom favored us with a call, being very much absorbed in the concerns of his vines and olive trees, but he was always accessible and kind when sought for. His knowledge of scripture, we were told, was remarkable, and he evidently took delight in repeating scripture incidents for the instruction and entertainment of present company. For an example, one evening as a number of us were together in his receiving-room he began to narrate some events in the history of Daniel.

"The king of Babylon had been pressed by his people to put Daniel to death, and he finally consented to have him cast into a den where there were *seven lions*. There the prophet remained without food *six days*. To make sure that the lions should devour him, nothing was given them to eat for all these six days. Daniel, by this time, was nearly dying with hunger. Now there was a certain prophet in Judea called Habbakuk, who had prepared a dinner for his laborers in the field, and was about to take it to them, when an angel from heaven appeared to him and said, 'Take this dinner which thou hast prepared and go to Babylon, and give it to Daniel the prophet who is shut up in the den of lions.' '*Go to* Babylon!' exclaimed Habbakuk, in astonishment. 'Where am I, and where is Babylon, that I should go from here to carry a dinner to the prophet Daniel?' But while he wondered the angel took him up by the hair of his head and flew with him through the air to Babylon and set him down with his dinner beside the den of lions, and so Daniel was fed and relieved."

Some doubts being expressed (though it were a pity to spoil an entertaining story) as to whether these facts were to be found in the Bible history of Daniel, the Bible was brought and examined, but the story was not there. The good Rey-is Simeon had read it in a book called "The Idol Bel and the Dragon," one of those "divine books," as the Maronite patriarch styles them, which the Bible men are cursed for leaving out of the Bible.

On the 8th of November a French corvette brought news of the terribly destructive battle of Navarino, in Greece, where a Turkish fleet of more than one hundred vessels, nearly all of them vessels of war, was destroyed by a combined force of twenty-four vessels of the English, French and Russians, the allies not losing a single ship. So tremendous a blow upon Mohammedan power could not fail to make itself felt through the nation. But in what way would this feeling be manifested? was the inquiry. Would it be by the sudden cry of revenge or by the sullen acquiescence of the fatalist? Turks as well as Christians were all taken by surprise and were without any matured or general plan of action. Through the country generally there were no serious insurrections heard of, no thirst for the blood of Christians, but rather a silent waiting to ascertain and follow the course that should be indicated by the government at Constantinople.

While the foregoing events were transpiring in the north of Lebanon, the elements were not much less disturbed with the brethren and friends at Beirut. The exciting causes were political as well as religious. A few extracts from letters received from that quarter during the summer and autumn fall naturally in place at this point of our narrative. Mr. Goodell, August 7, writes: "Sheikh Naameh arrived here last evening, and we were happy to hear of your prosperous voyage and journey. That which has happened since your arrival [the excommunication] is nothing more than was reasonably to be expected considering the relation of the two sheikhs' families and our own relation to the patriarch. We hope, however, the Emeer Ameen will give you due protection; if not, you will perhaps do well not to stay long at Eh-heden.

"As to Beirut affairs, the Greeks (corsairs) have been here the most of the time since you went away. Mr. Abbott lately had an express from Cairo in eleven days. This was understood by all the people of Beirut. The next morning early the consul sent several camel loads of furniture to the mountains. This too was known to all the people of Beirut. And the very same morning a Greek privateer came in with several prizes. This also was known, and all Beirut was in an uproar. But the express in question brought no political news whatever, and the general excitement is now calmed down.

"We were much pleased with Deir el Kullaa, which we lately visited, and took a house of the monks close by the convent. We go up probably this week, so that by next week you may perhaps hear of some such explosion in this quarter as you have had in yours. I do not intend *myself* to dispute with any of the monks, but I will get the consul to disputing as often as I can and will be his dragoman, taking the dragoman's liberty to explain, enlarge and help on his argument."

A letter from Mr. Abbott, the consul, of the same date was as follows: "It was almost of course that Sheikh Bootrus would avail himself of every advantage to trouble and annoy Sheikh Lattoof, and he found the patriarch's anathema very fit for his purpose. Naameh related to the emeer at Gebail the occurrences at Eh-heden;* the emeer laughed at it, but gave him an order which he said would set matters right. Naameh, thinking it was not sufficiently strong and explicit, particularly as to what concerned himself, brought it to me. I have directed my dragoman to represent the matter in a strong light to the emeer, and to require that he would permit no such scandalous transactions and insist that Naameh should be properly protected in the execution of the service for which I have employed him with you.

"We propose to move to Deir el Kullaa as soon as everything is prepared for us."

Four days after his first, Mr. Goodell writes: "We wrote to you by Sheikh Naameh, who, I fear, will lose his letters and his life before this reaches you. The next day after Sheikh Naameh was gone I wrote you

---

* Simply the anathemas, not the outrage in the evening.

by express, and the consul sent a second letter which he had received from the Emeer Besheer. These letters, I fear, will fall into the hands of your enemies.

"By your letters from Tripoli, received this morning, it would seem that, like Paul and Silas, you have been exposed to assaults of violence for the name of Christ, and have had to flee hither and thither to save your lives. Think it not strange concerning this fiery trial, but rather rejoice. . . .

"The Emeer Besheer advises me not to go on the mountain with Mr. Abbott, as it may be the occasion of something scandalous. The Maronites appear to be quite resolved to fight 'for their altars.'

"We deeply sympathize with you all, but we know who governs the world, and that he can cause even these commotions to turn out for the furtherance of the gospel. The poor monks of Deir el Kullaa have just sent word to Mr. Abbott that if I go up with him they must flee, for the patriarch has threatened them with something terrible in case of their receiving me."

Mr. Goodell, August 22: "The Allies have agreed on a course of policy. They do not declare war against the Porte, but they acknowledge the independence of the Greeks, and require a stop to be put to the war against them. The Turks at Constantinople, as might be supposed, rave and bluster and threaten, but it is not expected that they will fight.

"Mr. Abbott has written a very strong letter to the emeer respecting your case, but without avail, and redress could hardly be expected either at Acca or at Constantinople. You know what fanaticism has done at Malta, and in 'dear Ireland' occasionally. The mountaineers feel very sore. Our fare, for aught I see, must be at times like that of the apostles, when persecuted in one city, fleeing to another. The patriarch did all he could to prevent Mr. Abbott himself from going to the mountains.

"Where I shall flee, in case of war, I cannot tell. But the Lord will provide. There is great consternation in Beirut among Muslims as well as Christians, and Franks are leaving the city or sending their effects to the mountains."

Consul Abbott, August 29: "The alarm and consternation in the present crisis of politics are at such a pitch that I am extremely puzzled how to get on. Neither of my dragomans would dare write another letter to the emeer for me after what has passed, as they would be placed between two fires, and they are turning their faces toward the mountains for an asylum, whither they have already sent their valuables for security in the event of an uproar, so you may imagine in what a situation I am placed. Ever since I came to Deir el Kullaa, near a fortnight now, I have been perpetually teased, and have been thrice obliged to leave my family for days together. The noise and stir at Eh-heden has prevented Mr. Goodell's family from going with mine to the mountain. His children have been very unwell, and Mrs. Goodell lies in a sick bed, but I hope, by the mercy of God, she may soon be restored to her accustomed health."

Mr. Goodell, September 7: "Your long and affectionate communications were truly welcome. I became so affected in reading Mrs. Bird's that I had to give it to Mrs. Goodell to read. I assure you we deeply sympathize with you, rejoicing in all your joys and sorrowing in all your sorrows. I have much confidence that all that has befallen you will tend to open the eyes of many, and will thus promote the cause of the gospel. This week has been full of terror to Franks as well as the native Christians. The latter fled in such numbers from the city on Sunday and Monday, with their baggage, that the Turkish authorities put a stop to it, and sent to Acca to know the cause of all this consternation, saying that the Franks had frightened them all. Mr. Gabriel Chasseaud (English vice-consul) fled with his bed and gun, and is happy as a king on the mountain—happy to escape with his life, though all his property should go.

"The cause of this fear apparently is the very great number of messengers that have passed lately without bringing any letters and without bringing any news, except, it is said, that one of them threw out a dark hint. Some surmised that the sultan had been killed by some of the opposers of his new system, and that there would be a massacre of all Christians, natives and Franks; some supposed that war was declared, . . . and my Armenians were almost sure that their heads would be demanded. Mr. Abbott wrote to me to send him, without delay, all the fearful and faint-hearted, and I sent him yesterday Mrs. Goodell and the children, and the Armenians, Carabet and Wortabet, with their wives and baggage. Mrs. Goodell's removal increased the consternation of our neighbors to the highest pitch. The people had kept their eyes on us, saying that we had always heretofore stood at our posts while consuls and other Franks went away. . . . Assad Yacob has come and slept with us every night the week past. Michael Trodd and Hanna el Khoory also pass their nights with us. Tannoos el Haddad appears truly like a Christian."

Mr. Goodell, September 10: "Last night Priest Antone (Greek) came out and passed the night with us. Several of the people were with us also. We read the Scriptures as usual, and I prayed in Arabic. The priest broke out in the midst of my prayer, saying it was good and beseeching God to grant all my petitions. After this we had much interesting conversation till quite late. The priest was very zealous, talking and sweating and preaching, and the last generally in a very orthodox manner."

Mr. Smith, September 23: "G—— M—— (an Arab servant) has just returned from the mountains, whither he has been to see the patriarch. He was at Canobeen when his Blessedness first heard of your arrival, and saw his rage. He says it was reported to the patriarch that you began immediately on your arrival to disseminate your sentiments. The first message of his Blessedness to the Emeer Ameen, he says, was unsuccessful. He then sent a bishop,* who had not returned while G—— was there.

"Only one English subject remains in the city, and there is not a single European vessel in the harbor."

Mr. Goodell, September 24: "The pasha and the authorities at Beirut are doing all they can to allay the fears of the native Christians and to assure them of protection and safety. All the Muslims of the city have their arms with them, and during the night take turns in patroling the city. Those who sleep have their arms at their pillows.

"My Armenians are, I think, doing much good on

---

* This was the bishop that was rude to Sheikh Naameh at Gebail, but afterward, at Deman, called the patriarch a *beast*, and encouraged Naameh to defend himself boldly.

the mountains. All sorts of people call on them to converse on religion. It is apparently much better for the cause than if I were there. Yacob Aga also has, we think, done good at Joon, and Yoosef Lufloofy is useful at Sidon. Our Tannoos is of great use here. More or fewer Arabs are always present at our evening prayers and on the Sabbath."

September 25: "Soon after the messenger was gone yesterday, Galeb Shidiak came and brought another letter from Phares for you. He says it is true, as we have heard from a sheikh, that Assad's moustache and hair have fallen off through the excess of his sufferings.

"The number of those who read the scriptures with us increases. Priest Antone is very friendly to Tannoos and to us all. Our conversation is always of the spiritual kind, and the children of his church rejoice greatly to see him with us, reading the scriptures with us and hearing our prayers. We carefully avoid all disputes, and so does he, and so do all that come.

"There is at present the prospect of a wide door being opened to us among the Druzes. They all appear to look upon us as friends, and I am inclined to think will tell us all about their secret religion. I should not be surprised to find their religion more like Protestantism than like any other religion in this country. As to war, the probability of it seems to have passed, and every day makes it appear more unlikely to happen."

Mr. Smith, October 4: "I have received an invitation from the Beirut convent, since the arrival there of the Greek patriarch, to come and make them a visit. We have here little that is new, except that the Christians of the different sects seem to be less afraid of us than formerly. I suppose the news of the day, by almost turning their brains, has made them forget, in some measure, the threats and anathemas of their priests. Priest Antone continues very friendly. Finding at his last visit some one with us who, he feared, would inform the renowned Nicola Trodd, he has not been here of late. He, however, often sends his salutations, and the other day he urged Tannoos to come to his church, saying that he need not worship the pictures nor do anything contrary to his conscience. Tannoos continues with me, and, so far as I perceive, gives good evidence of being a true Christian."

Mr. Goodell, October 16: "The naval battle that took place lately off our coast was heard here and at Sidon and Soor, but no one can tell between what ships it happened. The plague is raging in the mountains in several villages. A Greek cruiser came in yesterday and took a French vessel out of the harbor. To-day they are parading backward and forward before the city. The Emeer Besheer lately sent a private message to Consul Abbott to say that, in case of war, he must not trust himself to the mountains for safety, as he could not take it upon him to deny his being in his princedom if the pasha should demand him. The consul returned for answer that it was no wonder he could not protect *him*, for he could not even manage that infamous petty priest at Canobeen."

Consul Abbott to Mr. Goodell, dated Deir el Kullaa, October 19: "At last, this evening, I have received an answer to my letter by express to Smyrna. Luckily the admiral was at that place when my letter arrived, and there is little doubt that we shall be taken good care of in case of any hostilities with the Turks, which do not at present seem very probable. By comparing dates and circumstances I am more and more confirmed in my opinion that all will go on quietly without bloodshed between us and the Turks on the subject of the Greek emancipation."

Mr. Abbott to Mr. Goodell, November 7: "I have received an express from my nephew, dated 3 o'clock to-day, saying that a French ship, just in, has brought the news that hostilities have commenced against the Turks by the united English and French fleets having attacked and destroyed the fleet of the grand seignor.

"Should this really be the case, I would advise you to remove all your most valuable property again up to this place, and as for yourselves, contrive to get up to Mansuruyah quietly at your leisure, where I have secured the Emeer Shedeed's house by an order from him just now put into my hands. When we all meet and put our dear ones in a quiet and secure place, we will consult upon the next measures to be taken for our own comfort or security. But before you take any decisive step you had better get every necessary information as to the authenticity of the report that has spread such a terrible alarm among our French neighbors.

"Let nothing disturb the quiet of your mind nor that of your dear family under the present or any other public alarms. Let us put our trust in Him to whom we belong."

Past 10 o'clock P. M.: "I wrote you more than two hours ago on the subject of our trials. Send Mrs. Goodell and what is dear to you up to us. I have told you of the place at Mansureeyeh. It will hold us all. I have stopped the messenger and sent my letter by Eleeas Fuaz, the weather being very untoward."

Mr. Goodell to us at Deir Belmont, dated Mansureeyeh, November 8: "We fled from Beirut hither this morning before sunrise. All the other Franks, consuls and their dependents, fled last night. A French corvette came expressly to bring the news that the combined fleets of Mohammed Ali and of the sultan fired upon the English and French fleets, when the latter sunk all the former to the bottom of the ocean, not leaving, it is said, a man to escape. Some of the Franks here have embarked on board the corvette, and the rest have fled to the mountains. I left everything behind, but hope yet to secure both your things and mine. This is to advise you to take good care of yourselves. We are in the house of the Emeer Shedeed, taken only yesterday (mark the Providence!) by the English consul, and before he heard of this war report. It is two hours from Beirut and one from Deir el Kullaa. The Lord be with you and preserve us all from the hand of the wicked!"

Mr. Smith, Mansur, November 10: "You will have heard that we have fled from Beirut. The consul's family will join us soon, and we hope to find ourselves comfortably situated. Mr. Abbott has informed the emeer of what has happened, at the same time telling him that he expects a man-of-war along soon to look after us. Should one come we shall not forget you. Mr. Abbott is in very good spirits and is very attentive.

"We did not hear of the late battle until after sunset on the 7th, and then dispatched Eleeas Fuaz to the consul in one of the rainiest nights I ever saw. After spending the night till late in packing, and having received, about 2 o'clock in the morning, an answer from Mr. Abbott, we set off on foot before sunrise, having been able to obtain only two donkeys for the children and Mrs. Goodell, the last of whom was sick abed when the news arrived, and thus, some on boards and some on broken pieces of the ship, it came to pass that we escaped all safe, Mr. Goodell and family to Mansureeyeh, and Mr. St. J. and I to Deir el Kullaa.

"All our houses are still undisturbed, and though we escaped with nothing except our money and the clothes on our backs, through the attentions of our Arab friends we have been able to obtain our most valuable articles."

Mr. Goodell, Mansureeyeh, November 12: "We have got into very fine quarters. I think it not improbable that we may winter here, even should there be peace. The priests and people are very friendly indeed so far. Mrs. Goodell's fright and flight entirely cured her. We are translating the official account of the battle, by the request of Mr. Abbott, into Arabic, to be circulated everywhere. I expect much good to grow out of all this. I am glad we wrote our joint letter to Mr. Jowett when we did. I am glad you have been kicking up such a dust in all your neighborhood. I am glad for almost everything and sorry for nothing, unless it be our own indolence. Let us go on laboring and praying fervently that by all these events the kingdom of Christ may be advanced. All the sheikhs and emeers and priests and monks and people in this quarter are in high glee at the news."

From the Armenian brethren, Carabet and Wortabet:

"We received a letter from you yesterday, and we enjoyed your desired love with great joy and comfort. We give thanks to God that keeps you and all true believers in him and his Son, and all who trust in the name of Jesus he delivers from every evil and every temptation as he has done for you. We are joyful very much, and our hearts are filled with comfort on God's gifts whereby all your family are in life and in health. Although you have had affliction in some respects, we hope you have comforts too from Him whom you trust.

"All we are very well, and stay with our beloved brother, Mr. Goodell, in Mansurie, giving praise to God for all his providence in this world. We are not neglectful to remember you and yours in our prayers in every time, and we ask you for this purpose, that is, to pray for all of us, and we, hoping to see you in a short time, remain your real friends,

"D. CARABET,
"J. G. WORTABET."

Mr. Goodell, November 29: "All is quiet in Alexandria. The pasha there offers a wager of fifty purses that there will be no war. Everything quiet at Cyprus. The Maltese families are returning from the mountains to Beirut. Letters from Constantinople say that the sultan received the news of the great battle with '*grandissima calma.*'"

December 8: "The Emeer Shedeed is now in this village. His mother came a fortnight ago. He is very civil and polite, and is also something of a scholar—is exceedingly kind and agreeable with Brother Smith, but very cautious not to speak my name, or to have any conversation with me. Since his mother came she has had constantly with her two or three priests who say I ought not to be here. Mrs. Goodell has been twice to see her with Mrs. Abbott. The emeer is also kind to Tannoos, and I think would not object to his going and residing anywhere in his district with Mr. Smith.

"Mr. Abbott thinks you had better move on this way soon."

December 17: "A few days ago the princess here received a letter from the bishop, saying he had heard that Mrs. Goodell had been twice in company with Mrs.

SYRIAN GENTLEMAN.

Abbott to see her, and that if she permitted Mrs. Goodell to enter her house again, he should be under the necessity of putting her under "the great excommunication."

The disturbances in consequence of the war news

having chiefly passed away at Beirut there seemed no reason for staying away from our proper station. We therefore came to a satisfactory settlement with our venerable superior, Priest Simeon, engaged animals for our goods, and made our way by land in two days to Beirut. Public feeling there, and in all the region, settled down from its apprehensions, but the late hurricane in the Morea had left many ominous clouds in the political horizon. All the great powers of Europe were agitated. Russia was seen to be threatening to seize the present occasion to weaken still further the Turkish power, and to wage a war with the Porte on her own account. Such a war was distasteful to the French and English, and in view of its possibility they withdrew many of their representatives in the Turkish dominions.

About the 1st of February the French consul, by order of his ambassador, removed his flag, and in a note to Mr. Abbott assured him that a similar order was prepared for him, which order came accordingly before the close of the month.

On the 14th of March war was actually declared by Russia, and though the fact was not then known in Syria, it was acted upon as if it were. Our circumstances became very embarrassing. The loss of our consul, war in the north, pestilence approaching from the south,* together with the cutting off of commerce and of our pecuniary resources, all moved us to a consultation whether the divine will were not sufficiently indicated that we should retire for a time from our field. After due deliberation and looking to the Father of Lights for wisdom to direct, we decided to charter for our use an Austrian vessel lying at anchor in the har-

* Scores were carried off daily in Acca by the plague.

bor, which was offered to take us to Malta. We commenced sending on board our goods April 24, carefully wrapping in flag-mats all articles known to be susceptible of the contagion of the city, for the plague had already begun its work there. Including the families of our two Armenians and that of Mr. N——, the English missionary, we made up twenty-one passengers.

When we were all safe on board we felt that we had much cause for gratitude for having been enabled to accomplish so successfully a work to which we had for weeks been looking forward with no little anxiety. It was at first doubtful whether we could find a convenient vessel for so large a company. It was also uncertain whether we should be permitted to embark *at all*, or at least without great molestation, especially as we were taking with us two families of natives. The consul himself had to steal away, leaving all his baggage behind him, to be taken care of by his friends.

At our departure not an enemy opened his mouth in triumph over us. As we passed through the streets, those from whom we might have expected scorn said to us, in all sobriety, "The Lord preserve and prosper you!" Our young friend Michael Trodd was anxious to go with us, though against the known wishes of his parents, whom he regarded with every appearance of due affection, and at the moment of our final separation he clung around Mr. Smith's neck and wept outright. Assad Khaiât, who had been persecuted and alienated from us, now came, and of his own accord confessed with tears his fault, hoped if we returned we should find him a different person from what he had lately been, and begged a constant remembrance in our prayers. Tannoos el Hadad could hardly be reconciled to be torn away from his old pupil and messmate. He also would have been glad to go where we went and lodge where we lodged until death should us part, but it was made to appear his duty to remain and serve Christ among his countrymen, and he patiently submitted. Priest Antone took pains to call and bid us farewell, as did many others not to be named. Some who we were persuaded were specially friendly to us did not call, either on account of the prevailing plague or because our sudden departure was yet a secret to them.

It was now about four years and a half from the time that the first missionaries still living came to anchor in the roadstead of Beirut. We had then no intention of staying at that place any longer than was necessary to obtain animals or a boat to take us onward toward Jerusalem. We were, however, prevented from proceeding, first by the season, next by the advice of brethren then on the ground, and afterward by a fruitless examination of the country for a better place for our work—an examination which extended from Beirut to Hebron, which answer to the Dan and Beersheba of Palestine. Every succeeding year strengthened the evidence that our remaining at Beirut was a well-advised measure, for in no other place, probably, south of Constantinople could there have been found a spot where there was so much readiness in the people to inquire after the truth, united with so much safety in declaring it.

At this pause in the progress of the mission, it is natural to recur to the events of its history to ascertain of what practical utility it has been. Those who, according to the notable missionary proverb, had been led to "*expect great things,*" were perhaps some of them disappointed. But if the things it had done were not to be called "great," it had accomplished *something*. It had made the Christian public more familiarly acquainted with the present condition of one of the most interesting portions of the globe. It had proved the practicability of Protestant missions under the Mohammedan government. It had exposed to view some important traits in the present character of Mohammedism and Popery. It had made known to thousands of Mohammedans that the worship of images and saints is not a part of Christianity. It had shown to thousands of nominal Christians that the English, or, in other words, all Protestants, are not the Free-masons and infidels which Jesuits and others had reported them to be. Above all, we could not doubt that it had accomplished one good thing against which money and human labor and sacrifices are not to be laid in the balance—it had increased the number of that happy throng who shall "ascribe dominion and glory for ever and ever to Him that loved them and washed them from their sins in his own blood."

CHAPTER XIV.

Operations in Malta—Messrs. Whiting and Dwight—Visit to the coast of Africa, to Greece, to Armenia—Labors at Beirut resumed—New curses—Patriarch excommunicated by Jos. Wolff—Death of Assad Shidiak—Brummana village—Druzes—Messrs. Parnell and Hamilton—Wortabet's labors in Sidon—His death—Two Jesuits—Lamartine eulogizes them—Outrage of soldiers—Traits of Ibrahim Pasha.

TO dwell on the operations of the missionaries while in Malta with any degree of particularity would not comport with the special object of these pages, which is to record transactions pertaining especially to Syria. Suffice it to say that in the absence of Mr. Temple, the official superintendent of the press, this powerful agent was kept in full motion, sending forth as usual its various tracts and books, and especially working off the Armeno-Turkish Testament, a translation to which Mr. Goodell and his two Armenian associates, while in Syria, had devoted the main portion of their time. An exploring tour on the neighboring coast of Africa was performed by one of the brethren, and also a similar one by another, in company with the Rev. Dr. Anderson, in Greece and the Greek islands.*

In the autumn of 1829 the war in Turkey came to a close; the English consul soon after returned to his post at Beirut; Mr. Goodell was detached from the work in

---

* A history of this latter tour, from the pen of Dr. Anderson, has been given to the public in a valuable little volume.

Syria, to continue his labors more directly in behalf of the Armenians in another field, and the Rev. Mr. Whiting, who arrived at Malta from America in February was substituted in his place. Mr. Smith, with the Rev. Mr. Dwight, another newly-arrived missionary, entered, in March, upon a tour of research in Asia Minor among the Armenian nation. Bishop Carabet was to be continued in the employ of Mr. Goodell, and Wortabet, having nearly lost the use of his eyes, left our employ, and, returning to Syria, entered into an employment by himself in Sidon, of which city his wife was a native.

Thus shorn of its strength, the station at Beirut was, after a two years' intermission, once more occupied. The separation of the two families who had been so long connected in Syria was attended with many regrets on both sides. On this subject we find our beloved brother who was left behind in Malta expressing himself thus: "Our dear brethren and sisters left us on the 1st instant and sailed in the Vincitore, a Maltese brig, directly for Beirut. Again and again have they been both publicly and privately commended to the care and guidance of the great and good Shepherd who gathers the lambs in his arms and carries them in his bosom, and again and again has his blessing been implored upon their labors. To those of us who for many years have been so closely associated in missionary work, who have passed together through so many scenes of trouble and of joy, who have seen so much of the goodness of God toward our families, who have so often been in circumstances to comfort, assist and encourage each other, and have so often borne each other's burdens, the separation was not a little trying. We had become exceedingly endeared to each other by numerous tender and affecting associations. But though we may never meet again at the table of the Lord or at the baptismal font, or be refreshed by each other's company again in this world, I trust that neither this nor any other created thing will ever be able to separate them or us from the love of God which is in Christ Jesus our Lord."

On the morning after our coming to anchor at Beirut we were visited by our old steadfast friends Tannoos el Haddad and Eleeas Fuaz, as well as by the English dragoman with a congratulatory message from the consul and an invitation to his house. Our friends gave us information of many events of a local character affecting the interests of our work. Maallem Aioob, one of our chief enemies in the Custom-house, had been displaced; Mansoor ed Dahh-dahh, another prominent enemy at Bteddeen, had been made to give place to a much more amiable and reasonable man, the Emeer Ameen. Encouraged by this last change, our young Sheikh Naameh el Ash-shi had indulged the hope of obtaining from the Emeer Besheer the restoration of his father's property, and he had been at the consul's now more than a month on this business. His long continuance with the consul had begun again to trouble the patriarch, and the latter was threatening to issue a new bull of excommunication against him for his prolonged contact with the English. Our young friend Anton Adam, who had formerly served as a translator, was also threatened for a like offence. Sheikh Girgis of Besherry had been down to have a consultation with our consul about some difficulty in which he showed himself willing to receive aid from a Protestant, an act strictly forbidden by the patriarch. An aid-de-camp of the Russian General Diebitsch, returning lately from a visit to Jerusalem, had publicly expressed his extreme disgust at the priestly farce of the Greek fire as exhibited at the holy sepulchre. Moreover, Eleeas Fuaz himself had come forth and taken a new and decided stand on the side of the Lord.

The day after we landed the Maronite priests repeated in their church the usual warnings and denunciations against the heretics. On the Sabbath we commenced once more our customary preaching service at the consul's. Tannoos and Eleeas were with us, though neither of them understood much of the English. They had both entirely ceased to attend worship at the Greek church, as they could not unite with the rest in all their ceremonies, and they were unwilling to disturb their quiet by appearing singular among them. Still the priests had passed no sentence of excommunication upon either of them. Eleeas in our Arabic meetings readily took an active part in the exercises and spoke with marked propriety. His change had been produced instrumentally by the faithful admonitions of his friend Tannoos.

Mansoor Shidiak had been bereaved of his wife and had himself been very seriously ill, both of which visitations he himself received as a judgment of God upon him for his ill treatment of his brother Assad. Sheikh Naameh informed us that in consequence of his alienation from the Maronite doctrines he had been obliged to give up his marriage contract with the daughter of Is-hoc Turbyhh. This gentleman was not only a relative of the Ash-shi family, but was a man of wealth, spoke and wrote well in French, and to become his son-in-law must have been an honor and a great worldly advantage to the young sheikh. If he really relinquished this honor and advantage from religious principle, it was what few mere men of the world would probably have done.

He gave us another piece of information, namely, that he had not long since had an interview with his Holiness the patriarch. Being on a visit to some friends in the neighborhood of Bkoorki, where the patriarch was residing, his friends took him in for a respectful call. Among other common topics his Holiness conversed about an excommunication which he himself had lately received from the Protestant missionary, Joseph Wolff, by which not only he (the patriarch) but all his people were laid under a curse. He promised to furnish the sheikh with the perusal of it, hoping evidently that, as one of the Maronite people threatened by Wolff, he would feel himself insulted by it.* Nothing unkind on either side took place during the interview.

* A duplicate of this paper of excommunication, written by Wolff himself, fell into our hands. It was couched in language by which his Holiness, St. Joseph, was probably not often addressed, and suggested thoughts which might well affect his conscience. Whether it was best to visit the patriarch with such an explosion, others, perhaps, beside his Holiness, might question. But it was doubtless the design of Mr. Wolff in this case to mimic and ridicule the proud style of the patriarch himself in his anathemas, as his countryman, Luther, ridiculed the pope in using papal language, saying, "I, Dr. Martin Luther, declare this or that," and quoting the pope's own Latin hexameter, "*Sic volo, sic jubeo, sit pro ratione voluntas.*"

The anathema of Wolff was this: "To our friend the Antiochian patriarch of the sect of the Maronites: The Lord renew your heart and drag you out of the Romish Church. After bestowing from our hand upon you and upon your beard the apostolic blessing, we give you information that we at present are in Alexandria preaching the gospel to the Jews, Mohammedans and Catholics, and it has come to my knowledge that Assad Shidiak is still in prison by your order. Therefore, I command you forthwith to set him at liberty, and if you do it not on arrival of this letter, and kneel down before him submissively and kiss his hand and beg his pardon, I will send a *herm* upon

A letter had been received by the Shidiak family at Hadet, signed and sealed by the patriarch, giving them intelligence that Assad Shidiak had died of fever at Canobeen on the 25th of September, after an illness of ten days. The family observed the usual mourning ceremonies, and the surrounding friends, including all the emeers, paid to the family in Hadet their visits of condolence according to the custom of the country. Reports of the death of this Christian martyr had often previously come abroad, but none of them with the apparent authenticity of the present. None had come with the signature and seal of the patriarch, and none had been received and acted upon as credible by the family and the public men of the village. Besides, from that day forward no man was ever found to say that he had visited the convent of Canobeen and discovered that the prisoner was living. We have therefore good reason to believe that his death actually occurred at the time specified.

As to the manner of his death it was strange that during a fever of ten days no word should have been sent to the family. It was more commonly reported by those who were in a situation to judge that the event was sudden and unexpected. In regard to a burial, it appears that he had none. He could not be buried in consecrated ground. His body was therefore taken out, it was said, a little distance from the convent and laid by the side of a wall, the stones of which were thrown down upon it. For a heretic, who deserved no burial at all, this was thought to be burial enough.

you, and upon all the Maronites, and upon the Pope of Rome, who is anti-christ, and you shall go to perdition. Repent, therefore, and believe in Christ.   (Signed)   JOSEPH WOLFF,
"The Englishman and missionary of Jesus Christ."

But neither the hand and seal of the patriarch nor all the mourning ceremonies of the relatives and friends of the Shidiak family could convince all minds that the man was really dead. He was at first decoyed into the patriarch's power by *fraud*, and it was believed that the same fraud would naturally be used to maintain that power, and that the story of the patriarch about the man's death was fabricated to rid himself of the trouble of constant watching to prevent efforts from without to liberate his prisoner. Even one of the mountain princes, though himself a Maronite, was a sharer in this incredulity as to the death of Assad.

As long as a shadow of doubt hung over the fate of this man of God, it was a thing to be desired, if opportunity offered, that the convent should be examined and the fact of his life or death ascertained. Such an opportunity was presented when in 1832 Syria fell under the power of Ibrahim Pasha. He readily gave leave to a young Scottish merchant to go, furnished with an escort of soldiers, and search the convent from top to bottom, which was actually done in presence of the patriarch. The soldiers went heartily and rudely to their work, paying no deference to the feelings of his Holiness, opening every cell and closet and striking every chest where he might be concealed, and calling upon Assad to "*come forth.*" But, alas, the patriarch had finished his work too early for them. "There was no voice nor any that answered." He will "come forth" only at the voice of the last trump, when "the trumpet shall sound and the dead shall be raised incorruptible, and we shall be changed." And oh how changed will he appear!—raised from the filth and squalidness of a three years' dungeon to the dignity of a martyr's crown, and arrayed in the "fine linen white and clean, which is the righteousness of saints."

During the summer of 1831 a residence was obtained by the author on the mountains, at the village of Brummana, under the government of Druzes. We were visited freely and treated with all respect both by the authorities and by the people. The Emeer Mansoor, the chief ruler of the place, was a man of sixty years, having a powerful frame, of more than six feet in stature and of dignified deportment. He had a large family; two or three of the sons were men and had influence in the government of the place; a daughter of his, Druze as she was, became the wife of the Emeer Besheer the less, of the Shehab family, and a Maronite. The family was therefore had in estimation. The sons had either professed Christianity or were about to do so. The father was not a Druze of the *initiated* class called aakils, neither was he careful to be thought a great admirer of the Koran. He had but one wife, and condemned the practice of polygamy. In conversation on the liberty which the Koran gives of having many wives, he said, "I tell my Muslim friends the angel Gabriel never brought such a precept down to the prophet; he brought that down himself." Even the aakils among the Druzes of the village were forward to court our acquaintance. When a short call was made upon us by the chief reader in their *khulwch* (church), he was found very affable and gentle in his manners, often giving his hand in token of assent and listening with attention to all that was said about the gospel. Four or five others were present to listen and to assist in the conversation. The aakil declared that the Druzes did not profess to have any new revelation from God; no inspired book had come from heaven since the Koran; the Druzes had their peculiar book of *prayers*, but no book from God like the Law, the Psalms, the Gospel and the Koran. All present said they believed in the gospel.

It may have been an hour that the conversation continued, and at the end the aakil begged a copy of the Bible and of the "Dairyman's Daughter." After this the brother of this man was at our house, and said, "Sir, it is your bounden duty to come and read to us the gospel at our Thursday evening meetings." Accordingly, on that same evening four or five women came to conduct both the missionary and his wife to their meeting. Their reader was present when we entered, and he and four or five others rose respectfully and pointed us to the "highest room" in the company. A few remarks only were made, and then the reader called upon a young man near by to assist him in commencing their services. The aakil placed himself near the light, and, sitting erect, began reciting the preface to the Koran. After this came two or three other books, partly, as it appeared, of poetry and partly of prose, including a few leaves of the Koran. There was no exercise but reading, with now and then a word of explanation; no rising, kneeling or bowing the face to the ground, after the manner of the Muslims. But evidently this meeting was not to be taken as a specimen of one of the more secret meetings, where aakils *only* are admitted. Many of those present at this meeting were of the uninitiated, whom they call *jah-hils*.

When their reading was finished a brother of the reader came and asked if we had brought our Bible. As we had not, a friendly Druze woman brought forward a

New Testament that had been given her, and they listened attentively to the reading of the Sermon on the Mount, with brief expository remarks.

At the close of this latter reading they were, of course, profuse in their professions of admiration at the doctrines of Jesus; wished to be learners of us; they were "very near" to us in regard to religion—that is, not having images, etc. It was told them in reply that in order to be *very* near to us it would be quite necessary for them to believe two things which the Koran denies—*first*, that Seidna Esa (the Lord Jesus) actually died; and *secondly*, that he died for our sins. They smiled, but made no reply.

After that evening, as long as we remained in the place, the Druzes came daily to our house to hear about the gospel, and on the succeeding Sabbath about a dozen came in to attend our evening devotions.

In our joint report for the year (1831) we wrote thus: "Some time since a Druze woman at Beirut was in the habit of coming daily to the house of our school-teacher to listen to the reading of the scriptures and religious conversation. Her face was often bathed in tears while she repeated ever and anon, 'That's the truth!' Her coming was interrupted by the prevalence of the plague among the people, and, as she never came again, the inference was that she was one of the victims of the disease. We have hope that she died a penitent believer. A man somewhat advanced in years, and who was one of the aakils, came also to the house of the same teacher, and, after hearing and opposing the truth for some time, at length gave up his opposition, and as a proof of his conviction offered to bring us one of the secret books of his religion, with which offer he has since complied. A considerable number among the princely families of the Druzes have within a few years become nominally Christian. Two or three families or clans that remain will very likely think it expedient to follow their example. But the common people do not as yet seem disposed to imitate their princes. Should our mission be continued, the experiment will no doubt ere long be fully tried, whether a pure gospel may not produce on this despised and uninstructed people results which the deformed Christianity of this country has never yet been able to effect.

"The Nusairîyeh of the parts beyond Tripoli, said by some to be a race of Druzes, but more erratic and uncivilized than they, have been furnished by us with a few copies of the word of life, which, as the agent assured us, they had begun to read with great satisfaction. A missionary station at Tripoli or Ladikeea seems desirable, not merely for the benefit of the *Christian* part of the population, but also in special reference to this half pagan people.

"In failure of all reinforcements of laborers from home, it has been with peculiar pleasure that we have enjoyed the correspondence and aid of a company of English brethren at Aleppo, who, though originally destined to a station farther on in the East, have hitherto been providentially detained on our coast. Two of them are at present with us at Beirut, imparting to us that strength and comfort which are the natural result of familiar Christian intercourse. For ourselves we should be willing their detention from their prospective field should be indefinitely prolonged, but we would not dare oppose what might seem to them to be a call of Providence. We are anxiously hoping for an addition of laborers in our section of the Lord's vineyard. May our hope not be long deferred! Alone we feel too weak in many respects to answer the natural calls of the work here and the wishes and the probable expectations of American Christians."

The two English brethren above referred to were Messrs. Parnell and Hamilton, the former the eldest son of Sir Henry Parnell, who occupied a distinguished position under the British government. They were members of a company who had set out on a missionary enterprise at their own charges, and, having arrived at Aleppo, were intending to proceed with Messrs. Newman and Cronin, their associates at that city, to unite with Dr. Groves, already at Bagdad. Mrs. Parnell had accompanied her husband as far as Ladikeea, near which place she met with a fall from her horse and died of the injuries she then received. These brethren came to make our acquaintance and witness our mode of operation. Mr. Hamilton, from his declining health, concluded to return to England. His companion, after a three months' visit, returned to his associates at Aleppo, having first shown his good-will toward us by ordering out from England, in behalf of our enterprise, a lithographic press and a munificent addition to our mission library. The company left Aleppo for Bagdad on the 19th of April. In four days they came to the large village of Aintab, where they were detained seventeen days waiting for a caravan. They sold here twenty-seven copies of the Armeno-Turkish Scriptures, and were told they might have found sale for two hundred if they had had them. Copies of Mr. Goodell's translation went off freely, though some were shy of them because they had not been authorized by the Church. The company, at the close of their stay, fell under the displeasure of the governor for selling a book or two to Muslims, and an order was given them to leave the place, which they had already engaged to do by a caravan that was just on the move. However, a popular excitement was beginning to rise against them, and they could not get free from the village without a few volleys of stones.

The visit of this little company to Aintab at this time may have been a distant exciting cause of that remarkable spirit of inquiry and great success of the gospel which have since made that place so remarkable.

Through the influence of Wortabet, our zealous Armenian brother in Sidon, an earnest inquiry prevailed about the scriptures and the way to be saved. A discussion of the Christian doctrines in writing was set on foot, and on account of Wortabet's want of familiarity with the Arabic we engaged our Arabic teacher, Tannoos, to go to his assistance. He returned in a few days confirming the accuracy of the reports which our sanguine brother had sent us. He brought at the same time a letter from Wortabet, saying, "My neighbor Nahass, since my answer to him, says to the people (who saw my proofs about the pope and who went to him to ask about the matter) that their fathers were mistaken in receiving the pope as head of the church of Christ. Two-thirds of the people here are not fasting, but are eating meat in this Lent openly, and the priests are not able to say a word to them. The people come to me always, and I am engaged with them daily in respect to the evangelical way. Many things there are to be written to you if they were not dangerous at these times of war."

Mr. Nicolayson also, who went to aid the native brethren at Sidon, writes thus: "As the press of business at Wortabet's magazine increases, conversations and discussions increase. By the blessing of God I trust much good will result from it. Yesterday we had a long and interesting discussion with a respectable Muslim from the camp of Acca, in which he frankly avowed that the more intelligent and reflecting Muslims now-a-days own that they have no solid hope of salvation, being well aware that such is the state of morals among them that they cannot possibly be received to heaven; and as to Mohammed's power to carry them there, this is believed by ignorant fanatics only.

"This morning the same Muslim came again, and with him an Armenian who had accompanied him yesterday and taken part in the discussion. The Muslim said, 'I am going to the camp to-day, but I leave you this man to be further instructed by you, for he is still in the dark.' A long conversation ensued between Wortabet and this Armenian, which the former closed at the end of four hours with a most affectionate and truly eloquent address on regeneration, telling him that without this all pretence to religion is *bosh*."

Subsequently Wortabet writes: "The keeper of the journal of Ibrahim Pasha, as he is my friend, came to my magazine and told me something useful to all nations which Mohammed Ali Pasha desires to do, but I cannot explain to you. Mr. Nicolayson, when he comes, will know and write it to you.

"Hannah Bah-hari [pasha's prime minister] sent me his salaam by the writer of the journal. He was coming from Acca and is going northward to join Ibrahim Pasha, and he asked me many things before many people here about the kingdom of Christ. I told him, before Jews and Turks, as much as I know, and he was very glad to hear me. He is a Turk truly, but an intelligent one."

Wortabet hints in the above letter that he is expecting the arrival of Mr. Nicolayson at Sidon, and that he will write on some important subjects more fully than he himself was able to do. Mr. Nicolayson's predicted letter was this:

"Could Wortabet write you himself, he would have much to tell you, but I shall condense it as much as possible. The work among Jews and Christians has continued as usual without change, but as it regards Muslims it has increased very much in importance and publicity. It is, indeed, such as to astonish very many.

"As to what he has hinted to you concerning Mohammed Ali's plans, as communicated to him by the chief journal-keeper of Ibrahim, it is to this effect: Wortabet had been explaining to him the expectations which the scriptures warrant us to entertain respecting the speedy establishment of the Messiah's kingdom in peace and righteousness. This led the above-mentioned personage to remark that should Mohammed Ali be questioned as to his designs if successful, he would declare his intention to be to dethrone Sultan Mahmood for his injustice and incapacity, and to place his son on the throne, with the condition that he should receive forty-four counselors, which would give the government the nature of a limited monarchy. The object of this change should be to put an end to all war and oppression and to establish universal peace and equality, and for this purpose he would have the new government formed by the advice and aid of the European powers, and its great object secured by mutual compacts and treaties with them."

Three days after the above Mr. Nicolayson writes:

"The Jews give me no peace till I scrape together whatever can be found in the shape of Hebrew Bibles and psalters, that they may purchase them. To-day we have been taken up almost all the time with Jews and Muslims. Among the latter is a certain Naseer Aga, a Damascene, who is often very useful to cut short some of the false reasonings of the rest. He does not allow them to assert that the gospel we possess is corrupted and different from the original."

Thus was our ardent and unwearied Armenian brother proceeding in his career of usefulness when we received an alarming letter from Mr. Nicolayson that he was dangerously ill. Two pious young men who were with us set off immediately to render him aid. But human aid was found to be unavailing. The first subsequent word respecting him was that he was no better, and the second was that he was no more.

The following extract of a letter from his wife is worth preserving. It describes a conversation with her husband after indications had begun to appear of occasional wanderings of mind:

"We asked him, 'Where are you?' He replied, 'With the merciful Jesus, and he is with me.' 'Where is Jesus?' 'He is present in every place.' 'Is he near you or afar off?' 'He is near at my side.'

"We asked him various questions, which he answered correctly, repeating some passages from the gospel. He remained in this situation, answering questions which we put to him, until sunrise on Monday, September 10, after which he was not able to speak. An hour and a half before noon his spirit left this world of trouble and went to Jesus his beloved, in whom he trusted."

At the time of the funeral services, to the disgrace of

humanity an altercation arose in the midst of the solemnities. The grave had been prepared in the cemetery of the Greek Catholics. It was consecrated ground, and according to papal law no heretical, unbelieving corpse could be permitted to rest in a place so holy. A number of men, therefore, united in declaring that the law of their cemetery should not be violated. What should be done? The procession had reached the grave and were waiting. It seemed as if they must take the dead back to his house. But Yoosef Lufloofy, brother-in-law of the deceased, boldly stood forth and asserted his right to at least as much of that cemetery as contained the bones of his own brother, long since dead, and declared that there his brother-in-law should lie. So saying, he seized the shovel and fell to work. The grave was soon opened without opposition, and the two dead were left, brother-in-law with brother, Protestant and Catholic slumbering together in peace, and no apprehensions are entertained that either of them on the resurrection morn will complain of having been defiled by the bones of the other.

There were two Jesuit missionaries, a German and a Frenchman, who, according to the established rule of the papacy for counteracting and neutralizing Protestant influence, were about this time commencing labors in the vicinity of Beirut. They were occupying the college establishment at Antoora, from which the Rev. Mr. Lewis had been formerly driven. Lamartine, the French poet, while for a time he was residing in Beirut, says of them: "The two young fathers often came to visit us at Beirut, and afforded us a society as agreeable as unexpected." In regard to their work and success he remarks: "They neglected no means or opportunity of propagating among the Druzes some ideas of Christianity, but the effect of their proceedings was confined to *baptizing in secret, and, even unknown to the parents, young children of families into which they had introduced themselves under pretence of giving medical advice.* I believe they will return to Europe without having succeeded in naturalizing in Lebanon a taste for more extended knowledge. The French father was worthy of a professorship at Rome or Paris." Speaking of their failure he says, "It was owing to this simple reason, viz., that *there are no politics* in the religion of the East, and therefore Catholicism *has no means of domination.* Now, as it is by HUMAN MEANS CHIEFLY that the Jesuitical system has acted and does act upon religion, this country does not suit it." *

One hot day in summer, while an encampment of the pasha's soldiers were lying near the walls outside the city, some of them strolled into our enclosure and began plucking the fruit and eating. Our house-servant went to warn them off, and a quarrel commenced between them in which stones were thrown very freely. One of the soldiers fell with a bad gash in the forehead, the others ran down to the camp. As a number of us were gathered about the fallen combatant examining his wound and binding it up, a little party from the camp, having got the news, came rushing into the garden armed with muskets and saying hurriedly, "Where is the guilty man? Where is he?" holding their guns in readiness to blow the man through if they could see him. The children were affrighted and ran, crying out with terror, while to increase their excitement the soldiers leveled their guns at them as if they would shoot them.

* Itinerary, Vol. II., p. 43.

The guilty man who threw the missile was a mile off ere this, and they, perceiving no one present that showed any signs of guilt, and supposing that the Frank who stood there supporting the wounded man and fixing on his bandage must have had something to do with it, seized him at a venture and conducted him by the arms out into the street and toward the camp. Along the street were crowds of other soldiers whom curiosity or indignation had brought out from the camp, who, seeing a man dragged out like a murderer, thought him to be the true culprit, and thought it good enough for him to receive a little chastising before he was crucified, and so began a sort of gauntlet execution with slaps and cuffs and such like from behind. One man broke a staff over his shoulder, the broken piece whizzing by and striking before him in the sand. Another came to the front, brandishing his gun and twisting his face and eyes into all the contortions of a fury. Being brought to the middle of the camp, they bound his wrists together behind him and seated him flat on the open ground. He must have been a ludicrous object to behold, in the midst of a thousand spectators looking on, squatted down without a sign of a seat (as a Frank never sits), without a carpet or a mat (as a decent Arab never sits), his coat torn open in the back, his hat crushed in at the side, his hands and arms drawn back out of position, and passers-by stopping to gaze, sneer and spit at him.

His position was not only ridiculous, but somewhat *uncomfortable* withal. To sit bent in the middle at an angle of ninety degrees, without arms before to balance and nothing behind to support, soon becomes wearisome. Then there was the scorching sand beneath and a midday summer's sun above; the tight ligature was painful, and soon destroyed all motion and nearly all sense of feeling in his hands. What some avenging brother of the wounded, possibly dead, man, coming from his bloody corpse, might do from behind, he could not see, but he could not help imagining to himself what kind of a sensation it would be to feel the plunge of a bayonet into his back, and what a tremendous change might in one moment more be wrought in the mode and place of his existence. But his hour had not come.

News of the occurrence had spread in all directions. Crowds of spectators from within and from without the city were collected about the camp-ground to witness the possible execution of a Frank. The first man that presented himself to attempt anything that looked like interference was our newly-arrived brother Dodge. As he attempted to approach he was rudely driven back, and stood with the crowd greatly embarrassed. Next the dragoman of the English consul passed by in sight, but was not allowed to come within speaking distance. The English consul-general in full uniform, with his mounted janizaries and other attendants, next appeared, coming at full gallop as if they intended to effect a rescue by a *coup de main*. Instantly the whole camp was roused, the drums beat, stones flew like hail, bayonets bristled and hedged up the passage. The strife was short. The consul, yielding to such immense odds, left the Egyptians masters of the field, and, drawing off his forces in good order, made his way by a circuitous route into the city.

The concourse of citizens, excited by these novel movements, continued to increase insomuch that the commander of the neighboring castle overlooking the camp-ground became alarmed for the safety of the soldiery, and was seen arranging his cannon so as to sweep in the direction of the multitude in case any violence should be attempted against the soldiers. At the end of about forty minutes the governor of the city was seen, accompanied by the American consul and other officials, issuing from the gate of the city and approaching the camp. The Egyptians, knowing their errand and not daring any further to trespass on the authority of the civil government, quietly gave up their prisoner. He was taken, bound as he was, to the governor's palace, where in a large open courtyard were sitting in solemn conclave all the European consuls, with their vice-consuls, dragomans, etc., as well as the governor, judge and other dignitaries of the city. The wounded man was also brought in in a senseless state and laid before them on the pavement of the court. They had just begun to interchange views as to what measures should be taken to repair the outrage of the soldiers when one of the subordinate officers, who had brought in the wounded man, glancing his eyes indignantly at the Franks and speaking in an undertone, vented his spite by threatening terrible vengeance in case the man should die. M. Jorelle, the French vice-consul, overheard the speech and immediately rose and said loudly,

"Gentlemen, I stay here no longer. If in the very palace of the governor of this city we cannot be secure from insult and from threats of assassination by these soldiers, it is time for us to look out for our own safety."

The judge looked up with open mouth as if thunderstruck. The whole company rose from their seats, and the consuls, agreeing to meet at the English consulate, passed out, and the whole assemblage dispersed. At this second meeting, the consuls decided to draw up a suitable representation of the insolence and violence of the Egyptian soldiery, and to demand proper measures to repress them, and that this document, with the signatures of the whole consular body, be forwarded to the pasha immediately. This being done all retired to their homes.

At the end of three months a court appointed by the pasha was organized at Beirut, and the soldiers were brought to trial in presence of the American consul. The sentence agreed on, and announced by the judges to the consul, was a punishment of the soldiers, graduated according to their different degrees of criminality, but the servant who threw the stone they left to the discretion of the consul, to be dealt with as he saw fit.

Soon after this Mr. Chasseaud received a communication from his Highness the pasha, officially confirming the sentence of the court in regard to the soldiers, but concluding with these remarkable words: "It is known to you that according to the decision of the court aforesaid, it was determined that the servant of the Frank, who threw the stone, be subjected to a punishment of *three hundred stripes*, . . . and you must know that this punishment will be insisted on." The consul was highly offended at the deception practiced by the judges, and determined to ignore their report altogether. The servant absented himself from the neighborhood for a time, and nothing was ever again said about him or about the report against him. He might have been to blame in the affray, but the witnesses in his case were never examined. This at least was to be said for him, he fought on his own ground and where his adversaries were interlopers and trespassers.

As for the soldiers, Ibrahim made sure that they

should undergo their sentence. Visitors at Acca saw them there laboring as convicts on the public works. The pasha was a severe, perhaps cruel, disciplinarian. Anything like disobedience or cowardice in soldiers, and anything like superstition or bigotry in priests, he could not bear with. His own coolness and daring in the face of an enemy were proverbial. He would be occupied in skirmishes with the enemy all day, and at night when he loosed his girdle balls would fall from it by the handful. So the natives had it, and even Lady Stanhope told it for a truth.* In the midst of the assault upon Acca, it is related that he met a man retreating to the rear with a bloody finger or something of the kind. "Coward," said he, giving him a severe cut with his sword, "go on, you're wounded now."

In religion he was quite an unbeliever, and of course had no patience with extremists. Had the prophets appeared under his government he would not have endured any of them. "They were all bad men," he said, "and *our* prophet was the worst among them all." On hearing of the imprisonment of Shidiak for his faith he entered into the project for his release with all the ardor of a partisan, ordered the Emeer Besheer who was with him to furnish a guard for the purpose, saying, "If you object to doing it, *I will send a band of my own Egyptians.*" When the pasha had obtained possession of Acca and the interior neighborhood, including Nablus, the time came round for the annual *hadge* or pilgrimage to Mecca. The usual caravan was forming at Damascus, and the pasha of that city sent to the Nablusians to furnish, as formerly, the usual supply of water-jars for the journey. The people sent to Ibrahim

---

*Eothen, chap. 8, p. 74.

to know if they should comply with the demand. He said, "No; let them ask of me." "But they are unwilling to ask of you." "Very well," said Ibrahim, "then *let there never be hadge.*"

The pride and bigotry of the Damascenes is well known. So holy was their city that no Jew or Christian could enter it riding, and when the English consul-general was appointed for Syria, with his station at Damascus, the Muslim population there, when they heard of it, rose with one voice, declaring that the English consul-general should never enter there alive. The consul, during the siege of Acca, visited the pasha, and inquired about the probability of his being able to occupy the station to which he was appointed. The pasha encouraged him, by *all means*, to take up his abode there. "But I suppose," said the consul, "it will be necessary for me, at least, to adopt the Arab dress in the city." "Wait a little," said Ibrahim; "I'll insure that you shall go there in *Arab* dress, or *English* dress, or *without any dress*, if you choose." And his promise was kept, for when the consul went there to hoist his infidel flag in that holy city he was met and welcomed by a vast cavalcade and crowds of people on foot, some of whom actually spread their garments in the way for him to ride over them.

CHAPTER XV.

Mr. Thomson sets off with his family for Jerusalem—Becomes isolated at Jaffa by war—Terrible earthquake—Horrors in Jerusalem—The city taken by the Arabs, and retaken by the pasha—Mrs. Thomson's death at Jerusalem—Mr. Thomson returns to Beirut.

OUR new associate, the Rev. W. M. Thomson,* to whom it was assigned to reoccupy the station at Jerusalem, set off with his family for that city in April, 1834. On reaching Jaffa by sea, without waiting for the landing and forwarding of his goods he hastened to see his family safely settled at their new residence, which had been prepared and waiting for them for some months past. Mr. Nicolayson, our English fellow-laborer, with his family, was already in occupation of a part of the tenement. The war-spirit was abroad in the land. The natives were rising to drive away Ibrahim Pasha and his soldiers from the possession of Jerusalem. Leaving his family in Jerusalem, and returning for his goods to Jaffa, Mr. Thomson saw on his way many of the *fellaheen* (Arab peasants) ready armed and equipped for the deadly strife, and found at Jaffa the pasha preparing to march against them. He, therefore, with all despatch put everything in readiness, and the very next day set off on his return to Jerusalem.

Evil tidings, like Job's messengers, had poured in

---

* Rev. W. M. Thomson, D. D., author of "The Land and the Book."

upon them at Jaffa, and the men they met to-day more than confirmed the bad reports of yesterday. Several travelers who had started from Jaffa the day before were returning in great terror, not having been able to get up the mountains. After passing these, there dashed by them an express bearing news to the pasha. "I was greatly struck," says Mr. Thomson, "with the appearance of the man. He sat erect, and firm as a statue on its pedestal. His countenance was fixed and steady, and every muscle and joint screwed down tight. With a firm grasp he held his cocked musket at arm's length and parallel with the horizon, and, dashing his heavy stirrup-irons into the sides of his swift Arabian, he flew over the ground like an eagle hastening to his prey."

When Mr. Thomson had reached Ramleh he was informed that a battle had been fought already between the fellaheen and a party of the pasha's cavalry, and that the latter had been driven down the mountains with the loss of their commander and many others. A reinforcement of two separate detachments of cavalry arrived at Ramleh during the night. Reports were every day more and more alarming. The whole of the hill-country of Judea, from Nablus to Hebron, was in commotion. The governor of Jerusalem had fled, and his father, who had been governor the year before and was displaced, was at the head of the rebels. It was confidently reported that the city had been taken by the native peasants and plundered. The consul at Ramleh and his family strongly urged Mr. Thomson to escape with them back to Jaffa, but in vain. They themselves succeeded in getting through safely with their goods, but a certain captain and his family, who attempted the same thing, under the same escort, becoming detached from the company, were attacked by robbers and stripped entirely naked, and in this plight had to walk all the rest of the way to Jaffa.

On the next day occurred a frightful earthquake. The people of Ramleh rushed forth into the fields to escape from the falling ruins of their houses, nearly every one of which was more or less injured. At night they ventured back, but at ten o'clock there burst forth again a tremendous screaming, as if from another earthquake. All fled once more into the open air, and remained out for hours, fearing to trust themselves within those threatening walls of stone. Two or three times subsequently, during Mr. Thomson's stay, the place was visited with these disturbances, and he became convinced that, both for safety and for comfort, Jaffa was better than Ramleh as a place where he might wait until these war-clouds should pass away. When, under the keeping of Providence, he reached Jaffa in safety, he found the city swarming with soldiers and vexed with the plague. A large addition to the Egyptian army was brought by five men-of-war from Alexandria. Six thousand men were soon on their march for Jerusalem. Mr. Thomson had nearly determined to set off with them, but was providentially, and, as it proved, very mercifully, detained. The pasha, on arriving at the first difficult mountain defile, sent one detachment of his forces to clear the adjacent heights, and another was stationed to guard the entrance, while the main body was to keep directly on its march. The defile was successfully passed, and the signal was given for the detachment in the rear to advance and join the rest of the army. But the commander failed to obey the order, and fell into the hands of the fellaheen. He and only two hundred of his thousand men found their way back to Jaffa, despoiled of everything but life. Had not Mr. Thomson been prevented from executing his purpose of accompanying the army, he would undoubtedly have been attached to this rear division of it, and have shared its perils and losses, among which latter might have been the loss of life.

The troops being withdrawn from Jaffa, the city was exposed to the assaults of the fellaheen. For some days a constant firing of musketry and of cannon was kept up with more or less fatal effect. The enemy without, not being in numbers sufficient to take the city, contented themselves with harassing the garrison and destroying the gardens of the suburbs. Great fear, however, pervaded the city, and the English and American consuls and many others packed up their goods and sought an asylum from the war in boats, intending to proceed to Beirut or Cyprus, or to some other port, or even to remain at sea till the troubles were over.

Mohammed Ali, being informed of the state of the country and the dangers to which his son was exposed, sent on from Alexandria fresh supplies for the war, and soon came to Jaffa himself in person. With an army of twelve thousand men at Jaffa, and as many more expected from the Bedawin by land, and with the ten thousand offered by the Emeer Besheer in case of necessity, Ibrahim could not fail to succeed. Accordingly, after a war of fifteen days the fellaheen forces were so far scattered and subdued that Mr. Thomson ventured to make a night-push for Jerusalem. He reached the city on the second day without molestation.

"But oh," he exclaims, " what horror, what faintness seized my heart when I came in sight of our house and saw that part of it which Mrs. Thomson occupied all torn to pieces by the cannon of the castle!"

He was permitted, however, to find the inmates all alive and joyful at his safe return. What had occurred at Jerusalem during these weeks of war and earthquake is graphically and touchingly described in the subjoined letter of Mrs. Thomson, addressed to her sister in America, dated Jerusalem, May 30, 1834:

"The last Sabbath was one never to be forgotten by myself and by hundreds in this afflicted city. My husband had nearly a week previous gone to Jaffa for the purpose of bringing up our things. The rebels marched toward Jerusalem, but the pasha's soldiers dared not leave the city to oppose them, for there is treachery within the walls, and they feared, with too much reason, that the gates would be shut upon them if they should sally forth.

"We were not greatly alarmed, however, until rising on Sabbath morning we received the assurance that we were literally in a besieged city. We are within a few rods of the tower or castle, and I saw, for the first time in my life, the cannon brought out to be mounted upon the walls, accompanied with other preparations for carrying on the work of death. We are staying in the house of the kind Mr. Nicolayson, from whom and his lady we receive every possible kindness. At 11 o'clock A. M. our two little families convened for reading the scriptures and prayer. Mr. Nicolayson's selections all had a bearing on our present circumstances, and were eminently calculated to inspire confidence in God. As he read some of those last conversations of our Saviour with his disciples, it seemed almost as if we were realizing the same scenes, and we felt every word to be applicable to ourselves. Still we were yet ignorant to what extent we were soon to be called to 'possess our souls in patience.'

"When our worship closed my babe was brought to be nursed, and I had scarcely taken him before the house above and around began to shake violently. 'What is this?' said Mrs. Nicolayson in consternation. Instantly the truth flashed upon my mind. I exclaimed, 'An earthquake!' and rushed out of the room. I descended the stairs amid a shower of dust and stones, a large one being precipitated from the top of the wall which narrowly escaped crushing little William's head. Everlasting gratitude to God for his preserving goodness!

"On gaining the garden I felt somewhat relieved. But, my dear sister, it was an awful sight to see the high stone walls of our garden shivering like leaves in a tempest, a part giving way and the whole threatened with the same fate, the house also shaking as if the next moment it would fall prostrate, and the very earth trembling beneath our feet as if no longer able to support its surface. What power but the Almighty can succor in such awful circumstances? To whom can we fly but to Him who holds all nature in his hands? To Him and to the blood of atonement that speaks pardon and peace I did in these terrific scenes endeavor to look; yes, to cast myself upon the mercy of God in Christ and await with resignation the result of these unlooked-for calamities. In a few moments the streets were filled with the weeping, lamentation and woe of afflicted multitudes who had fled from houses that threatened to bury them beneath their ruins. Several families, all Jews, came to take shelter in our large garden, and it was truly affecting to see these bigoted descendants of Abraham coming for protection in the hour of danger to the house of a Christian, really appearing to derive comfort from our composure and our confidence that God would protect us.

"The shocks continued through the afternoon and night, also on the next day and night, but not so violent as the first. It is predicted by the Latin monks that tomorrow, the seventh day from the first, will be the most tremendous shock yet experienced. But, poor mortals, they 'know not what will be on the morrow.' We must acknowledge, however, that present appearances rather indicate a return. . . . I was obliged by another shock, though slight, to throw down my pen, seize my infant and run out of the house just as I had written the word '*return.*' The weather is exceedingly hot and sultry, thermometer at 90° in the shade. In addition to this there is an uncommon dryness in the air. . . . What will be the termination of this season our heavenly Father only knows. Circumstances more appalling than these in which we are now placed I had hardly ever imagined. I hesitate to describe them. I have no wish to excite your sympathy at the expense of your comfort. But before this reaches you all these troubles will have been caused to subside, through the good providence of Him who has all events under his control; . . . or should he in infinite wisdom determine otherwise, we may be at rest where wars and rumors of wars shall never reach us more.

"Owing to the continued tremblings and quakings of the earth we thought it prudent to sleep in the garden. But here a new danger met us. The engagements between the soldiers on the walls and the peasantry without were carried on principally at night on account of the heat of the day. The fellahs got possession of a small convent without the city which enabled them to aim at the soldiers, and though they had no cannon, yet, because we were so near the castle, the balls from their muskets flew whizzing over our heads and around us in every direction. We lay thus for three or four nights, and then concluded that it was better to fall into the hands of the Lord than into the hands of men, and so returned into our partially-dilapidated dwelling. Perhaps you would not call it *partially* dilapidated were you to see the fissures in the walls and terraces, the half-fallen ceilings, the sunken floors, and other marks that tell of ruin and threaten to make it a mass of rubbish.

. . . "Through the mercy of God we are not yet left houseless. I and my little family have a small open room or house in the garden, but of so ancient a date that it would require no bad shaking to bring its rotten stone arches down upon our heads. Mr. Nicolayson's family find shelter in some lower rooms formerly used for lumber. Imagine us lying down at night with more than a mere possibility that our beds might be our tombs, endeavoring, but often without success, to compose ourselves to rest amid the firing of musketry and the roaring of cannon. Oh how different are our feelings in committing ourselves to God for nightly protection, under so many appalling circumstances, from what they were in our own peaceful country! How very trifling now appear many, many things to which I once attached importance! Even all that earth calls good or great dwindles into nothing when we encounter the horrors of war, earthquake and scarcity, if not famine. These things bring the realities of eternity near. Had not our dear Christian friends been most providentially supplied with stores out of which they have hospitably entertained us, I know not what we should have done in this emergency. You may think me selfish, perhaps, in dwelling so much on our *own* affairs and saying little or nothing about the state of the city, the war and the sufferings of others. The truth is we know nothing of things without, and are obliged to sit in our houses day after day in the most painful suspense. Rumors and conjectures—some of them frightful enough—we have indeed heard, but we question the truth of all. We are troubled with very few visitors. The disloyalty or disaffection to the pasha is so universal among the Muslims that they are said to be all quarantined in their houses. One thing is certain, that those who used to visit us come in no more. The streets are silent and deserted, patrolled only by a vigilant soldiery. It is said, and I believe this story at least, that several communications have passed between the fellaheen and the Turkish citizens. Some of these have been intercepted."

Another date.—"Several days, my dear sister, have elapsed since the close of what I last wrote. Many of these were days of such awful interest that I could command neither opportunity nor composure sufficient to describe the appalling scenes around me. Even after the danger had in some measure subsided I could not recall the past but with feelings of such horror that for the sake of my dear babe, whose health is much affected by mine, I have felt it my duty to keep my mind as calm as possible. In this endeavor I have been mercifully assisted with strength from above. I called upon God in my trouble; he heard my prayer and strengthened me with strength from on high.

"At sunset, May 31, Mr. Nicolayson ascended the terrace to ascertain the state of matters, and returned with the assurance that the walls were manned as usual, the gates closed and the soldiers at their posts. We retired to rest. . . . About midnight I was awakened by a loud discharge of fire-arms, and the balls whistled around us in such a manner that I was sure the engagement was within the walls.

"I hastily awoke Mr. Nicolayson. We all dressed as soon as possible, taking care not to awake the children. The narrow street that passed our front door led directly to houses occupied by soldiers. Mr. Nicolayson went there to listen, and found the soldiers removing their effects with the utmost expedition into the castle. That which we had anticipated and feared was now but too certain. The city was betrayed, and we were at the mercy of a lawless and ferocious multitude. The gates of the castle closed—morning dawned—the morning sacred to Him who came to bring peace and good-will to men; the day also on which, according to rule, you, with many of your beloved friends, were to commemorate the love of our Redeemer. Under what different circumstances was your sister to spend its hours! After the retiring of the soldiers we were not left long in suspense. The awful silence was broken by the shouts of the fellahs, the firing of musketry, etc., while from the streets were heard the breaking open of doors and the running of men to and fro. To add to our distress, our servant, who had been on the terrace, rushed into the room, pale with terror, exclaiming that the fellahs were murdering the people and plundering the city. Whither could we fly for refuge but to Him who said, 'Call upon me in the day of trouble, I will deliver thee.' We did call upon him, and sought him not in vain. Mr. Nicolayson read the scriptures, and oh how rich and appropriate seemed every line, especially our Lord's last conversation and prayer recorded in John, and many of the Psalms composed, ages ago, in this very vicinity, and under similar circumstances! They seemed written expressly to quiet our fears and confirm our confidence in God. If our hearts did not deceive us, we did not so much dread death. Oh no, I longed to leave a world of so much wickedness, cruelty and sorrow, and enter one where all is love and purity and peace. But nature—weak, terrified nature—shrunk from the possibility of personal injury and the terrors of a violent death. My infant too—my heart sickened when I looked at him. His smiles and caresses went to my very soul, and I was obliged to resign him to the care of others.

"During the day the soldiers made a sally from the castle and drove the fellahs into the lower part of the city, and, although again shut in, they kept up a constant fire upon the rebels. Our house being near the castle, we spent two days unmolested by the fellaheen, but within the constant sound of door-breaking and plundering. . . .

"Mr. Nicolayson afterward, finding the house was beginning to be robbed, hired ten men to guard it. They did their duty pretty well, still, on one occasion, a furious fellah rushed into the part of the house where we were and drew his sword to kill the dog, and next he seized our servant by the collar, and was going to run him through, on pretence of his being one of the nezzam soldiers. Being assured, however, that he was an Englishman and our servant, he let him go, and then left the house, taking with him, however, such of my clothes as hit his fancy. All this day and night, and the greater part of the next day, we were literally in the very din of war. We all stowed ourselves in a small lower room, where the walls were very thick, and heard the cannon balls whistle over and around us. One large ball entered the dome of the little room in the garden where I had slept and tore a large hole through it, scattering the rocks and mortar all over the place where I and the babe used to lie. At every discharge of the cannon from the castle the fellahs in the houses would set up a prodigious shout of defiance, and at stated periods they made signals to each other all over the city. I cannot tell you how this unearthly sound fell upon my ears. It was neither a yell, a shriek nor a shout, but a compound of all, and being prolonged while the voice could sustain it, was unutterably terrific.

"Near the close of the week our guard had become so exorbitant in their demands that we felt assured that unless relief should soon arrive our purses, at least, would no longer be in our own power. About noon, however, their tone altered, and we observed that the numbers assembled in our garden were decreasing. At 4 o'clock Mr. Nicolayson heard some one say very hur—"

At this point in her letter Mrs. Thomson, startled by a note of alarm, sprang to her infant and fled from the room, leaving as evidence of her fright a large blot where her pen fell across the face of her paper. She never finished the letter, but Mr. Thomson, on inquiry, supposed that the unfinished sentence ought to be concluded nearly thus: "Mr. Nicolayson heard some one say very hurriedly, 'They are coming—flee as soon as you can.'" It was probably the voice of some fellah calling out to his comrades below to flee from the face of the pasha, who was just entering the city. Immediately not a fellah was to be seen, and this was the last fright which those anxious mothers had to suffer from the war. The pasha once more had sole possession of the town. The peasants were, indeed, not yet subdued, but henceforth their fighting was all to be done outside the city.

It might be reasonably expected that a state of excitement so intense and so protracted could not have been endured by a lady of Mrs. Thomson's delicate sensibilities without a serious injury to her health. Accordingly, the month of June had not closed before she was attacked with a bilious complaint, which was soon succeeded by an intensely painful ophthalmia, accompanied by a high inflammatory fever. It was in this suffering condition that Mr. Thomson found her, when, on the 11th of July, by a night journey and with considerable risk, he arrived once more at Jerusalem. Her symptoms daily grew more aggravated. She became quite blind. No remedies seemed to give more than a partial relief, and she herself, from nearly the first, indulged no hope of recovery. She lingered for ten days longer, when her spirit, happy in God, was released from all the sufferings of earth, and welcomed, we cannot doubt, to a home where neither earthquake, nor war cry, nor cannon's roar, nor shrieks of terror, can disturb her.

The thought of death never alarmed her. She had for many weeks been in the higher, clearer regions of faith, ready to depart at any time. Her remains were deposited in the cemetery of the Greek church on the top of Zion, near the sepulchre of David.*

---

* Mrs. Thomson was a native of Baltimore, Maryland, and had

Another important loss to the mission, occasioned by this unhappy war, was sustained in the death of our old friend and translator, **Papas Esa.** He was taken off by a disease supposed to have been brought on by excess of labor in burying his chests and walling up his door at the beginning of the war.

Mr. Thomson, after his bereavement, found a temporary home with his brethren at Beirut, where he arrived on the 5th of August.

been successfully engaged with her sister in conducting a female seminary in Princeton, N. J., and afterwards in Jamaica, L. I. She was born in the year 1800.

CHAPTER XVI.

Work in Beirut—Arrival of a press—Decease of Consul Abbott at Ehheden—Station at Jerusalem resumed by Messrs. Whiting and Dodge—Death of the latter at Jerusalem—Druze excitement with little present result—Mrs. Bird's ill health compels the family to leave Syria—Mr. and Mrs. Smith's shipwreck—Death of Mrs. Smith—Triumph at Brummana—Earthquake at Safet—Jerusalem abandoned—Good reasons—Death of Mr. and Mrs. Hebard—New war at Beirut—Death of Mrs. Wolcott.

WHILE our friends in the south were suffering the horrors of war, we at Beirut were enjoying uninterrupted quiet, and our work went on in its customary routine. Mrs. Smith commenced a promising little school for girls in one of the rooms of the missionary house. Successful efforts were made for temperance reform, the consul himself, with a number of the natives, signing the total abstinence pledge. Books were given and sold to a number of Druzes, who seemed to be waking up to the inquiry whether our religion was one which they could believe in and adopt as a nation. Our printing press arrived, and was suffered to pass the custom house without any vexatious detention. A quarrel took place between the pope's new legate and the Maronite bishop of Beirut respecting their ecclesiastical rank and authority, and Maronites were forbidden the privilege of worshiping in the Latin chapel in our city. The watchful shepherd at Canobeen, in another general proclamation, warned his beloved flock against the ravening wolves in sheep's clothing, and a school teacher received a communication from his bishop, threatening him with penalties if he did not at once forsake our employ.

Four days before the death of Mrs. Thomson we were called in a similar manner to part with our respected, kind and steadfast friend, Consul Abbott. He was on a short excursion over the mountains for his health's sake. Arriving at the village of Eh-heden he was too feeble to proceed any farther, and at the house of his friend, Sheikh Lattoof, he in a few days resigned his spirit into the hands of Him that gave it, expressing a hope for mercy only through the blood of Jesus Christ. He was a high-minded, well-bred gentleman, foremost in dignity and influence among the Beirut consuls, and though an Episcopalian by profession and habit, he showed no sectarian prejudice, but treated both us and our message with uniform and unlooked-for respect.

The mission station at Jerusalem, once more vacant by the departure of Mr. Thomson, was again resumed by Messrs. Whiting and Dodge, the latter of whom, at the end of three months, was laid by the side of his American sister in the dust of Mt. Zion. He had been at his new station a little more than a month when he was called for to attend upon a case of dangerous sickness in one of the mission families at Beirut. In returning to Jerusalem his last day's journey was long and wearisome, and almost immediately after it both he and his companion, Mr. Nicolayson, were similarly attacked with fever. Mr. Nicolayson, after a serious illness, recovered, but Dr. Dodge lingered nearly a month, till his power of resisting the disease came to an end on the 28th day after its first attack. His colleague, Mr. Whiting, says: "Our departed brother had endeared himself exceedingly to us all. His example and conversation were highly honorable to the gospel and edifying to all who knew him. He had very enlightened views of the whole subject of education, and a happy talent for instructing and engaging the attention of the young. His medical knowledge, moreover, gave him peculiar advantages for intercourse among the people."*

As the Egyptian government in Syria became stable and seemed likely to be lasting, the Druzes were full of apprehension lest ere long the pasha should send orders and impress them into his army. To this event they looked forward as an insufferable calamity. They sought, therefore, most earnestly some foreign protection, and particularly that of the English. Many individuals from among them called from time to time to inquire all about our Protestant sentiments, for they knew we differed from the Christians of this country, and that our faith was comparatively unobjectionable. One respectable young sheikh in particular, of the family of Kadi, from the village of Bshamon, made us repeated visits. There was a marked difference between this man and most others of his nation. He had nothing of that fawning flattery and evident hypocrisy which are almost inseparable from the Druze character. He bore the evident marks of a man of candor, honesty, open-heartedness and prudence. Sheikh Kawsim, as he was called, assured us that a number of the first men of his nation had read our books and gave them their approval to

---

* Dr. Dodge was a native of New Castle, Me., and received his preparatory and professional education, both in medicine and theology, chiefly in Brunswick. His age was thirty-two.

that extent that they could subscribe to them as containing the religion of their choice. They would open their villages to our books, our schools, and our worship, and openly proclaim themselves Protestant Christians, on the sole condition that the English nation would guarantee in their behalf that they should have the same privileges as were accorded to other Christians of the land; in particular, that they should not be impressed into the army, but like them, serve only as militia when called upon to defend their own mountains. The sheikh had little doubt that if the chiefs of whom he spoke should lead off in the proposed movement, the whole nation would follow.

We gave the sheikh no definite reply as to what we could undertake to do in the premises, but when our brethren who were absent at Jerusalem returned we conferred together and concluded that we were not in possession of facts enough to give our Druze friends much encouragement. We could of course give them no governmental pledges, nor could we at present, with our imperfect knowledge of the state of the nation, undertake even to recommend them to English or American protection.

When the sheikh next appeared he was accompanied by some others of his people, and among them the Emeer Hyder and his son, of Shwifat, a large village near Beirut. We told them of our difficulties, and embraced the opportunity to explain to them fully what Protestantism was. They professed to understand the matter, and it was not unsatisfactory to them. They wished, they said, to become Protestants "*both in profession and in heart.*" They also expressed the hope that if the Druzes, as a nation, should decline to fall in with the proposed arrangement, the way might still be opened to any individuals among them who might be disposed to avail themselves of the privilege.

At Aaleih, a pleasant mountain village, which was made a missionary residence for the summer, these visits of the Druzes were continued and the conversations renewed. At our Sabbath-day preaching also we had Druzes among our auditors.

Respecting this temporary opening for the truth among the Druzes it may be remarked that no immediate and permanent changes were effected by it. It proved to be a season of mere seed-time. It furnished an invaluable opportunity for proclaiming the message of God to the nation. The intercourse of the missionaries with the people was free and familiar for many months. At one period their call for attention demanded nearly all the resources of the mission. To hundreds and thousands of them were the distinguishing doctrines of the gospel explained, and the people were made to perceive what they had never known before, and what it would have required long years in peaceable times to tell them, that the religion of Jesus Christ was not a religion of ceremonies, nor of image-worship, nor of laxness of morals, as was all the Christianity they had ever seen or heard of, but that it had its seat in the heart and its fruit in every good work. After bestowing much labor upon them by preaching, conversation, schools and scripture distribution, the missionaries were pained and not a little disappointed to find the door gradually closing against them, and to see so few individuals on whom the truths of the gospel had apparently made any permanent impression. They were consoled, however, by the reflection that they had done their duty to the nation, and, having declared to them all the counsel of **God**, they were pure from their blood.

But though it did not please God on this occasion to bless his word to them to the extent that was hoped for, yet it would be wrong hastily to conclude that the Druzes had received no lasting benefit. We cannot now tell how much good seed lies buried in the soil that may yet spring up and bear fruit. Indeed, one lasting benefit, evidently resulting from the occasion, was the thirst for knowledge and the increasing patronage of education which they have lately manifested. Numbers of their children have been more or less thoroughly instructed at the high school of the mission at Abeih, and lately, side by side with ours, they have themselves instituted a high school which is taught by a Protestant native and with the use of books printed at our Protestant press. Another important benefit has resulted from this Druze movement, which is the permanent respect which the missionaries seem to have won from the Druze community. The latter are thoroughly persuaded that the missionaries wish them well. They are ready, therefore, to befriend them in their turn when the other sects set themselves against them. One of the missionaries, speaking of the straits to which they have sometimes been reduced, lately wrote, saying, "I know not what we should have done had it not been for the favor of the Druzes."

The 23d of August was a very interesting Sabbath at Aaleih. Our service in Arabic was attended by not far from forty individuals. In the afternoon at our English worship, which was conducted by the Rev. Mr. Pease, late of Cyprus, we enjoyed the presence of our new neighbor Mr. Moore, recently appointed British consul in place of the late Consul Abbott. This was the last Sabbath spent by the author and his family on Mt. Lebanon. Twelve days afterward we bade adieu to our beloved missionary associates and embarked on board of a Greek vessel for Smyrna on our way to America. Of all our ten embarkations this was by far the most painful we had experienced. No charms of native land, or of kindred, or of early home and friends, were like those of the work and the associates that we were now compelled to leave. An exile from his country, or one who has failed in his chosen business of life and feels fit for no other, might easily sympathize with us in that sad hour. We yielded to the apparent will of God as indicated in the advice of the physician and a vote of the mission, but with the expectation of a return to the work in case of returning health.

The Rev. Eli Smith, during the summer, was supplying Arabic preaching at the chapel in Beirut with a small company of hearers, but which, later in the autumn, increased from fifty to eighty.

The press as yet had done but little, on account of deficiency in type. But measures had been taken to remedy the defect, and great expectations were entertained of the future usefulness of that instrumentality.

For the wider distribution of the scriptures and to enlarge the influence of the press it was concluded to send forth the trustworthy brother Tannoos El Haddad as a colporteur and catechist. With his knowledge of the scriptures, accompanied by his kind, modest and yet earnest mode of addressing his countrymen, no missionary probably could do better than he in such a work—perhaps not so well.

A boys' boarding-school was opened with six pupils,

which it was intended should be enlarged to become in time an institution for the supply of schoolmasters and preachers of the gospel. The boys attended the mission meetings for worship, formed a class in the Sabbath-school, were under daily religious training, and were giving great satisfaction to their teachers.

The female school at Beirut was highly prosperous, having about forty pupils, two of whom were Jewish girls. A large number from Mohammedan families had attended during the summer, but for some unknown reason did not return after the vacation in August. This school was originated and cherished particularly by Mrs. Eli Smith, to whom was added afterwards Miss Williams. A small school for Druze girls was taught in the summer on the mountains by Mrs. Dr. Dodge. A similar one was also opened for Mohammedans and others at Jerusalem.

The Sabbath-school at Beirut was attended by nearly twenty females and half as many males, all of whom were always present at Arabic preaching. A European Sabbath-school or Bible class was also in operation in the chapel of the American consulate. The common schools were five, with three hundred pupils.

In the early part of 1836 the mission was strengthened by the arrival of three new laborers, Messrs. Lanneau and Hebard and Miss Tilden. Mr. Hebard was retained at Beirut, the others were assigned to Jerusalem as colaborers with Mr. and Mrs. Whiting.

The desirableness of a more complete and elegant fount of Arabic type, one more conformed to the standard of native taste, was thought sufficiently great to justify a visit by one of the missionaries to Germany. Mr. Smith was accordingly deputed to accomplish this important object. The declining health of Mrs. Smith also seeming to require a voyage, they both embarked, with three English fellow passengers, in a Prussian schooner for Smyrna. For want of favorable winds, probably, their passage was made around the eastern end of the island of Cyprus. Coming to the coast of Caramania, the ship at nine o'clock at night ran upon rocks and was lost. The passengers and crew reached the shore, but of their goods Mr. Smith was able to save nothing from the wreck, with the exception of a traveling-bag, two mattresses and a small trunk containing money. The bag contained cloaks and shoes, but these, as well as the mattresses, had been soaked with water, and were useless. Mrs. Smith, in her feeble state, with a consumptive cough, had no resource but to spend the night in the open air, upon the damp sand, and with her feet thoroughly wet. In the morning they discovered a large Egyptian lumber-boat not far off, the captain of which received them on board, offering to take them to any near harbor which they might choose. But he proved himself a villain. About noon he brought his passengers into the desert harbor of Salefki (Seleucia). He had them now, as he supposed, entirely in his power, and could, for the rest of their voyage with him, extort from them whatever terms he chose. He made the most exorbitant demands, and insisted on being paid in advance. For the sole purpose, evidently, of carrying his point, he kept his vessel at anchor in this miserable nook forty-eight hours, the passengers spending their days under the shade of a tree, in a boisterous wind, and their nights in the open air. Their food was dry biscuit, saved from the wreck, some rice and oil purchased from the captain, and fresh fish caught by the

Prussian sailors. Their cooking dish was a copper wash-basin, and fingers were the knives and forks. On making the discovery of three other lumber vessels anchored at a distance, the passengers determined to have nothing more to do with their Egyptian, and to risk their chance with the other boats. They accordingly paid the man off, and he immediately quitted the harbor.

It was still two days before they could come to terms with either of the other boats, they also desiring to improve the opportunity to make a speculation. But at length, on the sixth day after the shipwreck, they were once more under sail. A company of twenty-two persons was on board; there was a great want of suitable food for any but hardy sailors, and for cooking and eating they had but one pot, one pan, one plate and a few wooden spoons. One of the three English passengers, who was feeble at his first embarkation, sunk under his exposures, and was buried in the sea. In four days they entered the harbor of Castello Rosso. Here they found a Greek vessel ready to sail for Smyrna, and immediately took passage in it. They were two days and two nights, with cold and sometimes tempestuous winds, in getting to Rhodes, during which time Mrs. Smith, rather than endure the filth and confined air of the narrow cabin, kept her place night and day on deck. As was to be expected, she took cold. All her symptoms were aggravated; and when, after three days' resting on shore, she was called to resume her voyage, she had to be carried to the vessel in a chair. Touching at Scio, Mrs. Smith was furnished by the missionaries, Mr. and Mrs. Houston, with a blanket to sleep under, instead of her cloak. Twenty-nine days from the time of their first disaster brought them to Smyrna, where they were joyfully received into the family of the Rev. Mr. Temple. Mrs. Smith was brought and laid upon her bed of languishing, from which she with good reasons never expected to rise. There we once more saw her wearing the same sweet smile as ever on her face, and wishing that all her friends when they called to see her would also bring their smiles; it would cheer and comfort her heart. Every care was bestowed upon her, but her life, which from this time was one of suffering, gradually wasted away till her release came on the 30th of September.

The character of Mrs. Smith is one of those which it is difficult to commend too highly. Such a full assemblage and such a perfect symmetry of Christian graces are very rarely met with in one and the same person.*

Mr. Smith remained in Smyrna and Constantinople attending to some preparations for the producing of the Arabic type, whence he proceeded to Egypt to accompany Dr. Edward Robinson in his celebrated Tour of Research in the Holy Land. Having accomplished this enterprise he repaired to Leipsig, in Germany, where he superintended the casting of the most beautiful fount of Arabic type the world had ever seen. In the mechanical preparations for this noble achievement, he was greatly indebted to Mr. Homan Hallock, the very ingenious missionary printer at Smyrna. Mr. Smith, after a visit to his native land, was once more found at his post in Beirut, after an absence of the greater part of five years. His types, together with Mr. Hurter, a new printer, had arrived before him. Meantime, however, the press, with all its deficiencies, had

---

* See the interesting biography of Mrs. Sarah L. H. Smith, by Rev. Dr. E. Hooker.

not been entirely dormant, but had turned off a million and a half of pages.

During the rule of Ibrahim Pasha in Syria, it was understood that men were to be left free in their religious sentiments; there was to be no persecution. The Emeer Besheer, in his government of the mountains, yielded tacitly to this law. The Maronite patriarch, however, did what he dared to do against it. He had not forgotten the visit to Canobeen made by the soldiers of the pasha. The priests no doubt shared in his feeling of resentment, and endeavored to shut out the Bible men from all residence in the mountains. Brummana was called a Druze village, and the English consul and the Protestant missionaries had more than once been freely admitted there. But the patriarch having gained one or two of the young princes, made at length a serious attempt to close up this place also. Mr. Thomson, having hired a residence there, was determined to assert his right, and moved up both his family and the boarding-school. The priests immediately set about their measures of annoyance. The people were enjoined not to have any intercourse with the new-comers. A girl in the family came home from the church one day bitterly weeping. The priest had excommunicated her, forbidden her entering the church, terrified her with the most dreadful curses, and ordered her immediately to quit Mr. Thomson's house. Moreover, the young emeers and princesses were rather remiss in exercising their authority for the church, and the priest was bold enough to address even them with insolence, and laid them under an excommunication. Meeting one day a lad that was bringing to the missionary family some articles he had been sent to purchase, the priest seized them and took them from him by force; in all which acts of annoyance he declared he was simply carrying out the orders of his lord the patriarch.

The princes did not long maintain any stand against their spiritual rulers. They sent a public crier one evening, proclaiming through the village, in the name of the emeers, that no one should speak to the heretics, nor sell to them, nor visit them, nor befriend them in any way whatever; those who spoke to them should have their tongues cut out, and those who sold to them should be bastinadoed, and have their houses burned and their orchards cut down. Copies of the scriptures that had been given or sold to the people were searched out and burned. One of the princes even went in person to a Greek school and violently took all the psalters he could find and destroyed them.

But there was a strong reaction among the people. The consul also, being informed of the proceedings, was highly offended, and procured an officer from the Emeer Besheer to put an immediate stop to them. The officer came to the village and instituted a formal examination of the complaints. The emeers and the missionary had leave to state their cases in turn before the commissioner. The emeers pleaded that they were under orders from their spiritual head to use their civil power to guard the church, and of course they must obey him. It was the business of the civil ruler to defend the true religion. Their chief speaker often repeated the maxim, "No sword, no church."

Mr. Thomson, on his part, defended the principle of religious liberty. The discussion had become somewhat extended when the officer, growing weary of it, took up the subject himself, and said in his own rough way,

"What! Do you dare say the sword shall reign over the conscience? No such thing. His Highness the viceroy will not allow it. Neither will his Happiness the Emeer Besheer permit the sword to be used in defence of any church. What! suppose I wish to change my religion; shall I have my head cut off for it? For example, I am a Druze, I wish to become a Christian; must I be killed for that?" This last was a home thrust, and put an effectual stop to the controversy. The emeers dropped their heads in confusion, for all of them, except the old father, had recently made this very change.

Thus, after four or five hours' animated dispute, the assembly broke up, the commissioner declaring that no one should annoy the family of Mr. Thomson in any manner; and lifting his hand and casting a stern look upon the princes, he said, "*Who is there that will dare rebel against the mandate of the governor of these mountains?*"

In the evening the officer gathered the people together at the house of Mr. Thomson, and in the name of the Emeer Besheer revoked the order of the village princes, proclaiming full liberty to all to visit the Protestant family, to trade with them, serve them, carry them on their shoulders if they liked, and that no one should be called to account for any such acts, either by the emeers of Brummana or by any one else. The triumph seems to have been complete. The Emeer Besheer would not formerly have done so much, but he had come under a new regime. He had become "learned in the wisdom of the Egyptians."

Mr. Thomson, some time after this contest had passed by, opened his doors to his neighbors for evening prayers in Arabic. Soon he had a room full of people every night, and had thus for weeks an audience of from twenty to forty persons, to whom he preached seven times a week with all the plainness of which he was master.

Mr. Thomson had had sad experience of the effects produced by an earthquake. But the account he gives us of the visitation that occurred on New Year's day of 1837 shows it to have been worse than any similar event in this land, perhaps in the past century, unless it were that of Aleppo in 1822.

In the present case, the shaking of the earth was perceptible all along the Syrian coast, but as a calamity, it was known only between Beirut and Jerusalem. Among other places that had specially suffered was the Jewish city of Safed, seated high up upon the mountains that overlook the sea of Galilee, which was almost wholly demolished. From the reports which came respecting the place, it was known that the necessities and distress of the inhabitants who had survived the first sudden destruction must be extreme. The good people of Beirut, therefore, were constrained to make a collection for their relief, and Messrs. Thomson and Calman * were chosen a deputation to carry and administer it. The journey was one of exposure at that unpropitious season, and among villages in ruins, where lodges are few and where storms are to be endured without a shelter, but it was one quite befitting the missionary office. Their work was eminently like that of the good Samaritan, to take care of those that were left " wounded and half dead."

On their way the two delegates ascertained at Sidon that at that place from seventy to a hundred houses had

* An English missionary to the Jews.

been wholly or partially thrown down, with the loss of some few lives. At Tyre, and in many villages in the interior, similar damages were witnessed along the way.

On the ascent of the mountain of Safed several fearful rents and cracks in the earth and rocks appeared, giving painful indications of what might be expected among the house-walls of the city above. But all anticipations proved to be as nothing when the reality burst upon their sight. "Up to this moment," says Mr. Thomson, "I had refused to credit the accounts that had come to us, but the first frightful glance convinced me that it was not in the power of language to overstate such a ruin. The Jewish portion of the city, containing a population of five or six thousand, was built around the slope of a very steep mountain, so steep and so compactly occupied that the roof of the lower house formed the street of the one above it, the streets thus rising like a stairway one step above another. Thus, when the tremendous shock came and dashed every house to the ground in a moment, the upper house fell with a double force upon the lower, and that upon another, and this seems to have been the true cause of the almost unprecedented loss of life in this calamity. Some of the lower houses were covered up to a great depth with the ruins of many others which were above them. From this also it occurred that a vast number of persons who were not instantly killed perished before they could be dug out, and some were taken out five, six, and one, I was told, seven days after the shock, still alive. One solitary man, who had been a husband and a father, found his wife with one child under her arm and the babe with the breast still in its mouth. He supposed that the babe had not been killed by the falling ruins, but had died of hunger endeavoring to draw nourishment from the lifeless mother. Parents heard the voices of their little ones crying, "Father! father!" "Mother! mother!" their voices growing fainter and fainter till hushed in death, while they themselves were either struggling desperately to free themselves or laboring to remove the fallen timber and rocks from their children. What a scene of horror must have been that long black night which closed upon them in half an hour after the overthrow! without a light or the possibility of getting one, four-fifths of the population under the ruins, dead, or dying with frightful groans, and the earth still trembling and shaking as if terrified with the desolation it had wrought.

"All around the hill," writes Mr. Thomson, "nothing is seen but one vast chaos of stone and earth, timbers and boards, tables, chairs, beds and clothing, mingled in horrible confusion. Men were everywhere at work, worn out and woe-begone, uncovering their houses in search of the mangled and putrefied bodies of departed friends, while here and there I noticed companies of two or three, each clambering over the ruins bearing a dreadful load of corruption to the narrow house appointed for all living. I covered my face and passed on through the half living, wretched survivors of Safed. Some were weeping in despair and some laughing in callousness still more distressing. Here an old man sat solitary on the wreck of his once crowded house; there a child was at play, too young to realize that it had neither father nor mother, brother nor relation, in this wide world. They flocked around us—husbands that had lost their wives, wives their husbands, parents without children, children without parents, and not a few who were the solitary remnants of large connections. The people were scattered abroad, above and below the ruins, in tents of old boards, old carpets, mats, canvas, brush and earth, and not a few dwelling in the open air, while some poor wretches, wounded and bruised, were left among the prostrate buildings, every moment exposed to death from the loose rocks around and above them.

"As soon as our tent was pitched Mr. Calman and myself set off to visit the wounded. Creeping under a wretched covering intended for a tent, which was the first we came to, we found an emaciated young female lying on the ground covered with the filthiest garments I ever saw. Her wounds were in a state of mortification, and when the poor old creature that was waiting upon her lifted up the cover of her feet a moment's glance convinced me that she could not possibly survive another day. The foot and the flesh also had actually dropped off from the leg, leaving the bone entirely bare. Sending for some laudanum to relieve the intolerable agony of her last hours, we went on to other, but equally dreadful, scenes.

"Not to shock the feelings by detailing at length what we saw, I will mention only one other case. Clambering over a pile of ruins and entering a low vault by a hole, I found eight of the wounded crowded together under a vast pile of crumbling rocks, some with legs broken in two or three places, others so horribly lacerated and swollen as scarcely to retain the shape of mortals, while all, being left without washing, changing bandages or dressing wounds, were in so deplorable a state as to render it impossible for us to remain with them long enough to do them any good. Although protected by spirits of camphor, breathing through my handkerchief dipped in it, and fortified with a good share of resolution, I was obliged to retreat.

"Convinced that while they remained in such a charnel-house as this, without air but such as would be fatal even to men in health, no medicine or surgical treatment could afford them relief, we returned to our tent resolving to erect a large shanty of boards, broken doors and timber, for the accommodation of the wounded. In this work was spent the remainder of our first day.

"We found the greatest difficulty in getting boards and timber, and when carpenters came they were without proper tools. In time, however, we got something in the shape of saws, axes, nails and mattocks, and all of us laboring hard, before night the second day the result began to appear. The governor visited and greatly praised our work, declaring that he had not thought that such a thing could have been erected.

"Some of the wounded were brought and laid down before us long before any part of the building was ready for their reception. After dark I accompanied the priest to visit the remainder of the Christian population of the village. These were never numerous, and having lost about one-half of their number, are now crowded into one great tent. Some were wounded, some were orphans, some were poor. To all of them we gave as we were able according to their need.

"During the building of the shanty the earth continued still to tremble, and once with so violent a motion that a cloud of dust was seen rising from the ruins, and the people rushed out from their remaining houses in dismay. Many began to pray with lamentable cries, and females beat their breasts with all their strength and tore their garments in despair. Even the workmen of the shanty threw down their tools and fled."

Having prepared their little hospital, collected the wounded, distributed medicines, furnished clean bandages for wounds and hired a native physician to attend in their place, the two philanthropists went on to the city of Tiberias. The calamity here had not been so sweeping as at Safed. Seven hundred only of twenty-five hundred had perished here, whereas at Safed the number was five or six thousand out of ten thousand. The only Jewish physician in Tiberias had his wife and children struck dead before him, and his own leg broken below the knee and held fast by rocks that had fallen upon it. So he remained two whole days, all around him being too much occupied with the cries and necessities of their own friends to notice his case. He endeavored to pull down upon himself the overhanging rocks to put an end to his existence, but could not effect it. He was finally relieved, and was now doing well. At the baths, a mile and a half from the city, no house had been demolished. Luby, where Mr. Thomson remembered to have slept some years before, was a ghastly heap of ruins. The old sheikh survived, but his whole family of eleven persons perished. In Segara every house was destroyed. Kefr Kenna (Cana of Galilee) was left unharmed, but Arana was a perfect desolation. At Nazareth the large Latin convent had suffered considerably. From this place the brethren went directly home, arriving after a twelve days' absence.

Here again Mr. Thomson is constrained to bear witness to the amazing absence of humanity and moral principles among the natives of the land. He exclaims, "There is no flesh in the stony heart of man. Nothing but dreadful punishments, oft inflicted by the government, preserved the ruined villages from becoming scenes of indiscriminate plunder. Taking advantage of the necessities of their neighbors, no man would work except for enormous wages. The head rabbi of Tiberias told me they had to pay about sixty dollars for every burial, although it required only an hour or two to accomplish it. He had paid out of the public purse upwards of seventy thousand piasters for this purpose alone. Nor were Jews a whit behind the Muslims in this cold-hearted villany. I never saw a Jew helping another Jew except for money. After our hospital was finished we had to pay a high price to have the poor wounded creatures carried into it. Not a Jew, Christian or Turk lifted a hand to assist us except for high wages."

The Syria mission originated in the cherished desire of American Christians to restore the honor and power of Christianity in the holy land, and especially in the city where was offered the great Sacrifice for the sin of the world, and that city was constantly held as one of the stations of the mission from the time of its being first visited by Mr. Parsons, and was regularly occupied, if war, sickness or death did not prevent, for the space of twenty years. The message of the gospel was declared there by Messrs. Fisk and King, and afterward by others to small audiences. During the hot months of 1841 the preaching service was transferred from Jerusalem to Bethlehem, at which latter place there was a considerable improvement in the number of hearers. To most of the Bethlehemites preaching was a new thing. Some had never before heard an evangelical sermon, and in general they listened with attention. A consid-

SAFEETA, A VILLAGE OF NORTHERN SYRIA.—See Page 397.

erable number of them were from the Latin Church. These often expressed their regret that they had no scriptural instruction from their priests, and that their public prayers were in an unknown tongue.

The ecclesiastics of the three large convents of Bethlehem were of course opposed to the residence of the Protestants there, and had it not been for the intrepid, independent spirit of the people, they would have been driven out of their coasts.

BETHLEHEM.

Bethlehem was found to be a cool and healthy place for summer residence, and, with the neighboring villages, presented an inviting field for the Bible work. A small common school was kept up here notwithstanding the opposition of the monks, and the teacher boldly avowed himself to be a Protestant. A similar school was opened in Jerusalem, against which the monks could in no way prevail except by opening a school of their own on the same plan, thus accomplishing one great object of the Protestant school and relieving the foreign treasury from the expense. The monks, however, got little credit for this forced charity to the people, for they thanked the Protestants as the real cause of it, and begged them to go on establishing schools in all the villages, that the monks might be roused up to go and do likewise.

A small school taught by Miss Tildin was attended by ten or twelve girls, mostly from Muslim families. Five native girls had been taken into the mission families with excellent success. It had softened the popular prejudice against female education, and many applications were received from parents both in Jerusalem and in Bethlehem to have their daughters taken for the same object.

In book distribution less was now done than in former years, on account of the disturbed state of the country and the fewness of the pilgrims. But in proportion more copies were sent to places at a distance, as Hasbeiya and Rasheiya villages, near Mt. Hermon, toward Damascus. Some went to Nablus, Nazareth, Jaffa and neighboring villages, and the books most sought for were Bibles and Testaments.

Two individuals who were brought into notice at this station deserve a special mention. One was Tannoos Kerm, a native of Nazareth, and claimed by the Latin church at that place. He had been a married man, but residing at Safed at the time of the earthquake, he was then bereaved of his wife and three children. He came in his solitariness and begged to be received as a helper in the gospel work. The missionaries had had some knowledge of the man by report, and his personal acquaintance confirmed their confidence in his Christian character. He was employed as school teacher with success, and to the great satisfaction of his employers, and not only so, but was also, to some extent, a teacher of the missionaries themselves. The other of the two persons alluded to was the son of Omar Effendi, the chief sheikh of the green-turban men, the descendants of the prophet Mohammed, the same man who in 1824 interposed in behalf of the missionaries in Jerusalem when accused by the Latin monks for "selling bad books." This young man seemed to cherish a high respect for the Protestant religion, as his father also evidently did. He had for some time shown himself specially friendly to Mr. Whiting, but one day in particular, at a call he made upon him, he addressed him in the following remarkable terms: "You know, sir, how Jesus and his disciples were at first persecuted, and how their teachings were rejected by almost all the people, and how afterwards they gained influence and prospered, and the gospel everywhere triumphed. So you now, though hated and despised by some, yet have no need to be discouraged. Have patience, and after a while people will be convinced that the truth is with you. And if you do not in *your* day see much success, those that come after you will. This is not the work of a day. It takes a long time to effect important changes in men's opinions and conduct."

"This man," Mr. Whiting remarks, "is in an interesting state of mind. He reads the Bible much. He assures me he has read the New Testament many times through. His frequent references to passages in both the Old and New Testaments show that he has read them both with some attention." Surely it was not to have been expected that so much could be said of a young Mohammedan brought up as he must have been, honored for his relationship to the prophet, and enjoying such enticing worldly prospects among his own nation.

It has been intimated that the labors of the mission ceased at the Jerusalem station in 1843. Through a part of this year, and nearly the whole of the previous one, Mr. Whiting was the only member of the mission occupying the place. He was seven days distant from his brethren in Beirut, Mrs. Whiting was suffering from ill health, and no American colleague was likely soon to be sent him to share his anxieties and aid in his labors. Meantime a loud call for help came from the thousands ready to perish among the hills and vales of Lebanon, and it was thought best that, for a time at least, Jerusalem should be left to the co-laborers from England, and that the American forces should be concentrated more in the region of Beirut and the neighboring mountains. Accordingly **Mr.** Whiting was transferred first to Beirut, and shortly after to Abeih.

The station of Jerusalem certainly, *in prospect*, presented many attractions for Christian effort, and perhaps no friend of Christian missions had questioned the propriety of making the trial of it. But in regard to the continuance or the reoccupying of the station, the following remarkable providences are worthy of special consideration. Of the first two missionaries destined to the Holy City, Messrs. Parsons and Fisk, the former was permitted to visit the place **one short winter only**, and he died. The latter made it three visits, amounting in all to a stay of six or eight months, and he died. Next an Irish physician was sent from the Jews' Society, England, to occupy the city as a permanent station. He resided there three or four months and died. After remaining vacant six years a resolute attempt was made to reoccupy the station by Messrs. Thomson and Nicolayson with their families. Mrs. Thomson was suddenly taken away ere she had become settled in her house, and her husband, like a man met by a club at the door, was driven straight back to his starting-place. The intended occupation, however, was immediately after carried out by Messrs. Whiting and Dodge. The latter was spared to occupy his post but a little more than a month when he was seized with a fever which carried him off. Mr. Lanneau joined Mr. Whiting in 1836, and was obliged to leave in 1840. Mr. and Mrs. Sherman, from America, arrived in the latter part of 1839, and departed in 1842, leaving Mr. Whiting alone. The most favored of the American laborers in the Holy City were Mr. and Mrs. Whiting, who were privileged, though suffering under much bodily infirmity, to hold their position from the close of 1834 to 1843; but they were obliged to seek summer residences in Bethlehem or elsewhere, and once to retire for two years to their native land.

To these untoward providences may be added those which removed by death the only three persons in Jerusalem who ever appeared to give promise of being essentially useful to the mission, namely, Procopius in 1822, Papas Cesar in 1826, and Papas Esa in 1834. The evangelical Bishop Alexander, from England, was removed by death after a few years' residence at his see, and his assistant, Mr. Nicolayson, did not long survive him. Thus this mission station, either by death or by permanent removal, sustained a loss of twenty laborers in twenty years. And may it not be considered a providence having the same unfavorable aspect, that the people of that devoted city have been so left of God that they are notoriously more debased in moral character, and less impressible by gospel truth, than almost any other people in the land, if not in the world?

All these things taken together form an assemblage sad to contemplate, and not a little discouraging to the hope of the speedy regeneration of Jerusalem. Some indeed may receive them as being divinely so ordered to try the faith of believers, but others may perhaps quite as reasonably understand them as part of the curse still resting upon the city, and as indicating that the "forty and two months" during which it "shall be trodden under foot of the Gentiles" are not yet fulfilled.

The mission station at Beirut was in 1840 further weakened by the loss of two more of its members, viz., Mr. and Mrs. Hebard. Mrs. Hebard died on the 8th of February.* From this time Mr. Hebard himself, from his anxieties and deep affliction, became incapacitated for the proper discharge of his missionary duties, and had virtually arrived at the end of his work. He visited Smyrna and Alexandria and other places in quest of health without avail, and finally set off for the United States. But while on his passage, near Malta, he was found too much reduced to proceed. He was accordingly taken on shore, and five days after died in the triumph of faith.†

---

* Mrs. Hebard came to Beirut in 1835 with the special object of aiding Mrs. Smith, who was her particular friend, in the duties of her female school. She arrived as Miss Rebecca W. Williams, originally from East Hartford, Connecticut. Her marriage with Mr. Hebard occurred in October, 1836.

† Mr. Hebard was born in Lebanon, New Hampshire, and graduated at Amherst College.

The discontent of the Lebanon mountaineers with the measures of the Egyptian government broke out into open rebellion, and the month of June, 1840, was mostly a month of war. The state of affairs at Beirut in the beginning of July was such that the newly-arrived missionaries, Messrs. E. R. Beadle, Keyes and L. Thompson, with their wives and Miss Tilden, retired for a time from the tumult of the region of Beirut to a more quiet residence at Jerusalem.

Mr. W. M. Thomson writes about this time, "The truth is that our good city of Beirut is not a very quiet abode in these days, and it has required an effort to keep from being swept overboard by the fierce tempest of war that has raged since the last thirty-five days. Messrs. Beadle and Thompson having closed their doors, I could not see a single friendly light in all the suburbs of Beirut. Every family has fled to town except those who have taken refuge in my house. Our native friends, Bishop Carabet, Tannoos el Haddad, Aboo Yoosef and E. Fuaz, with their families, I placed in our large book magazine in the city. As to my own house, I was thinking, as I went round at bed-time to see that all was quiet, that we very much resembled an encampment of Ishmaelites. Beside Mr. and Mrs. Wolcott, Dr. Van Dyck and other inmates of the family, we have forty or fifty others, with all the boys of the seminary whom we were not able to send home. Most of these people have wives and children, and have brought their goods and chattels with them. That which can be stowed away is but a *portion* of the whole mass, while the remainder is stationed, like the Arna-oot soldiers (Albanians), who are firing around us in regular confusion, in every nook and corner. Though one's heart bleeds to see the fear and distress and despair of this poor people, yet it would have disturbed the gravity of a much soberer person than I am to have walked about the premises and seen this strange congregation asleep.

"As to the city, it is about as full as my house. The whole population of the vast gardens has poured into it from the land side, and the pasha from the other side has emptied in from his ships many thousands of his troops. Since the area within the walls is very small at best, the town with the men on the housetops resembles a North River steamboat as she leaves the wharf. You will be able to unite with us in devout gratitude that in the midst of such scenes we are all kept in health and in safety from the violence of evil men."

The commander of the English squadron at Besika Bay, near Smyrna, having heard of the insurrection of the mountaineers against Ibrahim Pasha, sent vessels of war to Beirut to reconnoitre, and it was soon understood that a fleet of the combined powers of Europe was ready to appear to compel the pasha to give up his hold on Syria and return into Egypt. In these circumstances the missionaries at Beirut availed themselves of the invitation of Captain Latimer, of the American corvette Cyane, to embark on board his vessel for Cyprus till the war should be ended.

The Cyane was anchored directly opposite the town in full view of all that was passing both on the water and on shore, and it was no common relief to our friends to find themselves seated and safe from war's alarms under the ample awning of one of their country's ships. The very next morning there appeared in the west an immense fleet of ships sweeping round the cape, led on by the flag-ship of the British Admiral, Sir Robert

Stopford. These vessels, added to those already collected in the harbor, made up a fleet of fifty-one sail. Beside the twenty-four Turkish transports there were only six war vessels with Turkish and Austrian flags, all the rest being English. "They anchored," writes Mr. Thomson, "in concerted positions, and the whole harbor through the day presented a scene of the highest excitement. The stern command from the harsh-tongued trumpet, the heavy plunge of the strong-armed anchor, the low but mighty murmur of thousands in active preparation, spreading over the whole surface of the sea, the boats with officers in full dress flitting across the water in every direction, in prompt obedience to the mysterious signals of Admiral Stopford flying at the mast-head of the Princess Charlotte, united with all the din and hurry and confusion of a large armament of different nations, customs and costumes coming to anchor, composed such a scene as is rarely beheld and never forgotten."

The cannonading of the city began on the following day and continued daily for nearly a week, when the main body of the fleet was withdrawn. In the midst of this season of cannonading, however, the Cyane left the scene of war and came to anchor before Larnaca, in Cyprus, and after landing her passengers proceeded toward Jaffa to look after the missionaries in that direction.

Solyman Pasha was obstinately determined to hold possession of Beirut to the last extremity, and it was after a month, in the night of the 9th of October, that he evacuated the city. The allies took possession of it the following day, and on that day it so happened that Mr. Wolcott arrived from Cyprus, being deputed by his companions to ascertain the progress of the war and what had happened to the mission property at Beirut.

He came first to the house of the American consul in the city. It had been thoroughly pillaged. The Egyptian soldiers had carried off whatever they thought proper, and the rest they had wantonly destroyed. Chairs, tables, mirrors, etc., lay scattered about on the floors all broken to pieces. The consul himself had but just landed from one of the ships where he had been staying during the bombardment. Mr. Wolcott met him at his house. He could give no information respecting the fate of the missionaries' houses out of the city, but it was discovered that the magazine under the consulate, where had been stowed most of the effects of Messrs. Beadle and Keyes, had not been broken open.

Having made these discoveries, **Mr.** Wolcott proceeded directly to the mission-house, some fifty rods out from the city walls, which had been the residence of himself and Mr. Hebard. As he drew near he was encouraged by seeing the American flag, which he had hoisted before his departure, still flying. Soon he met his janizary, who gave him the cheering assurance that he had kept his post through the whole siege, and that although the soldiers had encamped in his garden, yet, except by the cannon of the allies, the place had not been violated. The walls of the house had been pierced and grazed in a number of places, two bombs had burst in the yard, carrying away the stone gate-posts, and marks of the storm were visible in the trees and fences around, but the furniture within was entirely unharmed. The library-room with its delicate and costly apparatus for the seminary, its invaluable manuscripts and books, and especially the large number of folio volumes of the Christian Fathers, remained safe, just as when left. With a grateful heart Mr. Wolcott repaired to the house of Mr. Thomson. The wall in front of it had been raised to double its height by the soldiers and used as a breast-work. The consular janizary had fled, but another native guard, whom Mr. Thomson had placed in the house, had remained the only occupant. Though much exposed, it had wholly escaped injury. Its basement had been filled with goods which the natives brought thither for safety, and all had remained untouched. Mr. Smith's house remained to be examined. The field around it had been ploughed up by the cannon balls, but on entering the inclosure no traces of war could be seen. The beautiful cypresses were still standing in their places, and the orange and lemon trees were bending unplucked beneath their rich load. The basement of this house had been used for the printing establishment, and the press which might so easily have been broken, and the types which might so conveniently have been transmuted into bullets, were waiting in good order to be set forward again in the work of God.

A preservation so entire Mr. Wolcott and his associates had not suffered themselves to expect. The violence and rapacity of man seemed to have been restrained by the visible hand of God, and to him, therefore, they did not fail to render their grateful acknowledgments.

Egyptian rule in Syria was now near its end. Simultaneously with the loss of Beirut, Ibrahim Pasha, with that part of his army under his immediate command, suffered a signal defeat in the mountains near by, and in about three weeks Acca, the only well-fortified city on the Syrian coast, fell into the hands of the allies. From this time Ibrahim acted only on the defensive, and commenced a retreat in which he made no pause till he found himself again in his native Egypt. The Emeer Besheer, who was allotted a certain time to determine whether he would give in his adhesion to the conquering party or not, debated his conditions till his allotted time was past, and was taken and sent a prisoner to Malta, from which place he was transferred to Constantinople, in the vicinity of which city he died.

The missionaries now made haste to return to their station, but their schools were all disbanded, and it was a considerable space before their operations reverted to their former regular course. The greatest damage had been inflicted upon the boarding boys' seminary, from which a number of the more advanced youths, allured by offers of high wages, had been induced to join the army in the capacity of interpreters. As a counterbalance, however, to this loss, the seminary had been favored by the accession of a well-educated teacher from the patriarch's own college at Ain Waraka. The regular Sabbath-day worshiping congregation, which had been composed of near a hundred persons, had been scattered to the winds, but the sanctuary doors were again thrown open, and the free invitation to enter went forth to all who were athirst for the water of life; old faces and new faces were drawn together, and the place of preaching became again a favorite resort to a goodly number.

The long-expected fount of the improved Arabic type arrived from Smyrna in the spring of 1841, together with Mr. Hurter, the printer. The chief superintendent, the Rev. Eli Smith, D. D., came soon after from the United States.

The youths' seminary was removed for the summer to Aa-raia, on the mountain, under the care of Messrs.

Keyes and L. Thompson. Messrs. Wolcott and Van Dyck were stationed at Deir el Kommer, a central position among the Druzes; it being a time when this people attracted almost the whole attention of the mission. They were awake as probably they never were before to inquire after the truth as it is in Jesus, and more tongues than could be had were needed to declare the true way of life to the perishing, yet it pleased God, whose judgments are unsearchable and his ways past finding out, to bereave the needy laborers of one more of their number. The lot fell upon Mrs. Wolcott. The heats of summer were past, and Mr. and Mrs. Wolcott had come down from their mountain residence in Deir el Kommer, when, after a very short interval, the latter was taken ill and sunk rapidly into the arms of death, expressing the deepest penitence and humility, and with the faith of Stephen, uttering among her last words, the martyr's prayer, "Lord Jesus, receive my spirit."

CHAPTER XVII.

Patriarch's ambition and defeat—Dr. and Mrs. DeForest—Death of Mrs. Smith—Case of Raheel, tried for her faith—Abeih occupied—Hasbeiya waking up—Fierce persecutions assail the inquirers—Alarming threats—Temporary retreat to Abeih—Dishonorable meddling of the Russian consul—The persecutors become advocates—The Protestants, after severe trials, fence off a cemetery, have a church of seventeen members and regular supply of preaching.

IN the time of the Sheikh Besheer, the proper chief of the Druzes, the interests of that nation had a powerful influence in the government of the mountains. But when that chieftain fell, and the Emeer Besheer reigned without a rival, the Maronite people, led by their hierarchy, assumed to themselves a new importance, and treated their Druze fellow citizens with disrespect, and sometimes with haughty contempt. A series of events in the course of years had conspired to increase in the Druzes their sense of degradation, and their envy and hatred toward their lordly Maronite neighbors became excessive. The Druze sheikhs, who still held the government over many villages in the mountains, perceived a growing insubordination in their Christian subjects, in which insubordination the patriarch was known to encourage them. The course of that ambitious prelate had become such as to leave little doubt that he intended to make himself virtually the chief ruler of the mountains, and to break down the power of the Druzes, if not even to drive them from the whole of Lebanon. They became aware of the patriarch's plan about the same time that it was discovered that he had been sending petitions to the Sultan to drive the Protestants out of the country as disturbers of the peace. The subsequent conduct of his Holiness had been but a further development of his plan. The large sums of money sent by France and Austria for the sufferers in the late war he had, as was generally believed, hoarded up for military purposes. A Christian prince (the Emeer Milhem), late governor of Beirut, was chosen by him to lead his forces, and ample funds were entrusted to him to hire retainers. The Christians were encouraged to look to the patriarch rather than to their Druze governors for the regulation of their civil affairs. He had required Druze owners of houses to refuse letting their houses to Protestants for temporary residences, and now he was interfering with the education of their children, and so effectually that to avoid an open quarrel the Druze chiefs in Deir el Kommer felt obliged to allow a school to be broken up which they had solicited to be established for their own children. By the patriarch's authority a committee of select men was appointed in Deir el Kommer who interfered boldly with the government of the sheikhs; and finally the ruling prince of the mountains, occupying the seat of the late Emeer Besheer, was surrounded with a council whose evident design was to strip the Druze sheikhs of the last vestige of their power.

The oppressed Druzes thought that they had borne these encroachments long enough, and one day in the month of October, 1841, soon after Messrs. Smith, Wolcott and Van Dyck had left Deir el Kommer, at a concerted hour the leaders of all the feudal families, at the head of their men, poured into that village from every side. About half the town was pillaged and burned, and the ruling prince was besieged in his palace.

The prelate of Canobeen was roused. He immediately proclaimed a crusade, armed two of his own bishops, and ordered them, in the true style of Peter the Hermit or of the belligerent popes, to march at the head of his troops. They assembled at the palace of the Emeer Milhem, at the foot of Lebanon, to the number of four or five thousand men. As they attempted to ascend, however, to meet the foe, they were confronted by the infuriated people of a single village, and driven like sheep down the mountain. This was but a specimen of the success of the Druzes in nearly all their subsequent encounters. The new crusaders found it impossible to penetrate to their own capital to relieve it from its besiegers. On one occasion, however, a detachment reached about half way toward it, and in a mixed village burned all the Druze houses found in it. The next visit was by the Druzes, who finished the desolation by burning all the houses of the Christians. From this time was inaugurated a system of mutual pillage and burning among all the border villages of the two races. Villages were destroyed by the dozen, and convents, some of them the richest the Maronites possessed, were plundered and burned. Deir el Kommer surrendered and gave up its arms. The chief prince and his suite were permitted to retire on consenting to leave the government chest behind them. But they were robbed and maltreated on their way, and the president of the new Maronite council walked the whole distance to Beirut barefoot and with only a single article of dress upon him. The

DEIR EL KOMMER.

villages of Hadet and Ba-abda, in the latter of which villages was the palace of the Emeer Milhem, the patriarch's commander-in-chief, shared in the common destruction. The war continued as it began, under the impulse of the worst passions. On the part of the Druzes, it was a war of defence for altars and firesides; on that of the Maronites, a war of intended extermination. Outrages were common on both sides, but in most if not all cases the Maronites were apparently the aggressors, and, where they had opportunity, conducted themselves worse than their enemies.*

The final result was decidedly in favor of the Druzes. They were left in undisputed possession of their mountain district. The patriarch's ambition was completely humbled, while all, even his own party, cast upon him the blame of the whole mischief. After the disastrous issue of this "holy war" of the patriarch, and his futile negotiations at Constantinople, he seems to have remained for a season in quiet seclusion. The Druzes, by their struggle, had lost nothing of their friendliness to the mission, but continued loud in their demands for schools.

---

* Of the spirit of the papists, let the following letter of a bishop to his men in the field serve as a specimen: "We understand you have been helped to a victory over the insolent infidel enemies of the holy faith at Meristeh, which victory has been by the favor of God most high, and *by the intercession of his mother*. We praise to the highest degree your zeal, only you have been faulty in not burning the village. The entire correct course was to have burned it. Hereafter, take good heed, if you are victorious, not to stop short of burning and entire destruction. Our only caution, beloved sons and honored brethren, is that you abuse not the women. Aside from that, burn, kill, plunder, hesitate at nothing whatever. Be ever constant in prayer and confessions, inasmuch as this is a holy war; go on and fear nothing: and we lift up the hands of supplication to the Father of lights that he may assist you and give you victory."

At this period the mission strength was increased by the addition of Dr. and Mrs. De Forest, and at the same time weakened by the death of the second Mrs. Smith. Among the many evidences adduced in proof of the peculiar fitness of Mrs. Smith for the position she occupied was "*her well-ordered household,* which, while it gave a comfortable home to her family, furnished a useful and impressive model to the natives of her own sex who frequently came to inspect it." She had the finishing polish to put upon the mind and spirit of a fine little daughter of the land, whom the first Mrs. Smith had taken to bring up and rescue from the poverty and impending infamy to which she was exposed in the house of her birth.

This youthful daughter became, particluarly by the kind treatment and religious instruction of the two Mrs. Smiths, so strongly attached to the family that neither parents nor relatives, nor the powers that be, civil or ecclesiastical, could persuade her to leave it. She became a member of the Protestant Church, and her case came to be made a matter of public examination and trial, and was remarkable as the one which brought to a favorable issue at Beirut the question whether native Protestants should be considered before the law as on an equal footing with native members of other Christian churches.

The father of Raheel (Rachel) had died, and the widow not sustaining a good reputation, the daughter had not for two years spent a night at the home of her childhood. Soon after her union with the mission church at Beirut the mother insisted on her return to her own family, saying that an offer had been made for her in marriage and she must come and get herself ready. Raheel was of age and was determined not to marry a Greek, and especially one whom her mother would be likely to choose for her. However, she went, in company with one of the missionaries, to visit her mother, and on that occasion was treated with proper civility, but on a second visit she was forcibly detained. Recourse was immediately had to the consul, who sent his janizaries, and, in spite of the family and the collected neighbors, effected her release. The mother and the son-in-law, with a party of Albanian soldiers, threatened to take the young woman by violence, and the Prussian consul living near by received her for safety into his family. The pasha was of course complained to by the relatives, but on hearing the full account of the case from the janizaries he seemed satisfied, notwithstanding, he said, it was important that he should see the girl himself and have an account of the matter from her own lips. He sent, therefore, a polite request to his Excellency, the consul, that he would favor him with the girl's presence under the escort of a dragoman and a janizary from the consulate. The request was readily complied with, and poor Raheel was taken to appear before the pasha and his full council.

"Girl," said the pasha, "what is your story?"

Raheel—"When I was a little girl my father gave me to Mr. Smith to be a member of his family. He has brought me up as his child. When my father died he left me with Mr. Smith, and now his house is my home. Yesterday I called to see my mother, and was forcibly detained contrary to my remonstrances and those of my friend who accompanied me. That friend hastened to inform Mr. Smith, who came, and then I escaped."

"Did he take you away contrary to your will?"

"No."

"Where do you now wish to live?"

"With Mr. Smith."

"Why do you not wish to live with your mother?"

"There are reasons which cannot be told here."

"But I wish to know what they are."

"They are sufficient; but as I have been taught from my childhood, I think it is not proper that I should mention them."

The pasha knew the reasons and told them quietly to his council, who sat by. Then turning to Raheel he said, "Well, girl, you may go to the place you have chosen." So the girl was conducted back, and the civil liberty of Protestants was so far vindicated. But this was not all the trial to which the poor girl was to be subjected. Another suit was brought against her by the Greek bishop of the city, and the pasha was induced to send a demand verbally that she should appear that very day before the bishop and offer her religious confession according to the custom of the Greek Church. Raheel was consulted as to what she would do. She replied that she was not a member of the Greek Church nor subject to the bishop, nor would she confess to him or any of his clergy. The English and Prussian consul-generals were consulted and their advice taken. Even the natives themselves protested loudly against the bishop for this interference with the rights of the laity, and not only the orthodox Greeks, but the Greek Catholics also, for once took sides with the Protestants against such a demand from a Greek ecclesiastic. When Raheel's answer was reported back to the pasha, he immediately replied that the relatives had been complaining to him that the missionaries were endeavoring to make the girl a Protestant *by force*, and now all he wished was, that she should go before the bishop as she had been before him, declare her mind freely, and then go where she chose. This liberal reply of the pasha was a great relief to the anxieties of the Protestant friends of Raheel. But she was quite reluctant to appear before the bishop at all. It would be a great trial to her own feelings, as it probably would be to his, and the missionaries were unwilling to use any constraint with her in the case. It was therefore concluded that she should return answer to the pasha that she acknowledged in no sense whatever the authority of the Greek bishop, and had no sort of connection with him; that the pasha was the person whom she knew as the governor of the country, and if he saw fit to command her she would again appear before him, as she had already done, and satisfy any doubts he might have respecting her ecclesiastical relations. This final reply of Raheel was given to the dragoman of the pasha, to be communicated in case the latter should again call up the subject. Nothing more was heard of the matter, and the missionaries were encouraged to believe that the right of a native Christian to become a Protestant if he chose would not again be brought in question.

The village of Abeih began to be thought of for the use that might be made of it for the mission work. It was situated in the Druze quarter of Lebanon, high on its western slope, overlooking the sea and the plain of Beirut, and contained about two hundred Druze and Maronite families. Among its buildings were two palaces of the emeers and two small convents. For quietness and safety, if not for health, it was preferable as a place of residence to Deir el Kommer. Besides, it had the advantage of being by half the distance nearer to

Beirut. The missionaries decided to make it one of their central stations, and to it they designated Messrs. Whiting, Thomson and Van Dyck. In a little time the shyness and reserve of the native residents disappeared, and both Maronites and Druzes began to look upon their new neighbors as their best friends. Even the Maronite priests and monks, perhaps constrained by witnessing the friendly disposition of their people, evidently sought the missionaries' good-will. During the first summer of their residence at Abeih, Mr. Thomson remarked that he had had more friendly intercourse with the Maronite priesthood than during all his previous missionary life. This was in the year 1843.

They had a good school in Abeih numbering fifty pupils, and these were taught by a Maronite who had lately embraced evangelical sentiments. He had suffered the usual denunciations of the Maronite bishop, but without any great annoyance. The Latin convent in the village had had no occupant for many years, but now, according to the established law of papal resistance, an Italian monk was sent to fit up the building and open an opposition school for teaching Italian and Arabic.

The mission-school in this village of Lebanon increased in importance, and at a later day became known as the Abeih seminary. Its pupils were here trained for work as evangelists, and have gone forth to preach the gospel all through Syria and the East. The seminary buildings were erected in 1849. They are of compact limestone, one story in height, and stand on sloping ground facing northward. Within its walls the intelligent young men of Syria are now preparing for the work of the ministry.

Beside this school at Abeih, others were at this time

ABEIH SEMINARY, MT. LEBANON, SYRIA.

in operation on the mountains, containing between three and four hundred pupils, of whom about one half were Druzes. The number of schools might now have been doubled had not funds unhappily been wanting.

Among the mountains of Anti Lebanon, near the foot of Mt. Hermon and the sources of the Jordan, northeast of Tyre, is a large village called Hasbeiya, inhabited by Druzes and a considerable number of Arab Christians of the Greek rite. In the infancy of the Syrian mission, in 1826 and 1827, we had there a flourishing school, as also in some smaller towns in the neighborhood. Through this channel, and from books obtained from the stations at Beirut and Jerusalem, the people had acquired some knowledge of a class of Christians called English or Protestants. Individuals among them had visited these new men at Beirut, and learned, to some extent, their peculiar articles of belief. It happened that there arose a dispute among the Greeks of Hasbeiya about taxation, and one party resolved to leave the Greeks and form some new organization. Accordingly they sent a deputation to Beirut to negotiate a union with the Protestants. The missionaries told them fully what Protestantism was, bade them go home, pay their taxes as good citizens should, become reconciled with their neighbors, and as soon as they could write and say they had done this, they would send them a teacher, and perhaps finally come in person. They gave them no encouragement to suppose that they could save them from taxation; nevertheless, the men still chose to carry out their plan of union with the Protestants, and left Beirut saying they would conform to the advice given them, but that to the Greek Church they never would return.

Unexpectedly, in a few days, word came from Hasbeiya that they had complied with the proposed conditions and begged that the promises made them might be fulfilled immediately. Two of the native brethren were consequently sent them, and after them Messrs. Smith and Whiting went to them in person. These last were gratified with the appearance of the men quite beyond their expectations, and were convinced that the excitement had its origin in something higher than mere earthly considerations or human agency. They were visited, from time to time, by different missionaries and by the native brethren, some of the latter, by long practice, having become very effective defenders and advocates of the evangelical truth. A good school was taught in the town by an energetic and decided young man, zealous for the gospel, apt to learn and apt to teach. He had, of his own notion, committed to memory the Assembly's shorter catechism, and was teaching it to his pupils. Many others, men and women as well as children, had learned and were learning portions of the catechism and scripture passages.

In the heat of summer, six months after the first steps had been taken, Mr. Thomson went to them accompanied by Tannoos el Haddad. Their arrival was most timely. The whole town was in commotion. Thirty horsemen, with five or six priests, had come to town the day before from Zahleh, sent, as was believed, by the patriarch to bring back his wandering sheep by force. They went to work with true persecuting zeal, leaving no measures untried. Entreaties, threats, bribes, reproaches and actual violence were all employed. In this work they were helped on by a band of youths, who had entered into a league like the Jerusalem Jews against Paul. The confusion and distress in the Protestant families were indescribable. At length an order, procured by Mr. Wood, the English consul at Damascus, came from the pasha, commanding the emeer of the place to protect the Protestants. The party of horsemen then retired, not, however, without some little success.

Notwithstanding the pasha's order, the five priests of the village, aided by the mischievous "Society," were still able to carry on a system of annoyance. The Protestants were repeatedly beaten, spit upon, turned out of their houses, and everywhere exposed to execrable abuse.

All this, however, did not prevent the two friends from holding a meeting for worship and instruction every evening, nor from interviews with the people during the day. Exhausted by the constant excitement and labor, and by the hot wind that blew, the missionary friends were compelled to seek a little relaxation. About midnight they set off toward Mt. Hermon. After riding eighteen hours almost continuously they came to the village of Jibbata. Here they were startled by a messenger, post-haste from Hasbeiya, bringing a hurried note from Shaheen, leader of the Protestants, imploring them to return immediately, "wherever they might be overtaken, by day or by night." The notorious "Society" had risen in arms, and sent Shaheen a written order to leave the town by three o'clock the same day, "*on penalty of death.*" It was now just midnight. Mr. Thomson mounted his horse at once, leaving his company behind, and, riding hard, entered Hasbeiya alone about nine o'clock in the morning. The town seemed deserted. The shops were shut, and neither friend nor foe was seen in the streets. The Protestants had all fled, and the "Society," having accomplished all they wished at home, had gone off on a foray against some neighboring Bedawin.

When Tannoos arrived they both went to the palace of the emeer, where they found a large assemblage of emeers and elders of the town. The chief emeer related a history of the material events which had taken place during the last thirty hours, from which it appeared that the whole power of the town was in the hands of those armed "young men," and that the emeer himself had signed a paper making himself their tool. He begged Mr. Thomson to use his influence to bring about some amicable arrangement. Mr. Thomson made no engagement, assured them all that the departure of Shaheen and his friends was without his advice or knowledge; that he had come to Hasbeiya as a spiritual instructor simply; that as his friends had now been driven away he should go with them, and that if they should return, and again request him to come to them on the same errand, he should undoubtedly do so. They all said that he *should be most welcome.*

For three nights Mr. Thomson had been without sleep, and after another wearisome day his fourth night commenced with his being thronged by anxious wives and mothers giving him messages to their sons and husbands, and charging him to protect them from injury. It was surprising and affecting to see what anxiety they evidently felt for their friends, while they expressed none for themselves, although left in the midst of their enemies, and some of them so poor as not to know how or where they should find their daily bread.

"At eleven o'clock," says Mr. Thomson, "we bade them farewell with many prayers and tears, and set forward to join Shaheen and his company. I had received a letter from them in the evening, informing me where I should find them, and begging me to come to them immediately. I reached the camp at daybreak, threw myself on the ground and slept until sunrise, not having closed my eyes for the best part of four nights, three of which had been spent in riding or hard work.

"I found the poor people on the open mountain without tent or bed or covering of any kind, half perished with cold, and very hungry. I had directed my servant to purchase what bread he could carry with him. This they devoured like locusts. We then set forward toward Abeih, but our progress was slow. The heat of the day was equal to the cold of the night, and some of the company climbed to the top of Lebanon with great difficulty. We reached Mokhtara after dark. We were nobly entertained by Sheikh Seid Jemblaut (son of the old sheikh). He made a feast for the whole company, and expressed the liveliest interest in their cause. I had been of some service to this young sheikh, in making his peace with the government after the last Druze war, and now that he is restored to his home and his authority his generous gratitude knows no bounds. The next day I divided the company into two parties, and sent one to Mr. Whiting at Aintab, and took the other with me to Abeih. They will remain with us a few days until some satisfactory arrangement can be made for their return."

The whole company was soon assembled at Abeih, and continued there many weeks listening attentively to religious instruction. When the way seemed open for their return, Bootrus el Bistani, a native assistant, went with them to their homes. On their way they met a company of three hundred Hasbeiyans going for some purpose to Beirut. They saluted the party, but received in return only revilings and threats. It was no good omen, but they kept on, thankful that they had escaped without suffering any violence. They found their friends in Hasbeiya still in great fear, but they ventured, notwithstanding, to have a meeting for public worship on the Sabbath, and about forty of them attended.

In a few days the patriarch made his appearance from Damascus. He came to try what his personal presence might effect. Of course, his coming increased the general irritation against them, and they sent word to the missionaries advising them not to visit them during the present excitement among their enemies, lest, if any disorders should occur, the missionaries should be accused as the cause. The party of three hundred, who were met on their way to Beirut, returned, and, after holding a council outside of the town with men from other villages, entered Hasbeiya with jubilant demonstrations, shouting, firing guns and chanting songs of vengeance against the Protestants. In this manner they went directly to the patriarch. They brought news that all the American missionaries had been banished from Constantinople, Smyrna and Greece, and that some had been stoned and murdered even with the connivance of the government. The patriarch sent to Damascus demanding of the pasha that the Emeer Khaleel, who had favored the Protestants, should be removed from the governorship of Hasbeiya, assuring him that if it was not done there would follow an insurrection in the province. The emeer was intimidated, and feared to punish anybody.

One Sabbath as our native brother, Eleeas Fuaz, who had come to aid them in their meetings, was going to the place of worship with three others, the men, women and children joined in mocking, cursing and stoning them; the place of worship was surrounded and the services prevented. The emeer was informed of this, but he talked loud and did nothing. "After this," Eleeas writes, "I am distressed on account of the unquiet state of our friends here; they are shut up in their houses and dare not go out. They cannot move from one place to another without being abused, cursed and stoned, and sometimes threatened with death."

Four or five days after, he writes: "I set out to go to our worship this morning, avoiding the road that passes by the Greek church for fear of another disturbance. I was met by a company of boys, who immediately surrounded me on all sides and began to stone me. The stones seemed to fall on me like rain, on my back and legs and head. One struck me below the eye, and with such force that it seemed as if my head had flown off my shoulders. I was struck almost senseless, so as not to know where I was, while the blood was flowing in a stream down my face. Leading men in the Greek community, and among them Girgis er Rey-is, Shaheen Da-oon and others, were standing in the bishop's yard looking on and laughing. Eleeas once more carried his complaint to the prince, all bloody as he was, but the most the prince dared do for him was to send one of his soldiers to see that he should not be set upon by the Greeks on his way to his house. But the house itself, when they came to it, was found to be surrounded by a company of young men and boys who were trying to break open the door, and who continued to occupy their place several hours, reviling, throwing stones and calling upon Eleeas to produce certain Protestants whose blood they "wished to drink." They cursed the religion of the English, called them water-dogs, and vowed to burn their religion out of their town though it should cost them thirty lives to accomplish it. With all the cursing and bitterness and bloody threats of these men, it does not appear that any man's life was directly taken by them, but the means of annoyance they used were so many, and so long continued, that eventually most of the Protestants made some compromise with their enemies and obtained leave for the present to dwell in quiet.

How much of this violent crushing down of the rights of conscience was owing to foreign intervention we may never certainly know, but there chanced to come to light, just at this time, the following significant diplomatic document, addressed by his Excellency the Russian Consul General to his Highness the Pasha of Damascus: "However I may desire to address your Highness on the subject [of the defections in Hasbeiya] in a friendly manner, I must remind you that I am a servant of the magnificent Emperor of Russia, and that we have the right of protecting the Greek Church in the Ottoman dominions. I should greatly regret it if I were compelled to change my language, and protest against every proceeding which may lead to the humiliation of the Greek church at Hasbeiya, and to the encouragement of the *pretended Protestants*, especially as the Sublime Porte *does not recognize among her subjects any such community*."

Did it comport with the dignity of a Russian Consul General to argue that because the Church of England, *i. e.*, the Protestants, had never been formally recognized by the Turkish government, therefore the Russian Church had a higher claim to protection than the English? Russia may claim a right to lord it over the consciences of her *own* subjects, and confine them by law within the pale of the Greek Church, but that she should claim such a right in Turkey is assuming a good deal for the nineteenth century.

Notwithstanding the conformity of the evangelical party, in some respects, to their former church, there were not wanting some among them who continued to declare that their conformity was a union "under protest," and that they never could consent to remain in that false position. They kept up a continued correspondence with the missionaries, and when the storms of war and persecution had somewhat subsided they renewed their calls for help. A native assistant was afforded them, but they earnestly desired a fully educated minister of the gospel. Accordingly, the Rev. Simeon H. Calhoun, who had not been long in Syria, went to them, accompanied by our able preacher, Tannoos el Haddad. They began with an audience of thirty hearers, and this number seems to have continued pretty regularly. On the eighteenth and last day of their visit Tannoos discoursed to them with unusual ability and effect. The little audience was melted into tears, some of them sobbing aloud.

They continued in comparative quietness for some months, having visits from the missionaries and their native helpers, till the governor, Saad ed Deen, was called by the pasha to render an account of his government for the past three years. It was probably a Russo-Turkish examination, particularly as to the causes of the failure of the measures against the new English (Protestant) church attempted to be set up in Hasbeiya. He could not show a clean record. He must be kept in durance for failure in the duty which he owed to the "magnificent Emperor of Russia," of whose right to rule over him he had never before heard. He could be released only when those "pretended Protestants" should be "burnt out."

Letters came from the emeer of a very threatening character. A council was held in the palace of the acting governor, where some proposed to crush at once the heretical intruders. But to this the Emeer Ahmed, eldest son of the Saad ed Deen, flatly opposed himself. He boldly declared that if anything more of that kind was attempted he would defend the Protestants with all his might, even to becoming a Protestant himself. They could not agree, and the council broke up. A second one was held, at which one of the speakers was Shaheen Da-oon, who, with Girgis er Rey-is, stood among the rest in the bishop's yard and laughed at the pelting of our Eleeas Fuaz. This man now stood forth more bold than Gamaliel and said,

"Why should we persecute these people? Why excommunicate them? Why not have dealings with them? Are they not Christians as well as we? Yes, and better Christians, too, than we. They do not lie, nor curse, nor drink, nor swear. Look at Nicola Haslab and Khaleel el Khoori; what were they once, and what are they now? You had better go and do like them. As for me, I'll have nothing to do with this business. I've troubled the people of God long enough, and if all my five sons were to become Protestants now, I would not oppose them."

One of the sons of this man Da-oon was already an open defender of the Protestants and of their doctrines. This council ended like the other. But the pressure

HASBEIYA.
A. The Protestant Church erected in 1854. B. The Greek Church. D. Palace of the Druze Sheikh.

was continued increasingly at Damascus, and the emeer wrote the most earnest letters, till the governor finally sent orders to the Protestants that they must positively conform to the Greek Church and attend that form of worship. They still refused and remonstrated, saying,

"Will your Excellency indeed compel us to violate our consciences, to do what is contrary to the holy Scriptures, to bow down before pictures, pray to dead saints, and such things? Send us away to Damascus, send us to the galleys, cut off our heads, but do not send us to the Greek Church."

The governor replied, "You need do nothing wrong, nothing against your consciences. You have only to go to the church and stand there and hear the priest read the prayers. This you *must* do, *voluntarily* or *involuntarily.*"

"*Voluntarily*, never!" said they. "Let all here present bear witness if your Excellency send us to the church it will be by *force*, but willingly we will not go."

The governor then called the priests, and called also a guard, and all were marched off together to the church; but the priests refused, in these farcical circumstances, to go through with the usual ceremonies, and the company separated and went to their homes. This manœuvre was repeated but twice, and they became sick of it; but though this kind of worship was too ridiculous to be continued, all were strictly forbidden by the government to assemble with the missionaries, and by special desire of the governor the missionaries temporarily left the place.

The Emeer Saad ed Deen returned to his post breathing out threatenings and slaughter against the new disciples, declaring he would rid the place of them if he had even to take their lives. He forged a bond against one of the leaders for the sum of eight hundred dollars, and put him into prison till he should pay the debt. The Prussian consul unofficially interposed his kind offices for the prisoner, and the latter, after paying forty dollars of the eight hundred, was set at liberty. The prince would have taken the same course with another man of property among them, but was prevented by the remonstrances of his two sons.

For many months this "wild boar of Hermon," as he was fitly called by Mr. Thomson, continued to waste the tender vine of Hasbeiya until after the imperial firman of November, 1847, securing the rights of Protestants, was published, when he sent to invite all those scattered men to return to their homes and pursue their occupations in peace.

But the Christian patriarch was not so ready to yield obedience to the powers that be as was the Mohammedan prince. He must try one expedient more. He first secures in some way the neutrality of the prince, and then issues a sweeping decree of excommunication against all the heretical English, and all that aid, abet or assist them in any way. The chief Christian population being of the Greek Church, it was easy for them to shun the excluded ones themselves, and to make it to consist with the interest of the Druzes and Muslims to shun them also.

Thus cut off from favor and sympathy with almost all their fellow-citizens, and obtaining no redress from the prince, they were soon reduced to an extreme of distress. But the Lord, in whom they trusted, would not give them up to despair. He gradually softened the hearts of the Druzes and Muslims, and even some of the Christians, who began in secret, and then more and more openly, to relieve their necessities, so that finally the net was broken and the fishes escaped. *One fish* was all that the patriarch and his hirelings had caught after so much toil. Not much of a draught for so much outlay!

For a term of almost two years these tried believers had been alone buffeting the floods of ungodly men. Their enemies had used every promising expedient, and had failed. The prospect of a long season of repose was now brighter than ever it had been. The prevailing cholera had disappeared, and the missionaries were constrained to make another visit to them and inquire into their state, especially as it was commonly reported that there were divisions among them. Mr. Whiting and Tannoos el Haddad, men eminently pacific in their dispositions, were sent to them to unite and comfort their hearts. They found them living in quietness with all around them. Most of the neighbors conversed freely and had business dealings freely with them. One important object, for which they had been laboring for years past against the opposition of governors and priests, they had at length obtained—it was a cemetery already set apart and fenced; and it was thought a remarkable providence that in these four years during which they had been held as schismatics and heretics, though they had had no cemetery, they had also had no *need* of one, for during this whole space of time not one of their company and no member of their families had died.

On the fifth of July, at Hasbeiya, a sermon was preached and a church of sixteen members organized. The next day being the Sabbath, after a discourse by John Wortabet, and after the admission of another member to the church, the Lord's Supper was administered. All these exercises were calculated to make a strong impression, and at the close the native brethren, inspired by one common feeling of Christian affection, began to embrace and salute each other "with a holy kiss," according to the Oriental method, breathing all the while some short prayer or hearty thanksgiving. Good Deacon Tannoos, with glistening eyes, repeated aloud the words of the devout old saint, "Lord, now lettest thou thy servant depart in peace." "This manifestation of fraternal love," says Mr. Thomson, "was so sudden, spontaneous and natural as to be very affecting and delightful. We who had known this people from their first steps toward evangelical religion could hardly recognize in these humble, devout and spiritual worshipers the rude, noisy, ignorant and worldly company that then caused us so much trouble." The sight must have abundantly rewarded this unwearied laborer for those exposures, those tiresome journeys and those successive sleepless nights through which he had formerly passed in looking after these sheep scattered and driven about among the mountains.

With the approbation of all concerned, young Wortabet was to remain to lead their meetings and minister to them the word. He was not only an acceptable and instructive preacher, but was considerably experienced also as a physician.

The early mission-schools in Hasbeiya, Deir Memass, Gedeideh and Rasheiya (Rasheiyet el Fkhár), had some little influence in introducing the Protestant name into this district of country. In the last of the above-mentioned villages the teacher's name was Yacob, whose son, Eleeas, came, from time to time, to Beirut to receive his father's wages. He was a pupil in the school, and there learned to read the Psalter and the New Testament as schoolbooks. He grew up, however, a heedless youth, and became a juggler, a sleight-of-hand trickster, and given to much wine. But it appears that his early impressions, received from the word of God in the school, had taken firm hold upon him and would not let him go till they brought him home to the fold of the great Shepherd. This is that Eleeas Yacob (or son of Yacob) mentioned by Mr. Whiting in his late visit to this neighborhood, and who united with the church of Beirut in 1843. "To this man's influence," Mr. Thomson says, "may be traced the first enlightening of Tannoos Kerm of Safed" (a native assistant of Mr. Whiting at Jerusalem who lost his family in the earthquake at Safed, and is now connected with the Jewish missionaries at that place). "Eleeas has also a disciple named Dawhir Ab-bood, in el Kheiam, and Dawhir also has a disciple in one of his neighbors, and so the leaven is spreading. These two men, Yacob and Dawhir, have a knowledge of scripture which is remarkable, and, being naturally shrewd men, they have a power of argument which their adversaries cannot gainsay or resist. They are both physicians, and are in the habit of making long tours through Houran and the parts east of Jordan as far south as Kerek, and to those parts they have already gone, and will continue to go, preaching the gospel of the kingdom. The results of that school are known only to Him who chooses the weak things of the world to confound the things that are mighty."

A few months more, and Mr. Thomson made another visit to this little community, and on the first evening after his arrival listened, with a hundred others, to an excellent sermon by the young preacher, Wortabet.

Most of those who attended were young men in the prime of life. The two preachers had discoursed every night to large audiences. The whole town was moved. Wherever they went religion was all the talk. All was perfect peace. The old emeer had become decidedly favorable, and no one presumed to move his tongue against the work. The various emeers, Druze sheikhs and elders of the town made their friendly calls. All the leading men who so vehemently opposed the missionaries at the beginning now sought their acquaintance and friendship. The ruling emeer let a man out of prison and sent him to Mr. Thomson, because the man pretended that he was a Protestant; and this was the same emeer who had sworn to exterminate the Protestants from all Hermon, and had labored for years to fulfill his oath!

One day Mr. Thomson and two deacons went up the side of Mt. Hermon to a solitary lodge where lived a poor man, a vine-dresser, and known as an humble applicant for admission to the Protestant communion. They had a joyful reception, and all three squeezed in to the lodge, finding space just sufficient to contain the four. For a bed there was a single quilt and pillow. On the latter lay the Arabic Bible, " Prayers for every Day in the Week," Thomas A. Kempis and Dr. Smith's work on the Spirit, all of them well worn by use. They discussed the whole history of redemption. At the close they knelt in prayer. Says Mr. Thomson, "It was good to be there on that mountain side, in that lodge beneath that olive, among those clustering vines, with that old man of humble mien and tearful eye, the voice of prayer ascending from full hearts to the canopy of heaven above our heads. Yes, it was good to be there. I crept forth from this humble lodge with eyes bedimmed with tears. In the afternoon," continues Mr. Thomson, "as the old man was coming to our preparatory lecture, I met him upon the stairs. Seizing my hand, he said, 'Ever since you left me this morning I have been looking up into heaven, and I see nothing there but Christ,' and gazing up into the clear blue sky, with a voice so earnest that it almost frightened me, he repeated, '*I see nothing in heaven but Christ, I see nothing in heaven but Christ.*'"

The next day (Sabbath) a sermon was preached, new members were admitted and the Lord's Supper was celebrated. Long before the time, the house was crowded with people, and those outside pressed together at the windows to listen. Three hours were spent in that meeting. No one moved from his place. All were silent and solemn. They listened as for their lives to the very last word, and many eyes unused to weep were bathed in tears. The number present was supposed to be about one hundred and eighty.

The following day Mr. Thomson went to Rasheiya, the village of Eleeas Yacob. Here he had a room full of people to whom he preached the word. About a dozen men here called themselves Protestants, and many more were examining and discussing the great question. Few men in the village could read, and Eleeas, having been taught formerly for a while at the mission seminary, was so far beyond the rest in respect to education that he was able to conduct worship very acceptably. By request the missionary visited the next day a family at Hasbeiya, and spent an hour in conversing with an old man and his four sons about the gospel. This was the house of entertainment for the Greek patriarch when, five years ago, he came to Hasbeiya to annihilate the Protestants, and this man was his right arm in the work of persecution. Now both he and his sons were declared Protestants. One evening the head man of the Maronites was present at the preaching, and his son was believed to be a sincere convert. Druzes were beginning to inquire what these things meant, and in the surrounding villages the truth seemed to be stirring up the people. Mr. Thomson was, on this account, looking for another storm to break out from some quarter, nor were his fears groundless.

Mr. Thomson next rode to Ibel and spent a few hours with Eleeas Yacob, and next to el Kheiam, two miles farther southward, where lived Dawhir, Eleeas Yacob's disciple. His whole soul was engaged in the subject of religion, into which he threw his accustomed energy and fearlessness. They had worship together, and afterward the leading men of the village assembled with them, and conversed about religion till late at night. About this time thirty new names were added to the number of Protestants in Hasbeiya, and forty-five persons at Ibel had petitioned the government to be enrolled with that community.

Such were the religious prospects of Hasbeiya and vicinity near the close of the year 1851, when there came over the whole region a new tempest of persecution, anarchy and war. Wortabet, however, maintained his stand firmly and reputably, and was ordained over the people as their regular pastor. Under his ministration the Protestant community became more compact, orderly and efficient. At their own charges they built themselves a house of worship, and when they heard of the opening of China for the word of God, and the resolve of English Christians to send to that heathen land a million New Testaments, they threw in their share, of about thirty dollars, for the same object.

Elecas Yacob made two successful tours to the east and south, in company with a native Protestant friend, preaching sometimes in the native churches, and gaining the assent of whole villages at once to enroll themselves as Protestants. In this work Elecas supported himself entirely by his own medical practice.

The Rev. W. W. Eddy, who had been stationed at Sidon, visited Hasbeiya in 1857, and also the village of Kheiam, where he spent a Sabbath and had an audience from five different villages, who showed great earnestness in inquiring after the truth. In a letter of still later date, Mr. Eddy speaks, with peculiar gratification, of some very earnest Protestants in Deir Memás. They had endured for many months a cruel course of persecution from the Greeks and from the Mohammedan government of the district, but, under all this, had been continually increasing in numbers. Mr. Eddy was with them several days, and was astonished and delighted to find gathered together each evening, after the severe labors of the day in harvesting, an audience of above a hundred souls, all eager, attentive and serious. The number of full-grown men professing Protestantism was above sixty, and though only a part of the women of their families had openly joined them, counting these and their children, the community numbered fully one hundred and twenty souls, the largest professed Protestant community at that time in Syria.

CHAPTER XVIII.

New flames of war in 1845—Druzes prevail—Maronite princes driven from Abeih—Greeks killed at Hasbeiya—Death of the patriarch—New election ends in quarrel and sacking of Canobeen—Greek patriarch in trouble at Beirut—Meshaka and his patriarch in discussion—Messrs. Wilson and Foote at Tripoli—Yanni—Messrs. Wilson and Foote driven from Eh-heden—Yanni unites with the church at Beirut—Abdallah Zeidan—Is-hoc el Kefroony—Safeeta.

THE civil war of 1841 resulted, as has been seen, in favor of the Druzes. The Christian princes of the Shehāb family, of whom the Emeer Besheer Shehāb was chief, were displaced, and on the ruins of the Shehāb dynasty rose the power of the Druze feudal sheikhs. The Shehābs, however, were still somewhat numerous, and bore their degradation with impatience. The Maronite sect were exasperated by their late defeat, by the plunder of their property and the burning of their homes, and having been deluded for some years by vain promises of remuneration, the people were more than ready to unite with these fallen princes in avenging themselves on their Druze enemies. The Maronite clergy also, whose authority had been greatly reduced by the late conflict, were by no means reluctant to see the question of power again submitted to the arbitrament of war.

In such a state of feeling the flame was easily kindled. Robberies and murders became frequent, and the Maronites did not refrain from open threats of a second appeal to arms. The collision came. After a skirmish on the

30th of April, 1845, below the village of Abeih, the Druzes descended in force upon Hadet, Ba-abda and the Wady, as it is called, drove the inhabitants to Beirut, and plundered their houses. Baadrán, Meristeh, Ammatoor and Bathir, places near el Muktara, with several others in the Shoof district, were burned, and after ten days the Maronites had all been driven a second time out of the Druze portion of the mountains, with the exception of Deir el Kommer and Abeih and vicinity. At the latter place remained some of the Shehâb emeers, and the Druzes insisted that they should go with the rest of their tribe. They were themselves willing to go, but their people in the village would not consent to it; and as neither party would accept the terms, an attack upon Abeih became inevitable. Sheikh Hamood, with his body of Druzes, was in the immediate neighborhood, at Kfer Metta, all ready for an assault. With a large force collected from the neighboring villages, he commenced the attack with great fury, and so continued till, through the intervention of Mr. Thomson with a flag of truce, the besieged consented to a surrender. The Maronite houses of the village, including their convent, had been burned, the people having fled for refuge to the palaces of the emeers. The chief monk of the convent was killed, as was also the Italian monk of the Latin convent, who had been sent to counteract the influence of the Protestant school. One of the two palaces had been captured, and all who were in it slain; the other contained five hundred and seventy-five survivors, who gave themselves up and were escorted by a guard, under the British consul general, to Beirut.

The war in Lebanon extended its influence to Hasbeiya. A regular battle was fought there, and many were slain.

The storm of war, however, soon spent itself, and in July (1845) the missionaries were nearly all again occupying their mountain residences at Abeih, Bhamdoon, Ainab and Bshamōn. At the last place Mr. Laurie, lately from Mosul, had a fine congregation to address every evening. At Ainab, Mr. Lanneau found the people quite ready to listen to the gospel, and at Abeih they had preaching three times every Sabbath to as large congregations as before the war, and the number of Druze hearers had increased. Applications for schools from surrounding villages were frequent.

The vicissitudes of the Lebanon war, which had been so harmless to the persons of the *missionaries*, proved of a very different character to their arch foe at Canobeen. Finding himself impotent in attempting to rule by spiritual power, he grasped after the temporal, and the bubble burst under his grasp. In the former of the late two wars, which his own people accused him of fomenting, so far from gaining any addition to his power, it is said that he even fled from his stronghold in the mountain cliff to some more secret hiding-place lest peradventure he should be found and taken to grace the procession of a Druze triumph. Again, in the second struggle he saw his people scattered and peeled as perhaps they had never been before. His once powerful prince, to whom he had looked to back up his measures, was gone from his country. Turks and Druzes now ruled over his great family. His sons and daughters, setting at naught his paternal counsels, which he had so kindly given them in his repeated *Manshoors*, were running madly after the Bible men, reading the scriptures—which it was not lawful to read except for the priests alone—and, moreover, using their own "private judgment" on what they read, actually *trying to understand* it!

He came to the patriarchal throne in the plenitude of power. The prince of the mountains was a son of his own church. No Christian sect in Lebanon claimed equality with his, either in numbers, wealth, dignity or influence. He doubtless expected that his term of administration would be one of ease and honor. From this high elevation, therefore, his fall was not only fatal to his peace, but also fatal, as it appears, to his life. He did not long survive this last defeat of his people, but died, as did his exiled prince, of a broken heart.

When the bishops came together to make choice of a new patriarch, it would seem that "Satan came also among them." The election was decidedly stormy. Two rival candidates were in the field, presented by the two extremes of the Maronite territory, the Gib-beh and Kesru-án, the north and the south. They met at a midway place, the convent of Meifook, near Gebail. Two ballotings were had, and no choice. Then Bishop Boolus, the Gib-beh candidate (perhaps without the consent of his party), withdrew his name, and Bishop Yoosef was chosen. Upon this the Besherry party rose upon the new patriarch and upon his bishops, beat them and drove them homeward to Kesru-án; then they turned back upon Canobeen itself, entered it and plundered it, and this notwithstanding the French consul was there to guard it.

This violation of the holy capital of the Maronite Church by the hands of her own sons was, if possible, more sacrilegious than that of 1832 by the armed force in search of the martyr Shidiak. The more scrupulous of the family would have revolted at such an act lest the holy father from the vault below, where they had placed him, should awake and hurl upon them his curses for such audacity. But these were the Besherry boys who had before this threatened to rescue Assad from his dungeon, who had dared to refuse water for the patriarch's gardens, laughed at his curses and cursed him in their turn; and now they were determined that if another patriarch of such an "unclean spirit" was to be forced upon them, he should, when he came to his house, find it *empty* at least, if not "swept and garnished."

The Greek patriarch at Damascus was in trouble at this time, not only with the secession of the little flock at Hasbeiya, but also with a powerful antagonistic party at Beirut. The bishop of Beirut had died, and the patriarch came from Damascus to consecrate another. His will was to put into the office one against whom the people had insuperable objections. They believed that he was moved in his choice by large bribes and by the fact that his candidate was a native Greek, while they wanted one of their own countrymen. His overbearing temper, his evident love of gain and his double dealing became so apparent that they could bear him no longer. They almost mobbed him, and in one of their gatherings, among the cries from the multitude was this: "Think not that you are in Hasbeiya now; this is Beirut." He was also advised to take warning from what had happened to the Pope of Rome, who had lately fled to Gaeta. Beirut became too uncomfortable for him, and he was constrained to seek his Damascus home, crossing Lebanon and Antilebanon in mid-winter on horseback, though more than eighty years old, leaving the people behind him quite satisfied to remain without either bishop or patriarch.

It may be remarked in this connection that the papal Greek patriarch, the only one of any note beside the two above mentioned, was subjected to a worrisome controversy with a powerful son of his church who lately left popery for Protestantism. This man was Dr. Michael Meshaka. Meshaka had been at heart an infidel, but had been converted by reading a translation of Keith on the Prophecies. He had come out with all boldness before priests and people to defend the scriptures against all the added perversions and traditions of men. "This," says Mr. Smith, "has brought on a controversy between him and his former patriarch, and, as Meshaka is probably the most intelligent layman in the country and the patriarch the most learned ecclesiastic, attention is directed from all quarters to what is going on between them. The doctor favors me with a copy of all the correspondence between him and his antagonist. It is deeply interesting both from the ability displayed and the deep Christian sincerity that animates him. Every word of the documents in my hand deserves to be translated and printed at home."

The city of Tripoli was occupied as a mission station in 1848 by Messrs. Wilson and Foote. They had the very efficient aid of Mr. Yanni, the American consular agent in the city, and the countenance at least of another young man, a decided, though not very active, Protestant, who had an honorable employment under government. The former was a relative of the late consular agent, Girgis Catziflis, who had some considerable acquaintance with Messrs. Fisk, King, and other early missionaries, and had to some extent adopted their sentiments. He had long been a Protestant in sentiment, and had been for many months in the daily habit of reading the scriptures and of private prayer. He was bold and zealous in declaring the truth to others, and had begun to draw upon himself the usual consequences of such a course. Yet his natural vivacity and excessive occupation in business rendered it doubtful whether the man's chief treasure was really in heaven.

As Tripoli was not considered a healthy residence in summer, the two brethren looked out for a more eligible place on the neighboring mountains. No situation could be more desirable than Eh-heden, if the fanaticism of the people would suffer it. They knew that twenty years before, a Bible man and family had been driven from the village by order of the patriarch, but the patriarch, and, as they thought, the disposition of the people also, had been changed since then, and they concluded to obtain a lodgment there if possible. They took all the advice and procured all the papers of protection that seemed necessary, hired their houses and took their keys. But when they arrived with their families and furniture, they found their houses opened and occupied, and they themselves refused admission. Under orders from the patriarch a mob had assembled, who first attempted to burn the houses and afterward began in earnest to tear them down. The two families camped out for the night in the open air and returned home the next day. The result of this uproar was a fine of seventy dollars upon the obedient sons of the patriarch and an official guaranty from the government for the missionaries to reside in whatever part of the mountains they might choose. The English consul, without the knowledge of the brethren, laid the facts of the case before the British government at home, and Lord Palmerston promptly administered a severe rebuke both to the patriarch and to the emeer for what had been done by their order or connivance.

For years after this the favorite summer residence for the Tripoli brethren was Dooma, about eight hours southeast of their station, where they gained the confidence and good-will of the people, and had schools and religious meetings among them, the latter of which even the priest himself approved and attended. In Tripoli Messrs. Wilson and Foote soon commenced a preaching service, in which they were assisted by young John Wortabet, who then resided as a physician in the city. Antonius Yanni was ever active, always present at the preaching and the Bible class, exhorting all to study the holy Bible, and stirring up the bishop and the priests to preach to the people in the churches. He himself, however, declined from year to year uniting himself with what he believed to be the only pure church in the land; but in June, 1855, when he could resist the voice of conscience no longer, he went to Beirut and publicly united with the mission church. When he returned home he told the family what he had done. They were wild with rage, and assailed him unmercifully with their threats and reproaches. No one should feed him; no one should bring him drink; his wife should leave him and take his two children with her, for it was not a Protestant that she married, but a Greek. The brother, his partner in business, predicted their common ruin, and the mother again and again wished that he and the beast that carried him to Beirut had been overwhelmed by the floods they had to cross, and that he had been swept into the sea. He had brought his whole house under reproach. In regard to *himself* she cared little. "Let him think what he chooses and believe what he chooses," she said, "and go to heaven or hell as he chooses, but let him not disgrace his family by openly forsaking the Greek Church."

The bishop took the matter more coolly. He said to the mother, "For several years your son has given us a great deal of trouble. When by any accident he has come to our church-worship, nothing has pleased him. Our supplications to the saints have been as rumbling thunder in his ears. Our sacred pictures are a staring abomination in his eyes, and the smoke of our holy incense is but a stench in his nostrils. He has omitted no opportunity to sow tares in the minds of our people, and, indeed, the devil in our church would give us less trouble than he. Better that he should be out of the church than in it." Through all these agitating scenes the man was enabled to maintain his self-control and to exhibit a spirit which commanded the respect even of his enemies. He very strenuously recommended the establishing of a mission station at Hums, a large inland village two days north of Damascus, and perhaps chiefly from his strong recommendation of the place Mr. Wilson removed thither in 1855. Previous to this Mr. Foote had departed for America, and Yanni was now left comparatively alone at Tripoli. But the grace of God was sufficient for him, and Dr. Jessup, who, with Mr. Lyons, came the next year, wrote of him saying, "He is a light shining in a dark place; he seems to have been raised up of God for some high and holy purpose, and his conscientious Christian course has been a source of great encouragement to Mr. Lyons and myself in this spiritual wilderness."

When told that the Hums station might have to be given up, Yanni was grieved and said, "Sooner than give up Hums, I would go there myself and preach the gospel four months in the year. Perhaps I could go also three months to Hamah. It would be hard for me to give up my business and leave my family, but I would do it sooner than give up Hums." He was offered the honorable and highly lucrative post of vice consul for Russia, but he promptly refused the offer, simply because it would bring him into too close relations with the Greek Church. Respecting Ishoc, the proud, hard-hearted brother, it is recorded that "his hostility to his brother's religious views grew more and more intense. He joined with the rest of the family in the growing persecution against him, and looked down upon him with cold contempt. But the time came when this proud brother was attacked by a mortal disease. The skill of the physician was baffled. Antonius was assiduous in his attentions to his loved and suffering brother. He spent nearly the whole of one night in the telegraph office, conversing with Dr. Van Dyck, at Beirut, about the case, but all without avail. From the very first the patient seemed convinced that his end was near, and his heart was softened. Every day he called Antonius and begged him to read to him from the Bible. He listened with all the eagerness of a dying man, and his brother explained more fully what he read, talked much with him and prayed with him. At length Ishoc said, 'Now read to me about some *great* sinner who was saved.' Antonius read to him about the publican and about Zaccheus. 'No!' said he; 'about some *greater* sinner than any of *them.*' Then he read to him of the thief on the cross. 'Ah! that comes nearer to my case. Read that again.' Again and again he read it over, and Ishoc seemed encouraged to imitate the thief in laying hold of Christ, and declared his belief in Christ as the only saviour of lost sinners. He then told his mother to take away those *eikonàt* (the sacred pictures) which had been hung all around the head of his bed through the superstitious zeal of his mother and his wife. 'Take them away,' he said, 'it is trifling to trust in pictures. Such a religion will never do to die by.' Turning to his brother he begged him to forgive him for having persecuted him so long, and said, '**Dear** Antonius, you have conquered me with love. You have never spoken an unkind word to me, and nothing but God's grace could have enabled one of your impulsive nature to be so calm and patient.' He begged and entreated his wife and mother to trust in Christ alone. Toward the last a company of priests, with their black flowing robes and swinging censers, came to burn incense and offer their prayers to the Virgin Mary on his behalf. He saw them entering the room and beckoned them all to stop, telling them and all the family that he had done for ever with such things, and could not allow anything now to come between him and his Saviour. They were astonished at the change wrought in him, but he called his brother and said, 'Bring the Bible and read to them, that these priests also may be profited.'

"Just before he died he called his whole family around his bed and spoke to them in a clear voice about his trust in Jesus as his Saviour, and raising both hands he called out loudly, '*None but Christ,*' and died."

The Rev. Samuel Jessup, writing of Antonius Yanni, May 11, 1869, says, "He always and everywhere *uses* his religion. I went with him to see his property at Ah-ba one day last summer, and as we were riding among the fig trees I noticed some on one side of the road with a ring of red mud around them. On inquiry, I learned that on the feast day of St. John the people thus paint all their fig trees, saying that St. John will then make them fruitful. Mr. Yanni forbade the workmen painting *his* trees. The workmen obeyed him, but assured him that he would have no fruit. Indeed, he expected none, because it was not the fruitful year; but there we saw before us *his* trees to be the only trees in the region that were bearing well. Those painted in honor of St. John *had no fruit* on them.

"A little farther on we passed under a beautiful little olive tree, and Mr. Yanni said to me, 'Do you see *your* tree?' 'What do you mean?' said I. 'Why, that beautiful tree is *consecrated* to you and your successors.' 'How so?' said I. 'Well, I will tell you. When I bought it last year, my farmer told me that for five or six years the tree had not borne an olive, and it was not worth the ground it stood on, and urged me to cut it down and plant another in its place. But I told him to dig about it and dung it another year, and if it did not do well, then I would cut it down, and if it bore well, then it should be henceforth dedicated to the missionaries in Tripoli, and now you see how God has blessed it for you.' In fact there was not another tree around us so loaded with olives, and my jars, from which I am eating every day, have been filled with its delicious fruit.

"Mr. Yanni spends considerable time at this place, and sometimes comes out to the village on Sundays. He has produced a very decided reform in the mode of keeping the Sabbath in the village, although all the inhabitants are Maronites. He always has prayers every night with his men, and they have become so, at length, that they do not like to have anything occur to keep them from the service. One old man, however, has given him a good deal of trouble on the score of Sabbath-breaking, and seems utterly incorrigible. He is very penurious, and owns a great many goats, upon which he quite sets his heart. One Sunday Mr. Yanni saw him mending his plough, and after arguing the matter with him, said, 'You try to cheat the Lord out of the time that belongs to him. This is *his* day, not yours. But you will gain nothing in the end. I should not wonder if a wolf should come and kill one of your goats this very night. The old man dismissed the matter, saying he was too old to learn. Sure enough, the next morning his shepherd brought him a dead goat from his flock and told him that a wolf had killed it only a few hours before, and that perhaps Mr. Yanni would buy a piece of the meat. The old man was not more struck with the circumstance than was Mr. Yanni himself. Some time afterward the man lost another goat, and Yanni said to him, 'Ah, you have been working again on the Sabbath, contrary to your promise.' He confessed that it was so, but said he could not learn easily.

"Mr. Yanni was building a house at Ah-ba, and had burned a lime-kiln. The lime was just ready to be removed from the kiln on a Saturday night when, from every appearance, there was a heavy storm preparing. Men could not be had to secure the lime immediately, as they were all busy about their own work, but they said to him, if the storm held off, they would come early in the morning and make a bee, and get all the lime in before it should rain. 'No! never! never!' said he. 'If I lose *all my property*, I will not work on Sunday.

The Lord says, "Them that honor me I will honor," and if the Lord spoils my lime I shall not have spoiled my conscience, and I know he will make it up to me in some way.' Then he rebuked them severely for thus tempting him after all that he had taught them. So he prayed in secret that the Lord would get honor to himself among that simple-minded people. 'I trembled,' said he, 'all the forenoon as I saw the storm thickening. But I knew I was right, and when the men came begging me to let them go to work, I detained them by reading the Bible to them. The storm came all around with great fury—thunder and hail and wind and torrents of rain. The little dry bed of a stream near by the lime-kiln became a roaring river in a few moments, but *not a drop of water fell on that kiln,* nor within an eighth of a mile of it. All around, the country was deluged with rain, but that little village got only a few scattering hail-stones.' The people were amazed, and from that time they have held Mr. Yanni in a sort of superstitious regard.

"These items," Mr. Jessup testifies, "*are all literally true.* What I have not myself seen I have heard from the mouths of many witnesses, and from some who would rather they had not been true."

Another prominent witness for the truth appeared in Tripoli in 1858, whose history is thus given by Mr. Lyons: "Abdallah Zeidân was originally of the Greek sect. Several years ago he was a merchant in Aleppo. Having failed in business from the dishonesty of his debtors, he invoked the aid of the saints, and particularly of the Virgin Mary, relying on their assistance. One man who owed him five thousand piasters having fled to Alexandria, Abdallah followed him. Meeting him in the street, he demanded that he should pay the debt or else make oath in the church before the picture of the Holy Virgin that he owed him nothing. The man chose the latter. The parties appeared together, and the unscrupulous debtor took a solemn oath before the picture that he owed Abdallah nothing. Horrified at the man's falsehood and perjury, and strong in his belief in the power of the Virgin, Abdallah seized hold upon her picture and shaking it with great violence implored her earnestly to interpose in his behalf. He expected to see the man fall down dead before leaving the house. But how great was his mortification and surprise, after all his prayers and imprecations, to see the perjured man walk safely and unharmed from the church into the street. From that moment his faith in the Virgin was shaken." At Beirut, on his return from Egypt, he was attracted by the sight of our Protestant book depository, and there found a book on popery and on the worship of pictures and saints. He begged the book as a gift and took it home. By comparing its teachings with those of the scriptures he was gradually led to understand and receive the truth. He afterward removed his family to Hums, where he was twice imprisoned by the bishop for his Protestantism. He then removed to Tripoli. In the spring of 1858 he applied for admission to the Protestant Church, where, after some months' delay, he was received.

Another notable member of the church at Tripoli is Ishoc (Isaac) el Kefroony, from a Greek village twelve miles north-east of Tripoli, called Sheikh Mohammed. Mr. S. Jessup says of him, "About nine years ago he heard the gospel and became convinced of the truth and declared himself a Protestant. From that day to this he has been the subject of bitter persecution." The Muslim beg chose him for his secretary, rejecting the applications of a large number of wealthy and influential Greek, Maronite and Muslim applicants, "because," said he, "you are the only man in all this region whom I can fully trust." The beg tells others that Ishoc's scrupulous honesty far surpasses anything he had ever heard of. Once his enemies went in the night and destroyed fifty dollars' worth of his property. The beg was very angry about it, and offered to destroy all that those men possessed. But Ishoc would not consent, saying, "I have learned not to render evil for evil." Ishoc was for years quite alone, but of late others have come out and stand by his side.

Safeeta,* an out station of Tripoli, nearly thirty miles from it north-eastward, is a large village inhabited by Greek Arabs and Nusairiyeh.* At first the come-outers were chiefly inclined by worldly motives to seek relationship with Protestants, and since then they have experienced a series of instructions and persecutions very similar to those of their brethren of Mt. Hermon. They were visited in 1865 by Dr. Post, then stationed at Tripoli, who found them gathered together again after having been dispersed like sheep by devouring wolves. The doctor says, "The family of tax-gatherers previously alluded to used all means of fraud and bribery to induce the Muslim governor to oppress them and steal their property, that they might be forced by starvation back to their old religion. Turkish soldiers were sent to the houses and ordered to break all that could be broken and to eat all that could be eaten, to beat the men and abuse the women.

* See Illustration on page 333.

"These cruel orders were so effectually carried out that the people were driven from the village, and in many of the houses all that they had laid by in store as provision for winter was stolen from them. Even the wheat on the threshing-floors was taken and the straw set on fire by these ruthless barbarians."

In October of the next year the same visitor reports, saying, "The Protestants are enjoying a rest after their severe distresses, and an abundant harvest has supplied their present wants. The young men, Hanna and Yoosef, who came from Safeeta to Abeih Seminary, as well as the two girls who studied in the girls' school in Beirut, have filled the minds of the youth here of both sexes with an ardent desire for knowledge.

"But again the tidings of evil came, that on January 22, 1867, the whole Protestant community of Safeeta were arrested—men, women and children—and thrust into prison in a small room, and a fire of cut straw was made on the floor to torment them with the smoke, but they were finally released by the influence of some whose hearts relented. On one evening they assembled for worship with Yoosef, the native preacher, and while there the government horsemen attacked the whole community, broke open their houses and plundered them, and dispersed all of their number without exception—old and young, mothers and children, boys and girls—into the wilderness, and this in the night-time.

"They despatched a messenger to Tripoli and Beirut for aid, and efforts were at once made to secure better treatment for these oppressed people. These efforts were finally successful, and the brethren at Tripoli were rejoicing in hope that now at last that suffering flock of the Lord might enjoy a permanent peace."

To the evidence already adduced, showing the power of the gospel in this northern part of Syria, may be added some facts in the colporteur's experience. One of these self-denying and useful helpers in the dissemination of the gospel, whose name was Ishoc esh Shemaa, after visiting various other places, came to the village of Sheikh Mohammed, where resided his namesake Ishoc el Kefroony, of whom he speaks thus:

"He is always ready to receive every brother who arrives at that place. He seems much advanced in spiritual knowledge. We spent our evenings in prayer and praise. Multitudes of the villagers assembled with us desiring to hear of the salvation of the gospel, and they seemed to rejoice in it. I rejoiced, too, to teach them the way of life, and I trust our meetings were blessed. Several persons, however, in the village opposed us, and broke into the house of one of the Protestants, beat him and robbed him, and took away his wife. Then one of the priests raised the cry, 'Whoever loves God let him collect wood to burn the house where this preacher is, and destroy these gospel men and their leader with them.' That was a fearful night. The whole Greek part of the village gathered in a mob with weapons, wood and firebrands, to come down the hill to Ishoc's house and destroy it. Ishoc himself was then not at home. But see how God protects his people! Across the little valley is a part of the same village, inhabited by Muslims, who are friends of our brother. A child, moved by some influence *not ours*, carried them word that the Christian people of the village were coming down toward the valley to burn Ishoc's house. In one moment all the Muslim agas and their men armed themselves, crossed the valley and stood before the house. The mob, as they came down, called out, 'Who's there?' The answer was, '*We* are here, and if you do anything to the owner of this house we'll burn *your* houses and *leave not one of you alive.*' When they heard this they fled, leaving us in peace. Had not these Muslims come to us the house would most certainly have been burned, and we who were in it might have been all killed. When Ishoe returned and heard what had happened he smiled and said, 'Not a hair of our heads shall fall to the ground without our Father.' After this the brother whose house was plundered went down to Tripoli and brought an order from the government to have the case tried and one of the Protestants to be in the court to try it. This so alarmed the Greeks that they immediately restored to him his wife and all his stolen property, and begged the man's pardon. Thus does God take care for his children.

"We went to Beit Millat to find an elderly man, a brother in Christ, named Hanna el Khoori. We reached the village very late, and nobody would tell us where he lived, for he was greatly persecuted. But providentially, as we were passing a certain house we heard some one reading aloud, and thought this must be the place. So we entered, and he rose to receive us, saying, 'You are very welcome.' And in this way our conversation commenced. I said to him, 'I thank Jesus Christ, my brother, who has given you this book.' He burst into tears and fell on my neck, saying, 'I am a poor sinful man; I am not worthy to be named in the same breath with the name of Christ.' And then he wept again, and I wept, and the brother who was with me wept. Then we began to rejoice together in the Lord, who had saved us with his own blood and granted us everlasting comfort and joy. Oh what a blessed, happy night was that!

"Hanna told us of all his trials and persecutions—how he had been excommunicated from the Maronite Church, and how priests had come from Tripoli to bring him back to them. But they could not convince him; and when he told me his answers to them, I was amazed at his knowledge of the scriptures. Then a company of the people assembled with us, and we spent eight hours that night in reading the scriptures and prayer. This brother, Hanna, was once president of the Papal Brotherhood, a society among the Maronites, and now he is so poor that he had no food to set before us. When he had learned the truth of the gospel he was put out of office and another man was chosen president in his place, and he, too, has followed Hanna in embracing the gospel, and nearly twelve men in their connection have been similarly enlightened. Hanna is indeed very poor, but he said, 'I am ready to die for the gospel; I must attend first of all to my soul's salvation.' Oh how my heart rejoiced at what I saw in the house of this brother of Beit Millat!

"I went to Meshta, where the people all know me, and they were greatly enraged when I spoke to them of the gospel. My grandfather and father were both very wicked men, and had often shed human blood. My father was a strolling singer and player on stringed instruments, and he used to bring me to Meshta from Hums when I was a lad to sing with him. So the people remembered me, and in the evening they crowded together and insulted me and threatened my life. One of the priests said, 'Far better rob and kill and stroll about, as did your father, than carry about those books and come to preach to us.' I assured them my father repented and died in the gospel faith, but this made them more angry still. I found I could not stay in Meshta, so I hastened next day to go to Kefroon, but in a forest, on the way to that place, a ruffian from Meshta, whom I had seen the night before, sprang upon me from the bushes and knocked me to the ground with a club. He then knocked down also my companion, a young man from Safeeta. I sprang up and ran, but he pursued me and bruised my shoulder and back with his club until I entered Kefroon, but as no one would allow us to stay there, I had to return to Safeeta. A man in Kefroon so far befriended me as to procure an armed man to go with me and save me from further violence. Yet in all this I rejoiced that I was counted worthy to suffer persecution for the cross of Christ."

A man from the village of Mahardee came from time to time to buy Bibles at Hums to sell again. The village is north of Hamath, contains four thousand inhabitants, wild and uninstructed. The only Protestant in it was a sheikh, who, for want of the cash or for some other reason, gave his *sword* for a Bible. In that half-civilized region, where most men wear arms and where he himself had found use for his sword in self-defence, he had chosen to give up his weapon of steel and trust to the sword of the Spirit. This sword of the sheikh was brought to the missionary at Hums and by him sent as a trophy to the American Bible Society. We may expect to hear something more hereafter from that village, Mahardee.

CHAPTER XIX.

Sidon—Messrs. Thomson and Van Dyck, laborers, with helpers, Tannoos el Haddad and Eleeas Fuaz—Sabbath services—The hearers are laid under ban—A Jesuit preacher—Meetings in Lady Stanhope's Joon—Petitions from Deir el Kommer—Church of seven members organized—Calls from Birteh, Kana, Alma, Rasheiya—Cruelty of the governor of Tyre—Deir el Kommer—Ain Zehalta out-station—Druzes attack Deir el Kommer June 1, 1860, and on the 22d utterly destroy it—Letter of Mrs. Bird—Wholesale butchery—A few saved by the missionary—Attack and massacre at Hasbeiya—Destruction of the city of Zahleh—Rush of people, wounded and impoverished, to Beirut—Task of feeding them—The part performed by the Americans—The mission transferred to the Presbyterian Board—Its present state—Letter of Mr. Dodge.

SIDON began to be occupied as a regular mission station by Messrs. Thomson and Van Dyck in 1855. They were accompanied by the two native preachers, Tannoos el Haddad and Eleeas Fuaz. Their way had been prepared to some extent by the residence here of Bishop Yacob Aga, and more especially by the zealous, though brief, labors of Priest Wortabet, with whom Tannoos himself had sometimes been associated. They commenced with two services on the Sabbath, with an average attendance of thirty or more hearers, though sometimes the number amounted to fifty or sixty.

Their chapel was repeatedly placed under the ban of the priests, spies were stationed within and without it, yet a goodly number of hearers would always attend. The enemy, in self-defence, suddenly introduced the novelty of preaching themselves. A capuchin friar was imported for that object from Beirut. Some said the friar was now attempting something beyond his reach; others said he was an eloquent preacher, only they *couldn't understand his Arabic*. The Greek Catholic bishop, who spent part of his time in the city, and sometimes preached about the Virgin or about the Protestants, could not satisfy his people. They demanded preaching about the gospel. In a time of great drought the Maronites not only joined the other sects in having prayers for rain, but got up a splendid procession through the streets, carrying on high a cross and a picture of the Virgin. The bishop refused to do this, saying, "We should only make ourselves a laughing-stock to the Protestants." Six men had been publicly recognized by the government as Protestants, and had paid their taxes as such. All but one of these had been subject to special persecution. Schools, visits, Bible reading, etc., were all employed to draw the attention of the people to the great subject of salvation, and not without effect. Religious discussions were rife in every direction.* Religious truth was spreading in the neighboring villages. In Joon itself, the village of the celebrated Lady Stan-

---

* Sidon is now (1872) a prosperous station of the Syria mission, and is occupied by Rev. Messrs. Eddy and Dennis. The view which we give is taken from a point south of the city, looking across a little bay which curves inward almost to a complete semi-circle just south of the seaside gate. Although much of the city is not visible from this direction, yet that which is seen is the quarter occupied by the missionaries and the scene of the mission operations in the city. Near to the mark over the large building on the left is the home of Mr. Eddy, while the highest building on the right, under the other mark, is that of the girls' boarding-school. The church-building and boys' school are not in sight, being hidden behind the buildings in the foreground. In the female boarding-school are about twenty scholars, who are trained here for future usefulness.

MODERN SIDON, SYRIA.

hope, a zealous Sidonian had obtained a residence, and his house was constantly visited by inquirers. They had regular meetings every evening for the study of the scriptures. Could her late ladyship have lived to see that fearful "rage of Bibles" spreading till it had reached her very doors, her hope of ever seeing her friend Barker again must have been faint indeed.

A brother of this same zealous Protestant at Joon was exerting the same kind of influence in the large village of Birteh, directly east of Sidon, on the mountains. A number of families there had combined together and declared themselves Protestants. Tyre and the mountains above it were in great need of a separate laborer. In Kana (given by Joshua to the tribe of Asher, Josh. xix. 28) there had been a decided movement among the most respectable part of the people. The same was true of Alma, higher up in the mountains of Antilebanon.

This general and increasing attention to the new doctrines was seen by the priests to endanger their interests, and they combined in a united onset upon the new followers of the gospel. Many of course were sifted out as chaff from the wheat, but more or less of the good seed was left. At Sidon particularly the number of new persons that continued to come filled up the place of those that left.

Repeated applications were made by some of the most respectable men from Deir el Kommer for schools and a laborer at that place. They were reminded of the treatment received there by our brethren, Smith, Wolcott and Van Dyck, a few years ago, but they said, "We are not such fools now as we were at that time. We have learned something since then both in regard to our hierarchy and in regard to yourselves." In a short time a Prot estant Church was organized in Sidon consisting of seven members, which was soon increased by others from the city itself and from neighboring villages.

The people of Kana sent out a deputation with a petition signed by twenty-six persons asking for a preacher and a school. Dawhir Abbood, who was immediately called from Kheiam, when he went and saw their earnestness, was greatly delighted. Mr. Eddy visited Kana and found all but one of the twenty-six petitioners still in the same mind and profiting by the instructions of Abbood. About forty assembled for worship and instruction. From Kana he proceeded to Alma. The people here had been assailed by persecution in vain. At this time Satan was using another mode of trial—that of internal division. Mr. Eddy spent three days with them, and succeeded in restoring harmony between the parties. After this, in company with his father, who was on a visit to Syria, Mr. Eddy made a visit to Alma, and on the Sabbath administered the Lord's Supper and baptized two children. The meetings were attended by from fifty to seventy persons.

At Kana the bishop and some of the most wealthy men of Tyre came out together, and had a formal meeting with the Protestants to seek to influence them, but all in vain. Next came the prior of the convents and tried his skill, and the effect of all this effort was that two more of the papists came out and added their names to the list of Protestants. The number soon increased to forty, who were considered earnest and hopeful inquirers. The priests were exasperated. The French consul was appealed to, and the pasha was induced to grant leave to the good Catholics of the village to punish their heretical neighbors in any way they chose. So beating, fining with false claims for debts, etc., were duly practiced, yet the Protestant numbers continued to increase. The wrath of man praised the Lord. The same was true of the people of the village of Elecas Yacob, Rasheiyet el Fakhár. But the Kana Protestants, perhaps because they were nearer the rod of the oppressor, were pursued with a malignity surpassing all others. Several of the women had been unmercifully beaten. One woman had twice had her food poisoned by her Catholic cook. One mother was assailed so furiously that her child was dashed from her arms and killed; another was herself nearly killed. The men, after paying their taxes for the year, were called upon to pay them a second time. The head man of the village called on the governor of Tyre, showed him his receipt, with the governor's own signature, acknowledging his payment of all government dues for the year, but this only seemed to enrage the tyrant, who ordered him to be beaten and put in prison. The other Protestants were sent for, but only two could be found. These were brought and immediately put under the bastinado and then into prison. They had been beaten in the most merciless manner with the staff upon their feet, and besides that, had been kicked and trampled on to make them lie still. Two of them were beaten again in the morning, and then all were let go. They laid a complaint against the governor before the notorious Kurschid Pasha (nicknamed *cursed pasha*) at Beirut, and after a pretended examination into their case and after a detention of two months, all the while out of business, they received an award of twenty or thirty dollars, from which, however, they must pay their two months' board and the surgeon's fee for attending to the healing of their wounds. Mix Pope and Turk together after this sort, and we see what kind of civil government comes out of the compound.

Deir el Kommer.—After the occupation of this city and capital of Lebanon for a short time by three or four of our missionaries in 1841, it was left vacant for some years, but in the latter part of 1855 it was again occupied, with the view of making it a permanent station, by the Rev. William Bird, son of the author, who, with his wife and Miss Cheney, had joined the mission two years before. He was accustomed to have a Bible-class in the morning of every Sabbath, and regularly a preaching exercise in the afternoon to about twenty-five persons. He saw much of the people in private interviews, and found them very accessible in conversation. But the schools were the most prosperous department of the station. In about a year the number of schools was seven and the pupils two hundred. Four schools, one of them for girls, were in the city itself. An examination of the three boys' schools was publicly appointed for a certain day. A friend offered a large room in his house for the occasion. The day was rainy, but there was an attendance of a hundred and fifty spectators, among whom was the Turkish governor of the mountains. The exercises passed off well and gave great satisfaction. The female school commenced with twelve pupils, but in less than six months had over fifty, and required a second teacher. When the missionary arrived there was not more than a half dozen Christian females who could read; in 1857 half of these fifty scholars were good readers.

"Fifteen years ago," wrote the missionary, "a man of my calling could hardly be permitted to buy his necessary food in the market, and when he finally left the place he was followed with stones and curses; now the same kind of man is welcomed and honored. Then fear kept many even of his friends from calling on him; now even the priests return his calls, and the bishop himself has done it. The old Emeer Besheer, once leagued with the patriarch in persecution, is passed away, and his ruined palace is used as barracks for soldiers. His second prime minister, who did much against Protestantism, and whose mansion was a stronghold of the enemy, is no more, and what remains of the habitation of this Ahithophel is now the abode of the missionary, and furnishes apartments for scripture schools and a Protestant chapel. His sons-in-law were leaders in the movement which brought us hither, and are among our firmest friends. His grandchildren learn the folly of popery within his own walls. Time was when every one trembled at the anathema of the clergy; now the latter dare not show their weakness by uttering such an announcement."

At the near out-station of Ain Zehalta there was a small Protestant community, and five persons were church members. Khaleel, a native helper, held regular religious services with them, and with an audience larger than that at the capital.

Such was the state of the mission-work in Deir el Kommer, and such its prospects, when there came on the desolating and barbarous war of 1860, which swept that city, for the time, out of existence. The indications of war had been many for a number of months, both Maronites and Druzes giving out mutual threats and mutually committing murders. On the 25th of May, the Druzes of Bshamōn sent down a small party to escort to the mountains some of their own men, who were occupied in their silkworks on the plain. One of these men was murdered by the Maronites, and two others wounded. About the same time twenty Maronites from Deir el Kommer set out for their homes from Beirut, and hearing evil tidings turned back for fear. One of these, however, being in the employ of the governor, joined himself to a troop of Turkish soldiers going toward the Deir, supposing that a servant of the governor would be as safe as his soldiers; but he was, notwithstanding, recognized by Druzes on the way, and boldly shot, the Turkish soldiers apparently conniving at the deed. Such a murder immediately before the eyes of a Turkish guard naturally excited in the city the most violent resentment. The cry through the streets was loud for vengeance. The reports of musket shots were heard in different directions, and it was not known but that each of these discharges killed a Druze. But the elders and the more cool among the people succeeded in quieting the tumult, one Druze only having been killed and only a few others wounded.

At this time, in the Kesru-ân district, a Christian army of some thousands was already collected, and was advancing to annihilate the Druzes, as they said, or drive them from the mountains. They commenced their work about the 27th of May, at Beit Miri, burning all the houses of the Druzes and driving their owners away. This village being situated on a high and conspicuous elevation, the fire was seen that night far and wide, and served as a war signal to the whole of Lebanon. Fire and sword at once began their work of desolation, and did not cease till all the important villages in Southern Lebanon were, either by flight or by the sword, emptied of their Christian inhabitants.

For two days the mountains were covered with smoke,

the smoke of consuming villages, extending from the northern boundary of the Druze region to the villages south of Sidon. In these two days also the imposing army of Maronites from the north was met by the furious Druzes and scattered to the winds. There remained within the Druze limits but three villages from which they could apprehend any further annoyance, namely, Deir el Kommer, Hasbeiya and Zahleh. These, according to the programme, came next to be destroyed.

Operations against the Deir were commenced on the 1st of June. It so happened that at this eventful moment our missionary was away from home. Quieted by the peaceful assurances of the Druzes and of the Turkish garrison, and fearing for the safety of the little community at Ain Zehalta, Mr. Bird had gone to see if their village had shared the common ruin. We are furnished with a graphic account of the situation of the mission family in these times from the pen of his wife in a letter to her friends in America. On the morning of May 31 she writes:

"The whole Deir is enveloped in a cloud of smoke. Exactly where it comes from we cannot tell, for we can see nothing at a distance, but we were told yesterday that villages were burning in every direction. We have many fears for Ain Zehalta, our out-station. Two of our church members from that village are staying with us, Khaleel, our native helper, and Assad his brother. For aught they know their houses are burned, and they made penniless and their wives and children homeless. There seems less probability that the Druzes will dare to attack this place.

"June 1.—Mr. Bird has gone to Ain Zehalta with a guard of soldiers from the governor. The object is to find out the state of the poor Protestants there and to see if he can do anything for them. As to ourselves, we have of course been and are still in danger, but not like the native people. Both parties here are friendly to Franks and would not harm us intentionally, but there is no knowing what a party of enraged Druzes would do in a fight. The people of the place all tell us they will do their utmost to defend us. Whenever there is an alarm, women and children flock to us for refuge. Last night five families, beside single persons, slept on our premises. We have thousands and thousands of piasters belonging to the people concealed in our house, and a great amount of valuables of all kinds. We have many opportunities of doing good by showing kindness to the distressed. The people call down blessings upon Mr. Bird as he passes through the streets. The 'old men' (sheikhs) have invited him to attend several of their deliberations, and when he enters the room they all rise to receive him. Twenty years ago missionaries were stoned out of the town. But hark! I hear firing. Yes, the whole place is full of excitement."

"Ten days after writing the above I once more, at my first leisure hour, open my portfolio. God be praised, we are all safe. The firing we heard was no false alarm. In an hour after I had put up my pen, which I had been using all unconscious of danger, the Druzes were upon us and the battle had commenced in earnest. It lasted about six hours, at the end of which time the victorious enemy had set nearly every house in our part of the town on fire. I will not attempt to describe my feelings in being alone amid such horrors. The firing was dreadful, the bullets whizzing and screaming over our heads, rattling down into the court, and even entering the house. One of our teachers, while standing near a window, received a ball through the fleshy part of his shoulder. We barricaded our most exposed windows, stoned up the outside gate, and gave the strictest orders to all that not a single gun should be fired from the premises. Then we dressed up three men in Mr. Bird's old clothes and distributed them about the house to show that it was inhabited by foreigners. Then we shut ourselves within doors, and I tried to look to the Lord for deliverance. He sustained me wonderfully, and I did not once lose my self-control. There was one anxious moment, I assure you, when we saw one of the Druzes jump upon our study roof. We knew not then but *our* turn had come. But Khaleel, our good native helper from Ain Zebalta, opened the parlor door and cried out to him that it was an English house, and asked if he did not see the flag. The Druze bowed politely and said we should not be harmed. Oh what a moment of relief it was when we saw him retire! Shall I ever forget it?

"Our men, who were all armed, then stacked their guns and said, 'Now we are safe.' But the Druzes were still as thick as bees all around us, and it required our utmost efforts to keep them off, as they came from different directions. They entered a house opposite ours and set it on fire, after regaling themselves with a supper that was cooking on the fire. Our boys' school-house, next house to ours, was nearly all burned, and the teachers, who lived in it, lost nearly all they possessed.

"It was a fearful evening. I cannot with my poor eyes and hasty pen give you any idea of it. And then to have Mr. Bird away! I feared for him lest his alarm for *us* would make him push on to reach his home even in the face of the bullets. You can imagine how he must have felt as he came in view of the town, and looked in vain for his loved home amid the curling flames and clouds of smoke. He stayed with the soldiers that night at Bteddeen, and reached us at early dawn in the morning.

"As soon as he returned some of the men of the place wished him to go to Besheer Beg, chief of the Druzes of this district, with a flag of truce and ask for peace. So we fastened a white handkerchief to a cane and he started off, with one of our Frank-dressed Arabs for an attendant. They found the beg about a mile distant, sitting under a tree and surrounded by his bands of armed men. He made many fair promises, but the sequel showed how little we could rely on them.

"About an hour after this interview the Druzes poured down upon us once more, all ready for battle if resistance should be offered, but the people were destitute of ammunition and food, and not a gun was fired. The Druze men were followed by troops of women, and together they went from house to house, plundering and carrying off on their backs beds, mats, divans, indeed everything they could lay their hands on that was portable. This plunder-work was carried on for two days.

"The number of Christians killed and wounded on the day of the battle was about eighty, and of the Druzes double that number. Four hundred houses were burned.

"The anxious and care-burdened days we have passed since the attack, I cannot describe to you. When the people found that the Druzes did not touch *us*, they came in upon us with a rush, bringing goods and chattels also till there was no room to receive them. For a number of days we had seven entire families, beside enough others to make up a hundred persons. Since then the number has been reduced to thirty. Even the aged bishop took refuge with us for two nights and a day, bringing with him, for safe keeping, his *golden mitre;* and the French Jesuit, who has been zealously teaching the people here that it was a mortal sin to come to our house, sent a note requesting permission to come himself."

The Turkish garrison, placed in the town for its defence, did nothing to prevent or interrupt the mutual slaughter. To them it was evidently as the entertainment of a Spanish bull-fight. They did indeed send orders to stop the incendiarism, but permitted the work of *plunder* to go on. The main suffering fell upon the suburbs of the city, the population of which, being purposely hemmed in by watchful Druzes close around them, were crowded to the centre, where the houses remained mostly unharmed. Here they were kept under guard as prisoners of war.

Two weeks after this bloody struggle the mission family were in part removed from these scenes to the neighboring station of Abeih, and they were followed by the missionary himself two days after. One of these two days being the Sabbath, Khaleel preached to an assembly of fifty persons, to some of whom this was their first as well as last sermon. On Thursday of that week, death came upon the people like a sweeping tornado. "Every remaining house was broken into, and every man and boy that could be found was struck down and slaughtered with the knife or the hatchet. The few that escaped were but a small fractional part of the whole. The rank or the age of the victim made no difference. The murderers entered the governor's palace and hewed down by scores, if not by hundreds, those who had fled thither for safety. Blood is said to have run from the drain of the great court like water in a time of rain. 'Cursed be their anger, for it was fierce, and their wrath, for it was cruel.' The whole city has been blotted out from the face of the earth, and we are stationless, homeless and heart-broken." These are the words of the missionary, and he proceeds: "On the 22d, the day after the butchery, I went over and saw on my way crowds of widows and orphans, and mingled my tears with theirs as I passed them. Many of the poor children had been my scholars, and some of them members of my Bible-class. I have no words to express my horror and indignation at the sight of their misery.

"So far as we personally are concerned, we cannot complain. I was treated with the utmost respect by the chieftains and all. Our house and goods had not been touched. Those whom we left in charge at our departure and those who had fled to the house for refuge had not been molested, though all seemed in imminent danger. The chiefs gave me an escort to guard me and those with me on my way back Abeih, and thus it came to pass that the whole company of fifty were brought in safety from the impending slaughter." More than half of them were men and lads, who would most certainly have been massacred had they not come under the shelter of this Protestant wing.

Simultaneously with the first attack on Deir el Kommer and its surrender, the same process, as if by fixed arrangement, was going on at our other exposed station, Hasbeiya, where Druzes were the chief rulers. For two days the Christians defended bravely their houses and families, but on the third they were persuaded by Othman Beg, the commander of the Turkish garrison, to take refuge with him in the castle, with the most solemn assurances of his efficient safeguard. Sitt Na-eefeh, a sister of Said Beg Jimblaut, of Mokhtâra, at the same time invited the Protestants to come under her keeping. Her invitation was accepted by Khaleel el Khoori, Kosta Majdelani, the schoolmaster, and some others, after they had once entered the castle, but Shaheen Barakât (Aboo Mansoor), Nicola Haslab and some others of the Protestants who had entered the castle remained, trusting to the promises and oaths of the beg. Here he kept them many days on short rations, all the while maintaining an ominous silence as to what he intended to do with them, until a large force of Druzes arrived from the Hooran. This event was the signal for something new. In a day or two the voices of the Druzes around the castle door were heard chanting their war song. Every article belonging to the garrison was at the same time removed from the lower court, the men were all ordered to assemble below and the women and children above. Armed soldiers were placed at the stairs that no one should reascend them. When all was ready the outer door was thrown wide open, and what followed is too horrid to be described. It was a pack of famished wolves leaping into the sheepfold. The slaughter was complete. If two or three women were killed by random bullets, or two or three men, by leaping through a window or feigning themselves dead, were saved from the jaws of the lions, they were accidental exceptions.

"Just before the slaughter Aboo Mansoor, one of the leading Protestants, a man of faith and prayer, seeing the preparations going on, and that there was no hope of escape, called out in a loud voice to the assembly, composed of a few Protestants and multitudes of the Greeks and Maronites: 'My dear brethren, time is short. The Druzes are about to be let in upon us, and we are all going like sheep to the slaughter. We shall soon leave this world and stand before God. In whom will you trust? There is no Saviour but Jesus Christ. Look to him, call upon him, trust in him, and he will save. Repent and believe, and he will not cast you off. Let every one call on the name of the Lord Jesus, the Saviour.' Great numbers of them then called out with him to Jesus Christ to save their souls. Aboo Mansoor and others of the Protestants continued in prayer, and he, while in this act, was slain by the Druzes and literally hewn to pieces."

Some remarkable incidents in this bloody tragedy are contained in the French Roman Catholic periodical, "*La Revue des Deux Mondes.*" The source from which the account is here copied, aside from its inherent interest, will justify its insertion in this place.

"The population of Hasbeiya," says the writer, "was composed of a number of Muslim emeers of the house of Shehab, some thousands of orthodox Greeks, a great number of Maronites and a community of Protestants, cruelly persecuted by all the other sects. Notwithstanding the ill treatment, however, of the Protestants, they at the moment of danger made common cause with the emeers and their other fellow-citizens for the defence of their country.

"The aged Barakât (Shaheen, Aboo Mansoor), beloved and venerated throughout the mountains on account of his piety, chose to march to the combat (notwithstanding his age of seventy years), and to fight by the side of his son Mansoor. It was this Mansoor who, freeing a passage for himself through the ranks of the Druzes, seized the standard of the enemy, cut off the head of him that bore it, and waving the flag on high, returned with it as a trophy to his friends.

"The Christians were finally induced to give themselves up to the protection of Othman Beg. This man, having disarmed them, kept them ten days in the castle dying with hunger. The Druzes at last came and said that their chiefs demanded the heads of their emeers and the heads of a certain number of Christians, whose names they gave; with this they would be satisfied. . . . Then commenced a scene of carnage the horror of which no pen can portray. One thousand and fifty disarmed men, Christians and Mohammedan emeers, were slaughtered one after another, proscribed and unproscribed, all alike. The Turks took no active part in the butchery, but contented themselves with simply *maintaining order*.

"One of the first victims was George, the civil head of the Greek community.* The civil head of the Protestants was more fortunate. Passing through the midst of the living and the dead, he made his way to a small back room already filled with emeers and Christians, some of them bleeding and dying. Hastily throwing off his clothes, he besmeared himself with blood and stretched himself on the floor as one that had been killed and despoiled. The Druzes approached and slew upon him three or four others, whose dead bodies served still

---

* This man was called Girgis er Rey-is. He was in the service of the governor, the Emeer Saad ed Deen, and though professedly a Greek, he was nevertheless a strict keeper of the Sabbath, and from being a persecutor had become a staunch friend of the Protestants, by whom also he was held in the highest esteem.

HASBEIYA, ITS LOWER PORTION.
C. Castle where the massacre of the Christians took place in 1860.

more effectually to conceal him. The night came on. He rose and dressed himself with a bloody chemise and with a pair of wide Arab trowsers which had been left on one of the bodies, and having made a hole in the wall, he crept into an adjoining chamber where there was an opening through which he escaped into the garden and into the street, and so finally, amid many additional dangers, to the palace of the Sitt."

The enormities of this crusade of Turks and Druzes against Christians gave fury to the sympathetic fanaticism of the Mohammedans of Damascus, resulting in the sudden and utter destruction of the whole Christian quarter of that great city. Frank houses, convents and even consulates shared in the common destruction. The Franciscan convent contained many European friars and nearly a thousand refugees of the natives, all of whom were put to the sword. One Protestant missionary, Rev. Mr. Graham, was slain in the streets. The bold native Protestant champion, Dr. Meshâka, who was vice-consul for the United States, was attacked in his own consulate by some savage Koords, and fled into the street. He was shot at repeatedly and assailed with clubs and axes and swords. His Muslim servant stayed by him and warded off many a death-blow, and his master was finally rescued by a few Algerines under Abd el Kâder, and brought, all gashed with wounds and nearly naked, to the house of a faithful Muslim friend, who bound up his wounds and for a month took the greatest care of him. Many persons had fled from the desolations of Hasbeiya and vicinity only to meet death at Damascus. Yoosef Barakât, a younger son of Shaheen of Hasbeiya, was in a remarkable manner saved, with his whole family of seven. They were all Protestants, and two of them in communion with the church. The wife had been educated in the family of our missionary, Dr. De Forest. When the ruffians broke into Yoosef's house, the family were all scattered in every direction. The wife was several times a prisoner, but by giving up her jewels one after another she was let go, and finally came to the house of the English consul, where all the seven from different quarters were at last brought together.

Beside the four principal towns above specified, the large interior villages of Resheiyat el Wady and Jezzeen, containing together four or five thousand inhabitants, and with them two hundred smaller villages, were, in this Turco-Druze war, either wholly or partially destroyed, and their Christian population either murdered or driven away. Deir el Mokhollis, the chief convent of the papal Greeks near Sidon, was violated, its inmates slain and its goods and chattels, with its valuable library, plundered. Mr. Wilson's station at Hums became unsafe, and he removed to the region of Tripoli, but on his way was robbed and held in captivity for a while by the Arabs. How many of the smaller villages about Damascus suffered in like manner is untold.

Great excitement also pervaded all the cities of the coast, and it is confidently believed that massacres would have been perpetrated in them like those of the interior had not the Muslims been overawed by a few foreign ships of war on the coast. At Sidon whole companies of Christian fugitives from the mountains were denied entrance into the city, and were overtaken and slain by their Druze pursuers or shot down by the Turks themselves from the city walls. The governor of the city insolently refused a guard for the houses of the missionaries, and they were compelled to remove for safety to Beirut. Yet even in Beirut Christians, both foreign and native, judging from outward appearances, for a number of days considered themselves in danger of violence and death, and subsequent revelations have made it clear that a plot against the town had actually been matured, and failed only on account of ships in the harbor. A similar deliverance was vouchsafed by Providence to Acca and other maritime cities. That this wholesale slaughter of Christians was not disagreeable to the Turkish government was evident not only from their promoting rather than preventing it, but also from an authenticated declaration years ago of one of the most eminent pashas of Damascus, namely, that the Turkish government could maintain its ascendency in Syria only "*by cutting down the Christian sects.*"

The punishment awarded to the guilty in this bloody war was shockingly inadequate to the crimes committed. The governor and military commander at Damascus, three Turkish officers, superintendents of the Hasbeiya massacre, and one hundred and seventeen others were indeed all shot. Fifty-six Damascene citizens died on the scaffold. Eleven prominent men were exiled and their property confiscated. The Turk who presided and "kept order" at the massacre in Deir el Kommer, the pasha at Beirut, and four or five other Turkish officials were condemned to perpetual imprisonment, and several Druzes to death, but none of these latter sentences were ever executed, and hundreds of others, chiefly Druzes, who were proved guilty of murder, went scot free. Not a Druze was punished.

After this a body of commissioners from the European powers was sent to estimate the damages for which the Turkish government ought to make due reparation to the remaining Christians. These commissioners failed to agree among themselves, and the benefit looked for from their appointment fell very far short of the public expectation. It was well, however, that they came, and could as eye-witnesses officially report back to their governments the depth of misery to which the poor Lebanon and Damascene Christians were reduced, and could also in some degree supervise the distribution of the alms sent for the naked, the hungry and the houseless from sympathizing fellow-Christians in Europe. Crowds in thousands after thousands of fugitives from Damascus and all parts of the mountains, driven by fear and poverty, poured down to Sidon, and especially to Beirut, nearly all of whom were reduced to beggary, and must be fed or die, and all the contributions of all Europe and America were scarcely enough for them "that every one might take a little." So far had the supply fallen below the demand in the month of November that Lord Dufferin, one of the English commissioners, felt constrained to advance from his own private funds a loan of twenty-five thousand dollars to save many that were not only suffering, but actually pining away and perishing from want. The depth of wretchedness into which the Christian population of the country were thrown by this barbarian butchery, and the part taken by our missionaries in administering such relief as they were able, may be seen from the following extracts from a letter of Dr. Thomson:

"We are now spending for food, clothing, bedding, shelter, hospital and soup-kitchen at the rate of about sixty thousand piasters a week, and yet we seem to make little impression on the mighty mass of misery around us. The actual working of all these departments of charity devolves *wholly upon our mission*. I have the clothing, bedding, shelter and soup-kitchen under my special care; Dr. Van Dyck takes charge of the hospital and the sick in general. Mr. Jessup has the enormous business of distributing bread to about six thousand persons daily, and two of our native brethren, Bootrus Bistany and Micha-eel Aramon, have the daily distribution to about two thousand five hundred poor.

"The English merchants devote much of their time to our committee meetings, and cheerfully help in managing the large financial business connected with this vast charity. . . . The extent of the calamity is bewildering. Yesterday we had an appeal in behalf of three or four thousand refugees from Baalbec and adjacent regions who fled over Lebanon to Besherry, near the cedars, and are there naked and starving; that is four days to the north. Word also came from Mr. Ford that fifteen hundred of the escaped from Hasbeiya and regions about there had just reached Sidon, and more were coming, while thousands are wandering about in Belad Beshára, three days to the south of us. Again, to the eastward going from here to Yabrood, two days beyond Damascus toward Palmyra, the whole region has been scathed and burnt over and the Christian population ruined. The victims far exceed one hundred thousand. The killed alone in Damascus are more than five thousand. And then remember that in all places the killed are *men and boys*, the *stamina* of the population, who find the work and furnish the support. This country has no factories where women can go and find employment and gain a living.

"I went to distribute clothing yesterday to one room. There were six women, all newly-made widows, with no male child or friend to comfort or care for them. Another room had five such widows. A friend of mine has taken nine women into his family, *all widows*, made such in the slaughter at Deir el Kommer. None of these widows saved *anything*, and they are in rags, except so far as we have clothed them. Mr. Calhoun, through scenes of great anxiety, still holds the important position of Abeih. But Mr. Ford, after working himself almost to death here, has gone to Sidon to do the same there for Hasbeiyans and other thousands there and to the south of Sidon.

"In regard to the effects of this desolating war, or rather massacre, particularly on the interests of the mission, it has been ascertained that among the victims that fell scarcely a dozen were from among those that had professed themselves Protestants. Very few of the stations or out-stations were more than temporarily interfered with, and most of them not at all. Every missionary, and nearly or quite every missionary teacher and helper, was spared; and when peace came, many of them were immediately and intensely engaged in the very work that occupied their divine Master—in feeding the hungry, as he did, by thousands at once, in preaching to them at the same time the gospel of the kingdom, and in healing, so far as means could go, 'all manner of sickness and all manner of disease among the people.' Lord Dufferin, in speaking of the part borne by the Syrian missionaries in this work of humanity and religion, awards to them unmeasured commendation, declaring that 'without their indefatigable exertions the supplies sent from Christendom could never have been properly distributed *nor the starvation of thousands of the needy been prevented.*'"

Thus in the most favorable circumstances possible were the missionaries introduced to the personal knowledge and acquaintance of multitudes of the natives whom they came into this land to benefit, but who otherwise would never have seen them, and probably never have heard of them, except it might be in priestly proclamation, styling them "*wolves in sheep's clothing and enemies of the human race.*"

In less than two months after the assassin's hand was stayed the missionaries were able to say, "The Beirut station continues its operations, the press is working, the female school is open as usual, and the boys' school would be but that the school-room is full of refugees, the translation of the scriptures has been resumed, the printing of the voweled edition of the New Testament is about to be commenced, and, what is more important than all, our chapel is crowded with hearers, and we have and are likely to have more direct missionary work to do in Beirut than ever before. Mr. Calhoun has remained at his station, where he has kept up his regular preaching service both in Abeih and in Aramûn, the congregations being as large as before the war, if not larger. The common schools at these two places have been re-opened at the urgent request of both Christians and Druzes, and we are inclined to think that even at Deir el Kommer, when the old settlers that escaped shall return and new ones come in, the door for the gospel will be open there wider than in the days of its prosperity. Mr. Ford has increased calls upon him for mission work, not only for the city of Sidon itself, but for his out-stations of Cana, Alma and the villages of Merj Aioon.

"So far from having nothing to do now in Syria," says Mr. Ford, "we never were so busy in our lives before. There is no lack of opportunity for the direct preaching of the gospel at nearly all our stations, and at some of them the congregations are very large and the people quite at leisure to listen to the truth."

Ever since the terrible visitation already described, Syria has remained in comparative peace and the mission has been steadily increasing in strength. This increase has appeared more especially in three particulars—in its *laborers*, in its *educational preparations*, and in its *press*. Its ministry has held its own in point of numbers. One strong man has been translated to a higher sphere, and others have left the field finally or for a time, but their places have been filled by new recruits, and in the female branch more than filled. Meantime, all have been growing *strong in speech*, so that it may be said now, as it never could have been before, that we have in the work a force of ten or twelve men able to announce the gospel message about as well in Arabic as in English. In this estimate, however, the men of the college must be included. The *theological seminary*, in its new organization, the *female boarding-school*, with its full complement of teachers, and the new *college* for literature and science will conspire to establish a new era in Arab thought in Syria, while the *press*, with its varied and elegant typography, and its power of turning out annually ten million pages of human and divine instruction, will contribute nourishment for the awakened minds and softened hearts of perishing millions.

This great and glorious enterprise for Syria lately passed, by mutual agreement, from the hands of the American Board of Missions to those of the Presbyterian Board. What the state and condition of it was at the time of the transfer may be seen in part by the following extracts from an account written by a laborer on the ground, the Rev. D. Stuart Dodge:

"The Syria mission was originally planted to evangelize the non-Christian sects, especially the Mohammedans; its work among nominal Christians was only a means to this end. Oriental Christianity stood as the chief stumbling-block to labors among the heathen beyond. This it was necessary to remove by exhibiting a Christian church with a purer faith and holier life. The gospel must be preached in the vernacular; only natives could do this to the best advantage and to the extent demanded. All efforts, therefore, have been primarily directed to the Oriental churches.

"1. The *Maronites*, dwelling principally on Mt. Lebanon north of Beirut, descendants of the ancient Syrians, and numbering two hundred thousand. They are papists, the common people ignorant, the priesthood educated and powerful, the patriarch ruling with a rod of iron.

"2. The *papal Greeks*, numbering fifty thousand, of pure Arab stock, the proudest, most intelligent and enterprising people of Syria.

"3. The *Orthodox Greek* Church, embracing one hundred and fifty thousand; its highest dignitaries foreigners, rarely speaking Arabic, and having little sympathy with the customs and wants of their people.

"In respect to all these sects, therefore, it is a significant and encouraging fact that, just as the mission is transferred, the people which it seeks to evangelize were never in a more favorable condition for enlarged and vigorous effort. The leaven scattered through so many years is not only apparent from a gradually-increasing spirit of inquiry, but unlooked-for events have now stirred up the whole mass to an unwonted ferment, and we are emphatically called to take advantage of the opportunity.

"The *material equipment* for this work is at hand. 1. *Churches* have been erected in many of the prominent towns and villages. The Sidon station has seven commodious and permanent buildings. All the stations have school-houses or accommodations for worship in desirable localities. Beirut, the strategic base of the mission, a city of eighty thousand inhabitants, the chief seaport and centre of influence in Syria, has now a substantial and graceful structure on a commanding site, with sittings for four hundred and fifty persons, and with a tower and clock, which stands up before all eyes a solid argument for Protestantism.

"2. *Educational institutions* have been established. The *theological seminary* has recently been re-organized. Mr. Calhoun, Dr. H. H. Jessup and Mr. Eddy are the efficient professors. The number of students is small, but no effort will now be spared to give this institution the prominence its vital work demands. The *college* is year by year attracting more widely the attention and confidence of the people. Drs. Bliss, Van Dyck, Post, Wortabet and others are absorbed in efforts to build it up on a basis of sound, systematic evangelical culture. It has *eighty* students in the literary and medical departments, with already extensive cabinets and apparatus, a hospital, dispensary and other appointments. It is not organically connected with the mission, an independent organization being deemed necessary. This, however, tends even more effectively to promote the objects of the mission. Its one comprehensive aim is to raise up men from among the people themselves to evangelize their own country.

"An *academy* is located at Abeih to prepare teachers for primary schools on the mountain and to fit students for the college. *District schools* exist throughout the field. A noble *female academy* flourishes at Beirut, with forty boarders and as many more day scholars. This school already exerts a wide influence, and is to become a centre for woman's work among women. A smaller *institution at Sidon* educates teachers for infant schools and wives for native helpers, whilst schools, chiefly primary, have been established at different places by Scotch and English societies.

"3. The *press,* also at Beirut and near the church, has long been felt in all parts of the Orient. It sends out annually from five to six millions of pages in various departments of religious and secular knowledge. The type and electrotype plates are made on the premises. Mr. Hallock is the able manager. Dr. Van Dyck has now issued six editions of the Old Testament and eight of the New almost wholly at the expense of the American Bible Society. A voweled Bible has just been finished for Mohammedan readers, and portions of the gospel have been issued for the blind.

"All these agencies are now in active operation. They need only such facilities as can readily be supplied, and then they should be pushed to their utmost capacity.

"The *field is ready,* the *machinery is provided;* let the MEN *be forthcoming.*"

THE END.

www.ingramcontent.com/pod-product-compliance
Lightning Source LLC
Chambersburg PA
CBHW051732300426
44115CB00007B/532